D0769477

Computational Organizational Cognition

Computational Organizational Cognition
A Study on Thinking and Action in Organizations

By

Davide Secchi
University of Southern Denmark, Denmark

United Kingdom – North America – Japan
India – Malaysia – China

Emerald Publishing Limited
Howard House, Wagon Lane, Bingley BD16 1WA, UK

First edition 2021

Copyright © 2021 Emerald Publishing Limited

Reprints and permissions service
Contact: permissions@emeraldinsight.com

No part of this book may be reproduced, stored in a retrieval
system, transmitted in any form or by any means electronic, mechanical,
photocopying, recording or otherwise without either the prior written
permission of the publisher or a licence permitting restricted copying
issued in the UK by The Copyright Licensing Agency and in the USA
by The Copyright Clearance Center. Any opinions expressed in the
chapters are those of the authors. Whilst Emerald makes every effort to
ensure the quality and accuracy of its content, Emerald makes no
representation implied or otherwise, as to the chapters' suitability and
application and disclaims any warranties, express or implied, to
their use.

British Library Cataloguing in Publication Data
A catalogue record for this book is available from the British Library

ISBN: 978-1-83867-512-7 (Print)
ISBN: 978-1-83867-511-0 (Online)
ISBN: 978-1-83867-513-4 (Epub)

ISOQAR certified
Management System,
awarded to Emerald
for adherence to
Environmental
standard
ISO 14001:2004.

Certificate Number 1985
ISO 14001

INVESTOR IN PEOPLE

A mamma e papà

Contents

List of Figures

List of Tables

List of Abbreviations

ABM   — Agent-Based Modeling
ABMO   — Agent-based models of organizational behavior
AOC   — Agent-based computational organizational cognition
DA(C)M — Dynamic Adaptive (Cognitive) Mechanisms
EDEC   — Embodied/Distributed/Extended Cognition
MOC   — Managerial and Organizational Cognition
MOR   — Management and Organization Research
OC   — Organizational Cognition
R   — Software for statistical computing
RECS   — Radical Embodied Cognitive Science
SDC   — Socially Distributed Cognition

About the Author

Davide Secchi, PhD, is Associate Professor of Organizational Cognition at the Department of Language and Communication, Director of the Research Centre for Computational & Organisational Cognition, University of Southern Denmark, Slagelse. His research is organized around (a) rationality in distributed cognitive environments by using (b) empirical data and advanced computational simulation techniques, especially agent-based modeling. He has authored more than 80 among journal articles, book chapters, and books. He is founder and convenor of the Agent-Based Models of Organizational Behavior Workshop Series and has presented his work more than 100 times at major international conferences (2002–2020). He sits on the editorial board of *Kybernetes, Team Performance Management* and, since March 2020, he is Editor-in-Chief of the *International Journal of Organization Theory & Behavior* (Emerald).

Preface

When I was invited by Flaminio Squazzoni at the University of Brescia in the North of Italy to give a lecture to his Master's students, I did not know what was going to happen. It was May 2018. The sun was shining, the futuristic look of the city provided a fantastic scenery, and the visit to the Ninth Century old San Faustino's convent in which the social science faculty is located simply blew my mind. "I miss this!," I thought, referring to what it means to breathe history daily, really unearthing sentiments of how much I miss Italy. And Brescia is not even *my* city! It just felt home. Anyway, I had the impression that the lecture "Implications of distributed cognition for leadership and team dynamics" did not go too well. I tried to do too much. I read the request from Flaminio for a lecture where I could present some of my research by connecting it to leadership, the topic of the course. In the first part, I talked about (bounded) rationality and cognition, and that did probably do the trick; students were engaged. The second part of the lecture was dedicated to a few of my agent-based simulations. I do not know why I decided to go on with such a review of my computational research. It probably was Flaminio, knowing who he is and what he does, the book he used in that course (it was Goldstein, Hazy, & Lichtenstein, 2010), or just my own ambition. That was probably too much for the poor students. But it meant the world to me. In an attempt to connect some of these simulations together, without purposefully planning it out, I outlined the very idea that is now this book.

There were a series of realizations (is "epiphanies" the right word here?) that made me understand what I was really aiming at as I was presenting my line of thoughts during the lecture. One was that 10 years had already passed from my book *Extendable Rationality*. That sounded like a long time. It felt a geological era, especially because many things had happened in my professional life. I was no more a young US scholar at the University of Wisconsin, with all the charm and vibrant force that such position brings. I was now back in the Old Continent, as I first landed in England and then in Denmark, where I currently work. When I wrote the previous book (published in 2011), I never thought it was something to be continued. To some extent, I was right, the message of that book is that there is a possibility to extend the way in which bounded rationality is looked upon and theorized. This is exactly the point. I find myself more and more dissatisfied with discussions around and criticisms of bounded rationality because I believe it is no more a starting point for me. Of course, as it is clear to those who will read this book, I still consider myself a scholar of bounded rationality. But here is the first realization of my lecture Brescia: I had moved on!

By giving that lecture and discussing my research, I connected a series of models and studies that had been previously published in papers and chapters. The connections were very easy to make, even though I never thought about them before. Not in that way, at least. But it all made sense. All this time, and with the help of my co-authors, I have been looking at the theory presented in *Extendable Rationality* to verify its consistency, robustness, and developments. Here is the second realization: this research is all connected and follows a rather consistent thread.

* * * * *

This book is not just the story of the last 10 years of my work. In fact, I think of the book as a way to reflect on some of the concepts, models, theories, and approaches that usually accompany my enquiries. In order to be able to fully engage with this declaration of intents, the book is made of three parts: Part I to discuss advancements on distributed cognition, Part II to assess the theoretical elements in Part I through agent-based modeling, and Part III to summarize and discuss an alternative view of organizational cognition.

Before everything begins, I have decided to write an introduction (Chapter 1) that discusses the aim and scope of the book and summarizes its content, offering a roadmap to readers who want to jump directly to one chapter or the other. The first chapter in Part I (Chapter 2) serves as a connector to more traditional literature in organizational cognition. This is something I decided to add after a comment from one of the colleagues who reviewed the book proposal. The reviewer was concerned that those who did not read my other book and come from a more traditional background in organizational cognition studies would be left out. The reviewer was referring explicitly to scholars affiliated to the Managerial and Organizational Cognition (MOC) division from the US Academy of Management (AoM). I thought that was a good point. I never intended this book to be of sole interest of MOC colleagues. My primary interest is the scientific community as a global project; of course, that includes colleagues from the AoM, but also those from all the other corners of the world and from other disciplinary perspectives.

* * * * *

As I did in the last monograph I wrote, a few words on what it means to write a book are probably warranted. Writing a book is one the most ancient ways in which scholars have communicated over the centuries. It is well engrained into the way European science has historically progressed. This means of communication is now entering a new phase, where its value, role, and effectiveness are questioned. Considering that a book should respond to the same criteria that apply to the evaluation of a journal article is one of the issues surrounding assessment of books as scientific outlets. Here are a few points, where I have tried to indicate how these two assessments differ (the list is not exhaustive):

- While journal articles have to strictly adher to the literature that allows them to be published in the journal of choice, a book may select this literature more freely, since it is not bound to a specific outlet (i.e. the journal). In fact, the book is an outlet in itself.

- Journal articles have page/word limits that make them exercises in succinctness and conciseness; books do not abide to such constraints. A book is more valuable if it can be concise, but there are plenty of examples of excellent academic books that are all but concise.

- Journal articles cannot digress or explore sideline stories, if not sporadically; books can and should be actively taking those sideline stories and digressions, as far as they contribute to building a stronger argument. In other words, more than anything, in a book the argument is king.

- A book is an exercise in exploring a topic in full; an article targets one (sometimes, but rarely, two) specific aspect(s) of a topic.

- The audience of a given journal article is predictable – not always, but fairly accurately – while that of a book is much more unpredictable, because it presents itself free from the outlet's (i.e. the journal's) constraints.

- Using traditional or innovative constructs in an unorthodox way is almost unanimously banned from journal publications. It is

possible, sometimes necessary, to do that in a book, because one
is more free to explore new horizons and has the time to explain
why, how, and when.

If one agrees with the points listed above, then one shall also start
reading this (and other) books with a slightly different mindset as of
when one reads journal articles. In fact, even though it refers to several
journal articles, this book is not a sum of possible papers, nor it is a
simple sum of its chapters, considered individually.

With these considerations in mind, I hope you want to keep reading
and I wish you a nice experience if you are going to.

Acknowledgments

The Italian academic environment is very formal or, at least, it was when
I used to live in Italy (now almost 15 years ago). Some of the junior
scholars used to refer to full professors by their titles, as in "Professor
X," and use the formal third person form. In some environments, this
behavior could have been more relaxed, depending on seniority. When
I was (very) young, my mother used to take me with her to some of the
classes she was teaching and, as a child, I have always had a fascination
with the academic environment. At that time, the old building where
the Faculty of Economics was located at the University of Cagliari had
giant black and white pictures of notable scientists on the walls, and
books, books everywhere. I never actually reflected upon the fact that
my mother was "Mrs" (Signora), and not "Professor," to some of the
junior faculty. She became full professor in Italy in a discipline and at
a time where 95% of her colleagues were men. Some of these men had a
difficulty accepting the fact that she was (still is!) a strong woman and
better than them. Not just a better published scholar, but better cited,
better with students, better in academic politics, better in attracting
funds, and better in establishing partnerships with local enterprises.
Not many colleagues had such a thriving and inspiring example at home.
I consider myself extremely lucky having been able to look up to her.
There are no words to express such an incredible intellectual debt. My
work embeds this inspiring upbringing of mine. Thank you, mother,
Professoressa Giudici![1]

During my early years, my mother was always taken by some academic project while my father was more relaxed in his work and philosophy of life. For many years my father used to receive phone calls from
colleagues who asked about various aspects of their work. He worked

---

[1] If you are wondering, of course, she read this book and provided feedback!

in the central administration office for the Italian Postal Services in Cagliari. These long conversations used to take him away from lunch or whatever he was up to. The calls did not stop after he retired. And he would still help! In fact, this service-driven mentality continues still today, after many years of retirement. He gives financial advice on how to navigate the intricacies of Italian tax law to those who need it and works as a volunteer for an association that is set to do just that. For many years, I failed to recognize how generous my father is and, probably, one of the reasons why I write about altruism is due to the example he set throughout his life. This is why there is another intellectual debt that I feel it is long overdue. Sometimes, actions speak louder than words and I believe this is a way typical of Sardinians to express themselves. Through his approach to life my father has taught me more than I have ever realized. Thank you, father.

As explained in the Preface, I owe this idea for a book to Flaminio Squazzoni and his invite to the University of Brescia for that seminar in the Spring of 2018. Thank you very much for serving as an inspiration.

I am extremely thankful to my colleague Stephen J. Cowley for our endless talks, seminars, workshops, papers, and conferences that made me realize the limits of my thinking and especially their potentials.

Dinuka B. Herath published his book *Organizational Plasticity. How disorganization can be leveraged for better organizational performance* with Emerald in 2019. He is the one who actually pushed me into writing this book. As a former PhD student of mine, I wish to thank him for the many things he has taught me. Daring to write another book is one of them.

All the colleagues with whom I discussed parts of what has gone into this book deserve a sound and wholehearted thank you. They are Billy Adamsen, Emanuele Bardone, Rasmus Gahrn-Andersen, Bruce Edmonds, Siavash Farahbakhsh, Nicole Gullekson, Dinuka B. Herath, Gayanga B. Herath, Fabian Homberg, Astrid Jensen, Martin Neumann, Laura Parolin, Raffaello Seri, and Yumei Yang.

The editor from Emerald, Niall Kennedy, believed in me since the beginning. Actually, since before I started to seriously think of this book. His nice emails and attempts to nudge me into a book project really worked as a motivation for me in that I would know that, once I had an idea, I could count on a publisher. His support has been exceptional, especially during the pandemic, when I could complete the work on my time as opposed to abiding to a strict deadline.

Last but definitely not least, an immense thank you goes to the love of my life, my wife Claudia. As we were all forced to work from home by the COVID-19 pandemic, she made sure I had some quiet time for myself so that I could write. I cannot fully express how fortunate I am to have such a patient and caring person next to me. My now 11-month old son Luca gave me the force to recharge my batteries very rapidly when I was off my (too many) projects. His smile and daily developments have been a blessing.

Davide Secchi
https://secchidavi.wixsite.com/dsweb

1

Introduction

This book is a very ambitious attempt to set new grounds for the study of organizational cognition. More specifically, it shows why cognition in organizations should be studied with computational means of inquiry, how this can be achieved, and what are the theoretical implications of such a scientific enterprise.

Organizational cognition is not a new expression, nor the area of interest and research is recent. In fact, it is almost 30 years that management and organization research (MOR) scholars have been concerned with it (Ilgen, Major, & Spencer, 1994; Walsh, 1995). Since its beginnings, the area has produced an increasing number of papers and other publications (Secchi & Adamsen, 2017; see also Chapter 2) and has recently started to diversify its perspectives (Hodgkinson, 2015). While the expression "managerial and organizational cognition" (MOC) is used to define one of the divisions of the American Academy of Management, there is no academic journal that is specifically dedicated to it. As Hodgkinson and Healey (2008a) showed in their review of the literature, this area of study was well alive and thriving a decade ago, and it keeps moving forward about a decade later (Healey, Hodgkinson, & Massaro, 2018).

With all that has been written on cognition in organizations, why this book then? Why should you read this book instead of one of the latest articles presenting a thorough review of the literature?

There are multiple reasons I can offer, not all of them equally appealing to all readers. Besides presenting a computational approach to the study of cognition, this book also represents a personal journey. It elaborates on the last 10 years of my research on cognition, what drove

Computational Organizational Cognition:
A Study on Thinking and Action in Organizations, 1–13
Copyright © 2021 by Emerald Publishing Limited
All rights of reproduction in any form reserved
doi: 10.1108/978-1-83867-511-020211001

it, how connected, and where it is headed. Through this process, the book tells the story of a theory as well as of a methodology.

1.1   A Theoretical Line

The book elaborates on the idea that people are *docile*, that is, they lean on information, advice, suggestions, recommendations coming from social channels and use them to make decisions (Simon, 1993). More than that, the book intends to show how any attempt to take cognition seriously as it manifests in organizations needs a re-definition of the way we think of cognition in general. A perspective that takes us close to this re-definition is the use of embodied/distributed/extended (EDEC) cognitive paradigms. But that is not enough. It is insufficient because these paradigms treat the *social* elements at their surface. Most of them do not fully elaborate on what, how, why, and when a structured social environment (such as an organization) affects cognition. I am generalizing here and, just like any generalization, I am partially at fault. There are instances in which the EDEC perspectives have referred to the role of the social (especially parts of Hutchins, 1995a). What I am referring to is that (a) this has not been taken as a constitutive element and as a starting point to understand, frame, identify, determine, and analyze cognition, hence (b) we do not have a proper theory of cognition in organizations. We do have adaptations of theories to fit organizations, attempts at matching cognition with organizational features, and wider approaches to cognition. However, there are no specific theories that start from what it means to cognize in an organizational environment.

   This is a big miss. It is because human life and work are organized around and within organizations. These social institutions shape our behavior, expectations, aims, motivations, the extent to which we experience satisfaction, as well as our knowledge, learning and, broadly, our thinking. In other words, much of what and who we *are* is inextricably tied to organized life and work. This is obvious and it has been within the realm of management knowledge for almost a century. Yet, and not surprisingly, it has not touched the way in which cognitive science has evolved and is conducted today. In line with this, and perhaps surprisingly this time, the implications of this simple truism – i.e. organizations shape human lives – have not been reflected upon by MOC scholars. As shown in this book, these researchers have been more concerned with applying (what they thought was) knowledge from cognitive science to various aspects of organizational research. As far as my knowledge is concerned, this approach has not produced theories of cognition in organizations, just applications of theories exogenous to the field. The fact that the theories of cognition used in organizational contexts were mainly generated by considering individuals (with the illusion that they were) working in isolation has not triggered much reflection. As if the cultural, interactive, normative, value-based, resource rich, and socially-bound organizational environment was, at best, an add-on feature of the individual brain. Maybe it is just like that, maybe one could juxtapose traditional cognition to a complex organizational context and gain some useful knowledge. After all, there have been advances in MOC over the past decades.

My reaction to this last consideration follows two threads. One is that advancements in a field that did not exist 30 years ago are typically large, if one considers that the starting point was a very limited knowledge base. The other is that these advancements have started to hit a wall (better, a ceiling). This is the same obstacle that has been hit by cognitive science decades ago, when many have started to question the brain-centered and the brain-only approach (e.g., Varela, Thompson, & Rosch, 1991). And this limit has started to surface among MOC scholars as well recently (Hodgkinson, 2015; Healey et al., 2018).

The main reaction, however, is of a more substantial philosophical nature. Do we truly believe that the instances of performing a task in isolation[1] or within the frame of an organization are the same? Let me rephrase: Is it fair to assume that the processes that inform human cognition are the same when performing a task independent of the context? And if they are not the same then, is the difference enough to warrant a different theory? This book is an attempt to answer these questions. An attempt to answer the first two negatively, and the latter affirmatively: no, it is not fair to assume that the processes are the same and yes, we need a theory.

The chapters included under Part I are dedicated to outline the backbone of *socially distributed cognition*, a general theoretical approach to cognition, that is tested through computational experiments in Part II and that informs what is called *theory of social organizing* in Part III.

1.2 Computational Revival

There is also a methodological story line that features in the title of this book and it is as central as the theory it outlines. The history of cognitive

---

[1] A quick note here to comment on the meaning of "performing in isolation." In its absolute interpretation, that is the independence of an individual from any environmental perturbation, isolation cannot be observed. As I am writing this footnote, I am supposedly doing it in isolation. Writing is a solitary exercise. And yet, it is not. Actually, writing is a social exercise because it is directed to a readership, to someone who will read and hopefully understand the content of the text. This implies that, while writing, one projects the activity to imagine how someone else (a potential reader) could receive the meaning. For example, every time I write "MOC scholars" in this book, I hope that the one MOC reader I will have will not be too disappointed by my findings and comments. In the end, one may argue, it is still me writing, although far from isolation.

science is intertwined with that of artificial intelligence and especially to
that of the first computers (e.g., Chomsky, 1980; Fodor, 1987; Newell &
Simon, 1972). After all, the computer metaphor of the brain was one of
the most widely used perspectives on cognition (as explained in Varela
et al., 1991) and, to some extent, it still is (Gigerenzer & Goldstein,
1996; Hodgkinson, 2015; Patokorpi, 2008). This view postulates that
the way in which the brain and the computer operate are very similar,
and it is the signature metaphor of the cognitivist approach. Much
has been written on the limitations of this view and of cognitivism
(e.g., Patokorpi, 2008; Varela et al., 1991; Ibáñez & Cosmelli, 2008)
and this book has not been written to counter that view. We are,
philosophically, theoretically, and empirically far away from cognitivism
today. This is why producing a counter to cognitivism is futile because
irrelevant. Put differently, this book does not use computation as a way
to describe the brain nor as a way to define artificial intelligence processes that mimic the brain. If not this way, how is computation used in
this book?

Before I can answer this question, I think it is necessary to reflect on
cognition in organizations, on what it is and then offer some thoughts
on how it can be studied.

1.2.1   Organizations as Complex Systems

Imagine you are coming from the Anarchic World, a society à la Proud-
homme where property does not exist, hence organizations take a form
that is different than the ones we have in this world. If you are tasked
with describing organizations, the first consideration would probably be
that they are constituted by a bundle of interconnected parts that stand
against each other in mutual dependence. Some of these relations can be
formally defined (e.g., power structure, titles, positions, functions) while
others are more informal and reflect behavior, common practices, habits,
in other words tacit knowledge. The synthesis of these aspects of an
organization's life defines differences and distinguishes one organization
from another. Of course, you may notice, there are also more standard
factors such as size, type of production, market and competition that
characterize organizations. Most of all, when observations are repeated
over a period of time, you may notice that change is probably the
constant feature of any organization. Not only they adopt different practices, hire/fire personnel, direct their attention to different customers
and markets, develop new products, procedures, routines, they also
adjust, sometimes abruptly sometimes more softly, to a mix of internal
and external pressures. Given the above, would you, as a visitor from

the Anarchic World, be able to predict an organization's state s_1 at time T given its state s_0 at time t?

This is notoriously very difficult. What I have described above as a generic path for an undefined "organization" fits the design of a complex system very well. This is a system where its constituent parts are interconnected and, at the same time, maintain a certain degree of autonomy such that the exact way in which they interact can be difficult to determine. This leads to indicate that a complex system such as an organization is, generally speaking, *unpredictable* because any state s_1 at time T cannot be fully derived by its state s_0 at time t. Well, it probably could ex post, almost never ex ante. This is because the functions that determine s_1 are only partially known. Moreover, the organizational system has only a loose dependence on the initial conditions s_0 at time t. This generates processes that lead the organization to define ways of action that *emerge* from the interaction between its social, material and immaterial components.

I understand the above is a rather abstract definition of an organization and its description as a complex system. A quick example may help understand what some of the concepts above mean in practice. Consider a small brewpub[2] – a company that has a micro production of beer and, at the same time, it has a restaurant – that employs about 15 people, with a simple structure made of one owner and CEO, an administrative person, one brewmaster with an aid, one chef, one sous-chef, three more employees in the kitchen, one maitre de salle, one barista, and four waiters. The company also sells their beer in bottles. There are processes in place that reflect the roles as briefly described. At the same time, unexpected situations may materialize and bring, for example, one of the waiters to pour beer from the tap or, even more wildly, make the admin person do that. The flexibility in covering each other's role may be done with ease or with a grumpy attitude, depending on what is "normal" for someone working in that organization. Early in 2020 the company faced a significant struggle, followed by the lockdown due to the COVID-19 pandemic. As a result of those circumstances and to stay alive, some positions were suspended but, with the closing of the restaurant, activity was also threatening the existence of the company. After a quick round of consultations, and without the restaurant, the owner realized that sales of bottles would not make the company survive. This led to the decision to sell mainly from the internet, offering take-home meals and, obviously, beer. The database of customers built over more than 10 years of business was used to send the message out. After a series of initial difficulties, business remained active, mainly because

---

[2]This anecdote is based on *Il Birrificio di Cagliari*, one of Italy's most internationally awarded companies in the craft-brewery business.

of loyal customers and special deals the company was able to offer (e.g., special containers that would bring the beer home as fresh as if it was drafted seconds before).

The pandemic took everyone off guard. If we consider s_0 for this company a time t placed somewhere in January 2020, there is nothing that could have predicted the lockdown and a move to turn temporarily off the restaurant, if we take late March 2020 to be our time T and state s_1. However, one may argue, this is a so-called shock and, by definition, these are unpredictable events that do not necessarily pertain to one single organization, they are market phenomena. Correct, this is something one cannot attribute to the single organization. Still, the way in which this particular organization re-structured to face the shock was unpredictable; many other organizations took a different path, with varying degrees of success. Suspending positions (who, when, how), how is take-home organized, which online platform, who is going to deliver, how is that management expertise built so quickly, and which parts of the menu can be transferred to a take-home business without losing the image customers have of the company? Moreover, interactions between members of the various teams – brewery, kitchen, restaurant – change significantly, being that the nature of business has changed. In the least affected part of the business, the brewery, for example, the decision was to suspend the brewmaster's aid, to freeze the production plan until the stock of beer could be sold. The lack of a restaurant made predictions on when the stock would be depleted very hard. So, the schedule had to change to something very flexible. The owner decided to step in and help the brewmaster. The production driver was now different, and making the beer became also different, with the brewmaster who needed to justify some of the choices in detail, now that the owner was stepping in. As a result, norms, practices, routines, as well as behavior, culture, forms of pressure, and roles in the organization emerged as the new configuration changed.

If we take the above to be a fair description of the way in which the typical organization behaves, then we can describe it as a complex (adaptive) social system.

1.2.2 Is Cognition Complex?

What about cognition? The question is more on what is the role of cognition and cognitive processes in an organization that is described as a complex system. There are some risks in a question such as this one that it is better to clarify.

One line would be to argue that, given the organization is complex, all of its constitutive elements are complex. This would be a logical fallacy called *composition and division* (Gabbay & Woods, 2009; Secchi, 2011), that of attributing the characteristics of the system to one of its components. Moreover, cognition has not been described (so far, at least) as a constituent part for organizations. So, let me take one step at a time.

Can organizations exist without cognition? This depends on what one means with the word "cognition." Inspired by the embodied, distributed and extended paradigms, in this book *human cognition is a way in which we use contextual embeddedness to make sense of the surroundings and inform action*. The expression "make sense" is vague and it is used here to refer to processes that involve conscious interaction with other human beings, material (e.g, computers, notebooks, buildings) and immaterial (e.g., ideas, concepts, models) artifacts. This process is embodied and embedded as well as dependent on the configuration of the environment, i.e. both the "contextual" and the "surroundings" in the sentence above. This points at a systemic or ecological perspective on cognition, that cannot happen in a vacuum. Finally, "action" refers to any activity that includes but it is not limited to behavior, at least, not in a narrow sense. Speaking, for example, is an action, probably not something one could refer to as behavior.

Hence, the question again: Can an organization exist without the use of contextual embeddedness to make sense of the surroundings and inform action? The answer is clearly negative. Or, one may argue using a hyperbole that an organization that does not use this feature is destined to nonexistence very soon (if it ever can exist in the first place).

But, if cognition is a feature of any organization – probably not exclusive to organizations but still a major feature – the following question would be that of asking whether organizations are cognitive systems then. This requires a more subtle reasoning. An organization may be part of a cognitive system, in the sense that it may become part of cognition as it happens within its boundaries. Organizational tools, resources, employees, as well as immaterial knowledge elements enable (or disable) and are functional (or dysfunctional, at times) to cognitive activities. However, even though it is clear that there is no organization without cognition, we cannot extend this feature as something describing the organization as a whole, the same way it would be difficult to argue that an organization is human because it cannot be without humans. It is the same logical fallacy mentioned above in its reverse capacity.

While organizations are complex systems by definition, cognition can be simple or complex depending on a multitude of elements. For example, when cognition involves repeated actions, such as the interpretation of the n-th invoice from a supplier, the convergence of stratified (long term) meanings and current numbers make it rather simple. On the contrary, interacting with multiple colleagues during a meeting to discuss the strategic positioning of the company with effects for the next five years to come make it complex. The two examples may be classified based on unpredictability of the consequences stemming from the action taken (processing the invoice vs speaking to colleagues), structural constraints (rules of interpretation vs rules of appropriate speech in a meeting, company history, meeting history), local constraints (the invoice vs colleagues, room, shared ideas, norms, etc.), personal connections (knowing the suppliers vs colleagues, allies/enemies, political games, etc.). From this perspective, not only the second instance is more complex than the first, but it is – I claim – more interesting from a scientific point of view.

By considering the complex nested sets of interactions that individuals find themselves in organizations it is possible to provide an additional layer in the understanding of organizational complexity and, at the same time, it is possible to further our understanding of cognition as essentially social.

The answer to the question in the heading of the subsection on whether cognition is complex is varied. It can be complex and, when considered within organizations, the most scientifically salient manifestations of cognition are those of a complex phenomenon.

1.2.3   How to Study Organizational Cognition

If organizations are complex systems that would benefit from the study of cognition, we are then in need of instruments that allow this agenda to come to life.

Tools for the study of complexity are not very popular among MOR and MOC. In spite of the many statements that substantiate organizations as complex systems, very few have followed up these conceptual declarations. There is no point to analyze the reasons why this is the case and how we got there. However, I can certainly mention the fact that I came to work on computational models because of the dissatisfaction with current methods.

Among circles of computer scientists and, more recently, computational social scientists, agent-based computational simulation modeling (ABM) has been developed and used to study complex systems (Edmonds & Meyer, 2017b). These models allow to replicate or create features of complex systems and are among the most suited to study organizations (Fioretti, 2013; Secchi, 2015). The tool is flexible enough such that it can take into account interactions, unpredictability as well as emergent properties of the system.

As apparent from the above, I am not applying ABM to the "making sense" part of the process, to the interpretation of cognition in an old-fashioned cognitivist approach. Rather, I am considering the cognitive system – a wider distributed system – where the ecology of different elements interact. This allows me (the modeler) to make various assumptions on cognitive resources, flows, dynamics, information, and content.

In other words, I am moving the epicenter of the study of cognition by emphasizing systemic synergies and eco-systemic features of the processes. This way, one can study how the different parts interact and explore the inter-dependent dynamics of cognition.

1.3   Setting the Scene

The field of organizational cognition has been rather static over the last two decades, with little or no movement from claims that are dear to the traditional information processing view. While MOR underwent a cognitive revolution, the field of cognitive science was also changing significantly with the advent of Hutchins' (1995a) distributed cognition and with Clark's (1998) extended view. Yet, after 20 years, MOR scholars still look skeptically at these views, with a few noticeable exceptions (see Michel, 2007; Heavey & Simsek, 2017, albeit only partially). Maybe this is due to the fact that the cognitive tradition in organization research is still considered "new" or too "tentative" to undergo another "revolution." Or, maybe, this is because research is conducted by scholars with a limited expertise in cognition. Another explanation could be that there is a level of content with the current state of research on cognition, due to the many advancements that this traditional approach has been able to provide.

One of the issues may be that a perspective, if not a theory, of organizational cognition is missing. This book aims at describing a perspective – that of *socially distributed cognition* – and a theory – that of *social organizing* – that takes on from the EDEC perspectives and moves on by highlighting its relevance for most organizational behavior topics, including teams, groups, decision making, problem solving, and leadership, among others.

This exercise has the potential to achieve two simultaneous strong goals. On the one hand, it aims at renovating organizational behavior by infusing a radically different perspective on some of its most traditional topics. The EDEC perspectives have now reached maturity and they are now relatively easy to operationalize. This makes the timing of this book particularly appropriate. On the other hand, the book talks to the community of scholars that work under the assumptions of that paradigm. By studying the "social" in its natural environment – i.e. the organization – one contributes to move the boundaries of the perspective on to uncertain adaptive and complex situations, where cognition is not reduced to performing one or multiple tasks.

In short, the book talks to both management and cognition scholars. And there is more to it. In fact, as the title makes clear, this work uses a computational approach to the study of organizational cognition, specifically *agent-based computational simulation modeling*. Computational simulation is not new in MOR – since the famous Garbage Can Model (Cohen, March, & Olsen, 1972) it has been an accepted (better: tolerated) method of enquiry. However, its use has been scarce and, over the decades, very few studies have appeared from within the field (for details, see Secchi, 2015). While cognition-related simulation models have appeared in other disciplines (e.g., Carley, Prietula, & Lin, 1998; Conte, 1999), they are yet to do so in MOR. Why agent-based computational simulation modeling? By answering this question, I believe I can also indirectly tackle the issue of the absence of cognition modeling in MOR.

There are two main reasons for the choice of agent-based modeling (ABM). One is that the theoretical framework that comes out from an EDEC perspective on organizational cognition is rather complex and articulated. At least, much more than the traditional input-output information processing view. This simply requires analytical tools that are capable of exploring, illustrating, validating, and unveiling emerging key aspects of complex social phenomena such as those around organizational cognition. Agent-based computational simulation has been repeatedly indicated as a technique that is capable of doing just that (see the selection of chapters in the most recent edition of the Handbook by Edmonds & Meyer, 2017b).

The other main reason is that "computation" is also used as a label for the traditional input-output information processing view. But this computational view of cognition in organizations got stuck very early due to the simplicity of the mechanisms that its founders envisaged (Simon, 1955, 1997/1947). By using computation as a root for generating complex adaptive systems where emergent unpredictable behaviors appear, one may read this agent-based-oriented approach to cognition in continuity with that tradition. More advanced techniques allow, however, to move the discussion much further, and away from a simple input-output matrix. The computation of agent-workers' cognition happens through interactions with other agent-workers. This unveils a cognition that moves its bounds while workers make sense of the local "reality," hence giving to the expression "bounded rationality" a whole new meaning – perhaps more tied to Simon's view but impossible to reproduce with the technical tools of his time. In other words, this new computational view has the potential to reinvigorate and infuse new life to a tradition that was almost abandoned in the recent past. I call it *computational revival.*

1.4 What to Expect

Organizational cognition (OC) is an expression that has been around for about 30 years, ever since the so-called "cognitive revolution" took place in the field of organizational behavior (Ilgen, Major, & Spencer, 1994; Walsh, 1995). From this perspective, there seem to be nothing new in that this book falls within the line of that same tradition (see also Hodgkinson & Healey, 2008a). However, most – if not all – of the studies falling under the 'organizational cognition' label take a very orthodox view on what cognition is. As Billy Adamsen and I show in a recent publication (2017), this view considers cognition as information processing, where the brain takes the whole stage to explain anything cognitive. This approach is in line with the tradition initiated by Simon, March, and continued by Kahneman, Tversky, Gigerenzer, Todd, Gavetti, Levinthal, and many others in MOR who take individuals as bounded cognitive processing *machines.*[3] This implies a simple input–output scheme, where information is disembodied, rationality is mostly achieved by aseptic cold reasoning, the situation in which something happens is only sometimes relevant, and time (and timing) is not a key feature but has an ancillary role at best. Even if seldom explicitly declared, all these aspects indicate a solipsistic view that has not abandoned the idea that the human brain works like a computer.

The many difficulties associated with the view above have been explored in another monograph (Secchi, 2011), where I present a review of the literature on bounded rationality and indicate how a wider view opens it up, making bounds more dynamic and more suited to organizational behavior research. The social side of cognition is the most relevant aspect that is missing in the work coming from the tradition mentioned above. There is some work by Weick (1993) and by Weick and others (Weick & Roberts, 1993; Weick & Sutcliffe, 2006) that attempts to overcome the focus on input-output and computation. This perspective – called *sensemaking* – moves to an "interpretive" approach (Lant & Shapira, 2000), but is still very much individual-centric (Secchi & Adamsen, 2017; Secchi & Cowley, 2020). In order to understand how cognitive mechanisms operate – emerge, develop, evolve, change, and disappear – in organizations, one cannot avoid interactions between people as well as with social and non-social artifacts. This leads to consider cognition as a *through doing* process (i.e. enacted; see Magnani, 2007),

---

[3]This word has not landed here by chance, see Chapter 2.

where a classic input-output scheme would not be sufficient because sometimes, for example, an input is such through behavior (e.g., writing an email) and an output can always be re-used as an input before it becomes the actual output of the process. It also forces us to re-introduce the role of feelings, moods, perceptions, and beliefs (or embodiment) into the mix when discussing cognition. This means that people exploit their bodily reactions, together with artifacts, and other human beings as part of their cognizing (i.e. they extend their cognition). The obvious consequence is that there is a situational milieu that affects the way a cognitive process is shaped; in fact, one may just write that cognition is always embedded in a given situation. And this points at an ecology of space/time elements (systemic aspects) that are to be considered any time one approaches the study of cognition in organizations.

These simple aspects are key to dismiss some of the claims of the traditional view and, at the same time, they can be used to improve some others. Part I, *In Search for a Theory of Organizational Cognition*, begins with Chapter 2 where I introduce the state-of-the-art in MOC research. Chapter 3 and Chapter 4 respectively summarize the original EDEC perspectives and some of their more recent advancements. The last chapter in Part I, Chapter 5 is a bridge to the following part of the book and frames *socially distributed cognition* to show the limits of traditional modeling.

Part II, *Agent-based Computational Organizational Cognition*, is then tasked with testing and developing the theory outlined in Part I. After an introductory chapter on agent-based modeling (Chapter 6), Part II presents four computational simulation models. Each one tackles with an aspect considered problematic in the previous one so that the model of diffusion presented in Chapter 7 suggests that socially distributed cognitive processes (conceptualized as docile) may be too much reliant on groups and encourage mindlessness. The model presented in Chapter 8 is a study on the limits of docility to understand which organizational, group, and individual conditions enable mindlessness. One way to extend the theory was that of breaking free from one of its underlying assumptions – i.e. that community (e.g., groups, teams) is a necessary enabler of virtuous behavior. Chapter 9 presents a model where some team members are not bound to their team but communicate with members of other teams in order to solve a problem. Another way conceptualize socially distributed cognition (docility) would be that of testing which one of the EDEC perspectives influences it more directly. Chapter 10 features a model that compares aspects of extended and distributed cognitive strategies as organizational teams take on existing and new tasks.

The final Part III, *The Larger Picture*, builds on the models presented in Part II to infuse what presented in Part I and outline a theory of cognition in organizations that is called the theory of *social organizing*. This cycle is explained in Chapter 11, where I move from theory to the models and then back to theory. The proposed theory is then presented in Chapter 12 while Chapter 13 outlines the advantages of employing *agent-based computational organizational cognition* (AOC) and define cognition around change as opposed to its bounds.

The material in the book is inspired by my work on cognition. By reflecting on previous work, I will summarize some of it and expand it to other aspects. Most of the theory outlined in the book have or will have appeared in various articles by the time the book is published. However, never such theory has been collected in just one place, nor its assumptions and underpinnings have been explained in such detail. In other words, the articles present a semi-disconnected partial perspective (at best) that is missing a general overview. This book serves the function of showing this unifying thread in my theory work. At the same time, the book presents a computational approach to organizational cognition that has not been fully articulated before.

Unlike the theory part, all of the agent-based simulations have been published in various articles. Apart from parts of the code, the materials presented in this book is completely original because it serves a purpose different than that of the articles. In fact, the purpose of the book is to build a consistent theory of socially distributed organizational cognition that is based on computational work. Three of the agent-based models can be retrieved online from OpenABM, an online platform for simulation modelers, while another is on Github. Given the scope of the book, all the models are presented in a new reinvigorating fashion, they produce sets of new results (when needed), and are used to discuss implications from the theory in the Part I and to develop the theory further (Part III).

Part I
In Search for a Theory of Organizational Cognition

2

Managerial and Organizational Cognition: What's Not to Like?

"A science that neglects its past is bound to repeat its mistakes and will be unable to visualize its developments."
– Varela, Thompson, and Rosch, (1991, p. 37)

The opening quote of this chapter is a warning that Varela et al. (1991) direct to themselves, when they start their review of cognitivism in cognitive science. It is a general warning for me, as I write this book, to look at the literature so far produced in organizational cognition (OC) with a critical eye. I hope this eye is not too critical, though.

This chapter is dedicated to an overview of research on OC performed by management scholars. As already mentioned in Chapter 1, this goes under the label of MOC, a division of the US-based Academy of Management. By presenting a review of this literature, I intend to isolate main trends, keywords, and understand where the field is going. Besides these aims, Chapter 2 is a foundation for what is to come. In fact, as it will become clear from reading this chapter and especially from Chapter 3 onwards, the views portrayed in this chapter are partially based on a dissatisfaction with some of the dominant MOC approaches.

Computational Organizational Cognition:
A Study on Thinking and Action in Organizations, 17–35
Copyright © 2021 by Emerald Publishing Limited
All rights of reproduction in any form reserved
doi: 10.1108/978-1-83867-511-020211002

In the following pages, I summarize the theory-inspired approach Billy Adamsen and I have used to identify the most common approaches to OC. A review of the literature that emerged in the last 20 years is then presented and analyzed. The chapter ends with a few "lessons learned" as a bridge to the next chapter.

2.1 Alternative Approaches to Organizational Cognition

In a book chapter written a few years ago, Billy Adamsen and I (Secchi & Adamsen, 2017) dissect the possibilities in which the topic areas of *cognition* and *organization* relate to each other. This is not done by reviewing the literature to determine how these two domain are framed. Instead, we take a conceptual approach and outline the ways in which the topic area of *cognition* (C), on the one hand, and of *organization* (O), on the other hand, can be considered. By the use of Venn diagrams, we isolated about four alternative ways to relate the two topic areas that can be said to belong to the field of OC:

(a) *Additive*: $C + O$ – The two topic areas are kept as separated domains, and they are simply added one to the other, depending on research enquiries. This is how one could frame Herbert Simon's research (Newell & Simon, 1972; Simon, 1979), for example, in that his attempt was to bring cognition research in other domains, without adaptation. The approach could be also called juxtaposition.

(b) *Combination*: $C \cup O$ – The two areas are still considered separate domains, but there is some cross-fertilization that make them share some common ground; the approach includes, for example, sensemaking and its derivatives (e.g., Weick, 1993). This is an all-encompassing approach where combination is sought at large, but there are no attempts to change one domain by means of the other.

(c) *Intersection*: $C \cap O$ – Similar to (b), with the exception that this approach only focuses on what the two share, without explicit reference to the topic areas as a whole. Research on shared cognition is a typical example (e.g., Cannon-Bowers & Salas, 2001).

(d) *Conditional*: $C \mid O$ – Cognition is one of the many aspects one could use to study organizations; this implies that typical organizational behavior research (e.g., leadership, decision making, team dynamics) is accompanied by a cognitive element. In their literature review, this is what Hodgkinson & Healey (2008a) mostly cover. It is a general approach that studies one phenomenon, typically within the organization domain, given another in the cognition domain.

There are other ways in which the two areas can be organized to conceptualize their relations (see Secchi & Adamsen, 2017, note 2, p. 313), but the four above are a good approximation of how scholars have approached studies in OC in the past decades.

Another way in which OC literature can be looked at is by taking a perspective and zooming in. This is what I do in the first part of *Extendable Rationality* (Secchi, 2011), where I present an overview of the two traditional research streams in bounded rationality: the biases paradigm and the heuristics paradigm. Bounded rationality is an approach, some claim a theory (Grandori & Cholakova, 2013; Rubinstein, 1998), to decision-making that posits humans have two sets of limitations. One is a limit on the access to information that is necessary to make a decision while the other is a constraint on processing cognitive capabilities. First introduced by Herbert Simon (1947 /1997, 1955), bounded rationality has been further developed (Gavetti, Levinthal, & Ocasio, 2007) and used by many (more on this in later chapters; Foss, 2003).

The biases paradigm was initiated by Kahneman, Tversky, and colleagues (e.g., Tversky & Kahneman, 1974; Kahneman & Tversky, 1979; Kahneman, 2003), while the heuristics paradigm can be associated with Gigerenzer and colleagues (e.g., Gigerenzer & Selten, 2001; Gigerenzer, Todd, & Group, 1999; Todd & Gigerenzer, 2003). These approaches have been and are still applied to organization and management in specific domains – e.g., negotiation (Neale & Bazerman, 1991), advice taking (Yaniv, 2004; Yaniv & Kleinberger, 2000), risk aversion (Benartzi and Thaler, 1999) – to gauge cognitive aspects of human behavior.

In this chapter, I am not taking either approach, rather I am building on them and using them as benchmarks. The following pages are an attempt to answer questions such as "what are the main streams of literature that have populated OC research in the last twenty years" and "has the field as a whole moved and in which direction." The intention is not to present a comprehensive literature review, but that of introducing literature that captures trends and most popular research areas.

2.2 Organizational Cognition in the Literature

Using one of the largest databases of academic scholarly work, i.e. Elsevier's Scopus, I have performed three simple searches. I looked for publications where variations of the the words "cognition" and "organization" appeared either in the title, abstract, or author-supplied keywords. The search has been limited to the last 20 years, from 2000 to

1999, excluding 2020, the year in which this book has been written. The other limitation concerns the subject areas. Even though it may seem difficult that the two search strings appear in areas other than management, they do. One of the most influential reviews of the literature, the one conducted by Hodgkinson and Healey (2008a), was published in a psychology journal. Hence, since it is difficult to make an a priori judgment about where authors may have published, the subject area of this search includes sources from the entirety of humanities and social sciences.

The search does not discriminate between journals, book chapters, or other publication types. Initial results show 438 documents of which 33 conference papers,[1] 1 retracted article, 1 duplicate, and 1 categorized as being of undefined type were excluded. Of the remaining 402 documents, Scopus identifies the following subject areas as the most populated: 202 from "Business, Management and Accounting," 141 from "Psychology," 140 from "Social Sciences," and 50 from "Arts and Humanities." There are other 13 relatively "minor" areas that are not reported here. As apparent from these numbers, there can be multiple subject areas for an article, such that the sum of subject areas does not coincide with 402. This is quite natural, since there are many journals that appeal to multiple disciplines. It still gives an idea of general trends.

Fig. 2.1 shows the annual trends for papers published on OC in the humanities and social sciences. The figure also draws the lines for the four most prolific subject areas indicated in the previous paragraph. Overall, the solid dark slate blue line seem to indicate there are two periods, one before and one after 2011. Before that year, annual publications reach the number 20 only once in 2007 with a mean publication-per-year of 12.5. After 2011 publications are always above 20, with mean = 31.6. The trend is driven by numbers in Management, Business and Accounting, represented by the dashed red firebrick line and by the publications categorized as Social Sciences, the dash-dotted dark blue line.

The following step in the analysis is that of understanding what is in the 402 articles to try and isolate common themes. There are many ways in which this can be done but, given the number of sources and the two questions above, the best way to proceed is that of using bibliometric tools for the analysis. In the next section, I focus on the entirety of the publications to understand most common keywords and trends.

---

[1]Excluded only because information on whether those are peer-reviewed sources and/or whether they are abstracts or full articles was not available at the time of the search.

Fig. 2.1. Organizational Cognition in the Literature (2000–2019; Publications Per Year; Scopus Database).

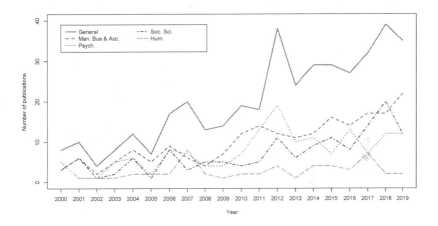

Note: *Base search string*: TITLE-ABS (organizat*) OR TITLE-ABS (organisat*) AND TITLE-ABS (cogniti*) AND AUTHKEY (organizat*) OR AUTHKEY (organisat*) AND AUTHKEY (cogniti*) AND SUBJAREA (arts OR busi OR deci OR econ OR psyc OR soci) AND PUBYEAR > 1999 AND PUBYEAR < 2020 AND (EXCLUDE (DOCTYPE , "cp") OR EXCLUDE (DOCTYPE , "tb") OR EXCLUDE (DOCTYPE , "Undefined")).

2.3 Bibliometric Analysis of General Publishing Trends in Organizational Cognition

The analysis is carried over by keywords first, then by co-citation analysis, and then by bibliographic coupling. In order for these analyses to be carried out successfully, the file downloaded from the Scopus database needs to be screened, for example, to align keywords that differ only by spelling and/or by expressions that are similar but not identical. The software, any software, would consider irrelevant differences as differences nevertheless, and this may ultimately affect the analysis.

Once this preliminary data preparation stage is finished, all analyses are conducted with the software `VOSviewer` (version 1.6.15) (Van Eck & Waltman, 2010, 2014) that allows to visualize different clusters, visible by different colors in a network, and classified either by author or keyword. Social Network Analysis (SNA) calculations are instead performed using `R` a statistical computing software (R Core Team, 2019), package `igraph` (Csardi & Nepusz, 2006).

2.3.1   Keywords Co-occurrence

Fig. 2.2 presents a map of the most recurring author-supplied keywords. The system indicates that there are 37 keywords that are used by authors more than five times. Some of these keywords are connected with other keywords, while some others may not be. In fact, of the 37, 5 are not connected to any other keyword in the map and, for this reason, they have been excluded from the analysis. Since they are relatively popular, it is worth mentioning them: *knowledge organization, organizational citizenship behavior, perceptual organization, cognitive organization*, and *depression*. The last two keywords are connected to each other.

Fig. 2.2. Most Recurrent Author Supplied Keywords (2000–2019, 35 Nodes, Scopus Database).

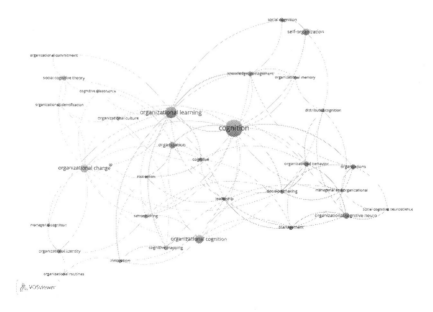

In Fig. 2.2, the visualization is such that the strength of ties between two keywords is a count of how many times those two appear together. The software `VOSviewer` indicates that there are five clusters, visible by different colors in the map. They are organized around keywords that occur the most. Table 2.1 specifies what is in the map by indicating the first three most recurrent keywords per cluster, then proposes a label for each cluster, and presents some statistics that summarize its influence. The statistics reported are the mean number of times a keyword occurs in a given cluster as well as how many links they have on average. Both statistics are accompanied by standard deviation, so that it is easy to understand how much dispersion is there within each cluster.

Table 2.1. Clusters, Labels, Average Occurrences and Links.

Clusters	Keywords (*first three by #links*)	Label	Occurrences		Links	
			Mean	*St.dev.*	*Mean*	*St.dev*
Cluster 1 (N = 8)	decision making leadership MOC	*micro approach*	6.33	1.77	8.38	2.56
Cluster 2 (N = 7)	organizational cognition sensemaking cognitive mapping	*processing*	5.29	2.43	9.29	4.96
Cluster 3 (N = 6)	organizational change organizational culture cognitive dissonance	*macro approach*	5.83	3.92	9.33	5.09
Cluster 4 (N = 6)	organizational learning distributed cognition knowledge management	*learning*	5.83	3.76	12.67	8.59
Cluster 5 (N = 5)	cognition cognitive organization	*cognition*	7.20	4.60	16.60	17.98
TOTAL (N = 32)			6.12	3.12	10.84	8.52

Note. MOC: managerial and organizational cognition.

First, let me exclude Cluster 5 from the analysis, because this seems to contain keywords that are obvious (e.g., cognition, cognitive, organization), given the selection of papers I have operated. Among the remaining four, Cluster 1 is the most populated and it also features the higher mean number of occurrences, 6.33, with a relatively small standard deviation of 1.77. Given the focus on the individual as a center of analysis, this set of keywords all refer to a *micro* self-centered perspective of cognition.

Cluster 2, Cluster 3, and Cluster 4 are all very similar when we look at the average occurrence of their keywords, but they differ as far as connections to other keywords are concerned. While Cluster 1 has its strength on occurrences, its keywords are the least connected to the rest of the network with 8.38 links on average. An approach that is, instead, very much connected to the rest of the network is Cluster 4, one that groups keywords that are very much concerned with *learning*. Not only this is done with a micro perspective similar to that of Cluster 1 (e.g., organizational learning, knowledge management), but it seems to include more ecological and systemic perspectives such as those belonging to distributed cognition. The average number of links for keywords in Cluster 4 is 12.67 (with a relatively large standard deviation = 8.59; see below for more comments on this).

Cluster 2 and Cluster 3 are very similar both in terms of occurrences and of links. They are also similar in the underlying constructs they use. Cluster 3 is more explicitly leaning toward *macro* approaches by referring to, for example, structural aspects of the organizational life such as culture and change. Cluster 2 also refers to some of these structural aspects, such as routines, but it probably takes a more micro perspective on them, by looking at the way these are *processed* by individuals (e.g., the reference on sensemaking or cognitive mapping).

Overall, the picture offered by Fig. 2.2 and Table 2.1 is still incomplete because it hints at possible influence of keywords by their location in the network and by the analytical data from the clusters. However, I believe the analysis still misses a number of more concrete indications of influence. For this to be done, one could use the tools of Social Network Analysis and try to understand how each keyword stands in relation to the others in the network. Table 2.2 calculates three measures of centrality, *eigenvector*, *e*, *betweenness*, *b*, and *closeness*, *c*. The first is a measure of the influence of each one of the nodes in the network, and ranks nodes in relation to their own links, especially if they are linked to other well-connected nodes. Since it is influence I am after, I have used this to order the keywords. Table 2.2 presents the first 16 keywords (50% of the total number), ranked according to the value of their *eigenvector* centrality, or *e*. *Betweenness* centrality, *b*, of a node measures the number of shortest paths connecting two other nodes and passing though the node. *Closeness* centrality, *c*, is just an average number of paths connecting the node to every other node in the network.

The picture that emerges from Table 2.2 sheds some light on what discussed previously. As expected, Cluster 5 features prominently in this

Table 2.2. Eigenvector, Betweenness, and Closeness Centrality Measures for the Most Recurring 16 Keywords in the Organizational Cognition Literature (2000–2019).

#	Keyword	Cluster	Eigenvector	Betweenness	Closeness
1.	cognition	5	1.00	85.61	0.65
2.	organizational change	3	0.77	70.30	0.60
3.	organizational learning	4	0.69	86.03	0.61
4.	organizational cognition	2	0.66	26.39	0.55
5.	decision making	1	0.65	13.63	0.54
6.	sensemaking	2	0.58	14.69	0.54
7.	organizational behavior	1	0.56	13.94	0.49
8.	man. and org. cognition	1	0.52	19.52	0.49
9.	cognitive	5	0.51	13.08	0.53
10.	leadership	1	0.51	33.47	0.56
11.	organizational culture	3	0.51	14.60	0.53
12.	organization	5	0.46	6.27	0.48
13.	cognitive mapping	2	0.46	13.53	0.54
14.	knowledge management	4	0.42	10.78	0.52
15.	organizations	1	0.41	13.49	0.47
16.	management	1	0.39	6.73	0.47

table with "cognition" being by far the most influential keyword with $e = 1.00$ as well as the closest one with $c = 0.65$. Surprisingly, it is not the most central by means of being in-between two other keywords, scoring a value of $b = 85.61$ that is second to the value for "organizational learning," i.e. $b = 86.03$. Overall, the study of how change affects cognition in organizations (Cluster 3) occupies a very high position in the influence scale with $e = 0.77$, followed by "organizational learning" (Cluster 4) with $e = 0.69$. The *processing* cluster comes next with the keyword "organizational cognition" and $e = 0.66$, but *betweenness* is particularly low $b = 26.39$, suggesting this is not a well connected keyword, but probably one that is connected to more influential others. Next comes "decision making" (Cluster 1) with $e = 0.65$, but showing the same problems of the previous keyword with an even lower measure of $b = 13.63$.

If one considers the 16 keywords together, we can confirm what we have seen from Table 2.1 and Fig. 2.2 in that: (a) Cluster 1 has a strong numerical presence but its keywords are not very influential nor well connected, (b) Cluster 2 has also a good presence with two keywords in the top 6 but overall low b and average c, (c) both Cluster 3 and 4 have very strong influence and at least one keyword that has strong b and above average c.

The conclusion that can be drawn from the analysis above is that there probably still is an emphasis on cognition as information processing and, at the same time, research strives to connect these micro aspects to more macro structural organizational phenomena. The question to ask is one about the theories that are used more often, in order to qualify this first reading of the literature.

2.3.2 Co-citation Analysis

The 402 publications count 25,781 references in total. Co-citation analysis serves the purpose of understanding the most relevant trends in this literature, by isolating the references that have been used most commonly. This allows one to infer something about the most popular theories in use. By using the software `VOSviewer`, I started with the number five, meaning that a reference should appear in the reference list of the 402 articles at least five times. There are only 22 publications that meet this threshold and that is unsatisfactory in terms of how much inference one could make. If the threshold is down to four, then we have 47, and if it is three, there are 157 references. For clarity purposes and following a need to focus on the most recurrent patterns, I have selected the 47 references that are used at least by four of the 402 publications. A portion of this map appears in Fig. 2.3, where those references that were not connected to the others are not shown in the network. These are Tolman (1948), a very early work discussing cognitive maps, Rafferty (2001) on knowledge in library classification schemes, Cacioppo, Petty, and Feng Kao (1984) on the assessment of needs, and Nicholson (2001) connected to another source that I was not able to locate.[2]

The image in Fig. 2.3 is not easy to read, because the references are truncated. However, these are all very well cited publications and it is not difficult to recognize both authors and source. I consider a most recurring reference as a proxy for wider tendencies toward the study of related topics.

Fig. 2.3. Co-citation Analysis (2000–2019; 42 Publications; Scopus Database).

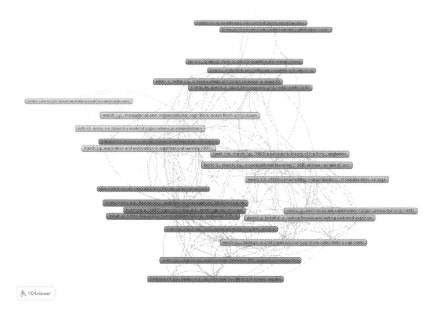

The first observation on Fig. 2.3 is that all the references belong to classic streams of management literature. Among the authors who feature most prominently are Weick, March, and Walsh. One may imme-diately connect them to a series of topics that feature prominently in the OC literature. In fact, from Fig. 2.3, it is apparent that sensemaking (Gioia & Chittipeddi, 1991; Weick, 1995), organizational learning (Cyert & March, 1963; Levitt & March, 1988; March, 1991), and organizational

---

[2]It appears cited as Azar, B., 2002. Advice for a Young Investigator.

memory (Walsh, 1995; Walsh & Ungson, 1991) are among the core topics.

By observing this map further, it is possible to identify four clusters. Some references (e.g., Walsh & Ungson, 1991; Walsh, 1995; Gioia & Chittipeddi, 1991) appear twice, due to difference in formatting that the software was not able to combine (in spite of the algorithm it uses to prevent this from happening). Nevertheless, the map is still telling although it makes clusters slightly less meaningful. For this reason, it probably makes sense to isolate main tendencies across these clusters. One such tendencies is represented by studies of *dynamic capabilities*, typically falling into the area of strategic management. Here, classic studies by Teece (2007); Teece, Pisano, and Shuen (1997); Adner and Helfat (2003) are among those that feature more prominently. As a partial justification as the reason why there is an apparently macro approach in OC studies, Hodgkinson & Healey (2011) indicate that there is a tendency to study the micro foundations of strategic managerial decision-making. This is also what Gioia & Chittipeddi (1991) try to do with their sensemaking approach.

Another tendency develops around the classic themes of bounded rationality (Simon, 1997/1947) and, more broadly, *decision making*. It is very interesting to see that Newell and Simon (1972) still has influence in the field after so many years from its publication. Clearly, Tversky and Kahneman (1974); Kahneman and Tversky (1979) have been rather influential, together with various topics of James G. March's work (March, 1991; Levitt & March, 1988) and of March-inspired work (Cohen & Levinthal, 1990). The stream of sensemaking, even though, according to Weick (1993) it can be considered as an alternative explanation to decision-making, is still related to this perspective and features very significantly among co-cited studies (Gioia & Chittipeddi, 1991; Weick, 1995; Weick, Sutcliffe, & Obstfeld, 2005).

From the above, one could attempt to isolate main theoretical trends as well. Among those that are cited more often is Ajzen (1991) and the *Theory of Planned Behavior*. This is not surprising, given the extent to which Ajzen's work features in management research in general and given the fact that, in the OC literature selected, there are many who look into cognition from an applied psychology perspective even among authors of this small collection (Hodgkinson & Healey, 2008a, 2011; Kozhevnikov, 2007). The application of *Social Identity Theory* to management (Ashforth & Mael, 1989) is another one that is among those cited. Again, this is not at all surprising, given how popular this theory has been among management scholars. I have already cited bounded rationality and, although that is not a theory (at least, this is what some argue; see Foss, 2003) the *Behavioral Theory of the Firm* (Cyert

& March, 1963) and *Prospect Theory* (Kahneman & Tversky, 1979) certainly can be considered as representative of this perspective on decision-making. The attempt to theorize on *Organizational Learning* (Argyris & Schön, 1978) and the other to theorize on *neuroscience* and their contribution to organization research (Becker, Cropanzano, & Sanfey, 2011) are among those that should also be mentioned. Finally, the influential *Cognition in the Wild* (Hutchins, 1995a) also features, if not among theories, certainly among the perspectives that have been co-cited the most.

To further confirm the results seen in Fig. 2.3 I have also performed a co-citation analysis by using author names instead of references. I have obtained a network of 169 authors that have been cited at least 20 times. This was done to make sure that the references in the map were not biased or too much prone to error. The map – not reported here – is consistent with the co-citation analysis as discussed in these pages. There are some differences in relation to co-authors, but the top cited names are in line. Just to give an example, top of the list are: (1) Weick, with 183 citations, (2) March has 142, (3) Simon 117, (4) Bandura and (4) Hodgkinson are next with 87 each, (5) Dutton has 81, (6) Kahneman 74, (7) Senior 71, (8) Gioia 68, and finally, (9) Nonaka and (9) Gavetti have 64 each.

There are at least two major considerations on this co-citation analysis. First, the mean year of the cited publications is 1991 and the median is 1992, not too distant from it. One may think that this is natural, since the range of publications selected for the analysis is 2000–2019 and it is just normal that citations refer, on average, to sources published before 2000. However, this is a faulty line of reasoning. For studies published in the first decade, it is probably natural to refer to research appearing in the previous decade and earlier. However, this is not a necessity. Authors should strive to cite up-to-date research as much as possible. Still, old theories are usually better established than newer ones, and I also use them in my writings, just like the authors that feature in this analysis. The point here is that, as shown in Fig. 2.1, most OC publications appeared after 2011. If the reasoning above is applied, then the second decade would still use mainly research appearing in the previous decade. And the weight of this second decade would be much heavier, simply due to their larger numbers. Instead, as already mentioned at the beginning of this paragraph, the median is 1992. To make things worse, the fourth quartile – where the most recent 25% of citations lie – starts at 2000, still 20 years ago. The most recent co-cited reference dates 2011. The conclusion is that there is a bias toward more established theories rather a tendency toward innovation.

Second, these results confirm what already argued in Secchi and Adamsen (2017). There we highlight how sensemaking is the most advanced theoretical approach in the OC literature. This is because this tradition has incorporated some aspects typical of the embodied cognition tradition, namely the situated and embeddedness perspectives. Cognition is, according to sensemaking theory, always circumstantial and related to a given context (Weick, 1993), hence it is situated. At the same time, understanding what happens in this situation needs artifacts and people to be contemplated, and this points at embeddedness (Weick & Roberts, 1993). The appearance of Hutchins (1995a) among the co-cited references indicates a possible movement forward, but it is hard to see it clearly. This is because, by simply counting occurrences and link strengths, prevalence is still coming from bounded rationality and more traditional approaches to cognition. These perspectives view cognition as pertaining to the self, an individual, as the core element of reasoning (e.g., Hodgkinson & Healey, 2008a) as well as they frame it as having the function of information processor (e.g., Argyris & Schön, 1978; Cyert & March, 1963; Newell & Simon, 1972). The vast majority of the co-cited references in Fig. 2.3 fall into this stream.

Overall, the OC literature seems to lean on relatively old references and their respective theories. This statement should not be interpreted as an a priori call for the new or as a way to interpret the old as eminently worse than the new. Some of the references above may be only ceremonial, meaning that authors use those references because they feel the pressure they should. Nevertheless, they indicate a field that is consolidating around past knowledge and is probably not reflecting enough on the directions in which to move its next steps. This is particularly relevant when one thinks of what happened to theories around cognition in the last 30 years. Much of the philosophical discussion is around the so-called distributed cognition revolution (starting from Hutchins, 1995a), a perspective that has evolved into different streams, by taking together the *embedded, embodied, enacted, ecological,* and *extended –* or simply *e-cognition –* approaches (more on these in Chapter 4 and Chapter 5). By stressing one approach or the other, different angles are highlighted although, at the same time, the need to consider them all together led some authors to propose a *systemic* cognitive perspective (Cowley & Vallée-Tourangeau, 2017).

Given the "Copernican" shift above, the impression that the OC literature gives is that of remaining still in the face of turbulence. Would this unconscious strategy pay off in the long run or would it condemn the area as we know it today to irrelevance? Of course, this is a provocative question and does not need nor it can be answered. However, the tendency already outlined after the analysis of keyword co-occurrence is confirmed. This is that the OC literature has been focusing on an individual micro/self perspective in an attempt to understand organizational phenomena.

2.3.3   Bibliographic Coupling Analysis

The final step of this analysis is that of running another check using yet another instrument. Like the one in Fig. 2.3, bibliographic coupling networks are made of publications that cite the same documents, hence they can be paired because they refer to the same underlying literature. These networks are useful to understand how central publications are in tackling the discourse in a particular area. The reasoning behind this is rather simple. When there is an increasing number of publications that use the same references, it is possible to identify a common ground on which scientific discourse is usually based in a particular field of studies. By looking at the most widely connected among these publications it is possible to have a clear representation of what is going on in a field.

The analysis is performed on the clusters that appear in Fig. 2.4, that is a visual representation of bibliographic couplings, and by using Table 2.3, that presents the top 20 publications (i.e. at the 0.95 percentile), ranked by influence in the network, i.e. *eigenvector* centrality, *e*.

Fig. 2.4. Bibliographic Coupling (2000–2019; 367 Publications; Scopus Database).

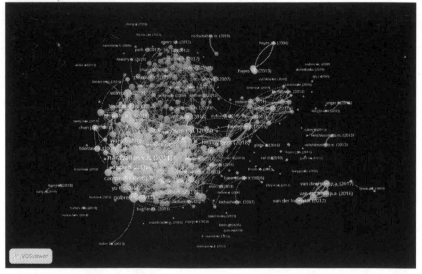

Let us start with Fig. 2.4. This is derived by taking the 402 publications appearing in the last 20 years and asking the VOSviewer software to connect those that cite similar streams of literature. This led to 367 connected publications, and leaves out 35 that were not. The software indicates the presence of 13 clusters and orders them by their size. The first five clusters count more than 20 connected references while the last three only have less than 5. From a visual perspective, Cluster 1 (99 publications) is made of red circles at the top of Fig. 2.4, Cluster 2 (75 publications) is green and is found at the right-hand side of the network, Cluster 3 (45 publications) is blue and distributed at the center of the figure leaning toward the bottom, Cluster 4 (38 publications) is yellow and it appears at the left-center, and Cluster 5 (24 publications) has a purple color and can be seen toward the bottom right of the cloud of circles.

Given the numbers involved in the clusters, Table 2.3 presents only the top 5% publications, classified by their relative influence in the network, *e*. The third column in the table connects it to Fig. 2.4 so that it becomes easier to map the papers to the cloud of circles in the network. The idea is that, by analyzing research in these publications, one could gather a clearer understanding of what has been covered in the OC literature in the last 20 years. As one may expect, many of the publications in the list are conceptual studies. In fact, the format of a conceptual study – e.g., model development, literature review, theory development – is more likely to elicit larger portions of the literature available to allow authors to fully elaborate their frameworks. This is the case of Narayanan, Zane, and Kemmerer (2011) where authors elaborate a model of the antecedents, structure, and outcomes of strategic cognition. A different example is that of Hodgkinson (2015), who succinctly reviews the main streams of literature in MOC starting from its history. Instead, Yu and Glynn (2015) present the theory of competitive memory by specifying applications of organizational memory. These three types – e.g., model, review, theory – repeat among the other publications.

Table 2.3 also includes empirical studies, some who are apparently well grounded in the bulk of research that constitutes the core of OC. For example, three studies in the top ten are empirical articles; Gnyawali, Stewart, and Grant (2005) describes knowledge acquisition through the informational and interactional processes of organizational members, Guiette and Vandenbempt (2013) explore how strategic change affects team mental model dynamics, and Thomas, Randolph, and Marin (2019) studies corporate entrepreneurship using an information processing paradigm and cognition-based trust.

Now, the question is whether the articles appearing in Table 2.3 and selected because of their centrality in the use of the most commonly cited literature confirm the previously outlined trends. The vast majority of these publications refer to a very standard paradigm of cognition as information processing, sometimes explicitly mentioned (Campbell & Armstrong, 2013; Thomas et al., 2019) while some others more implicitly so (Narayanan et al., 2011; Neill & Rose, 2006). The standard paradigm

Table 2.3. Eigenvector, Betweenness, and Closeness Centrality Measures for Bibliographic Coupling Analysis (at the 0.95 Percentile, 2000–2019).

# Keyword	Cluster	Eigenvector	Betweenness	Closeness
1. Narayanan et al. (2011)	9	1.00	1,137.73	0.59
2. Akgün, Lynn, & Byrne (2003)	4	0.96	3,806.37	0.60
3. Hodgkinson (2015)	9	0.94	1,029.70	0.57
4. Borghini (2005)	4	0.91	743.71	0.56
5. Gnyawali et al. (2005)	4	0.90	477.79	0.56
6. Guiette & Vandenbempt (2013)	3	0.90	670.66	0.57
7. Manral (2011)	8	0.89	455.24	0.55
8. Healey, Hodgkinson, and Massaro (2018)	2	0.88	5,940.04	0.61
9. Hodgkinson and Healey (2008a)	1	0.88	2,013.03	0.58
10. Thomas et al. (2019)	7	0.88	470.65	0.56
11. Campbell and Armstrong (2013)	4	0.87	395.68	0.55
12. Nobre and Walker (2011)	11	0.84	491.55	0.54
13. Secchi and Adamsen (2017)	5	0.83	767.74	0.55
14. Yu and Glynn (2015)	8	0.82	256.03	0.54
15. Weiss and Wittmann (2018)	6	0.79	1,271.31	0.55
16. Salaman (2001)	3	0.78	523.35	0.54
17. Nooteboom (2008)	10	0.77	1,910.77	0.56
18. Neill and Rose (2006)	9	0.77	254.86	0.53
19. Busby and Hibberd (2006)	3	0.76	266.26	0.53
20. Grewatsch and Kleindienst (2018)	6	0.76	357.02	0.53

takes many forms. For some, cognition is still the very classic computer-like brain of Simonian echoes (Campbell & Armstrong, 2013) while for others working on organizational memory (mainly inspired by Walsh & Ungson, 1991) cognition is still individual-centered but opens to some social processes (Akgün et al., 2003; Yu & Glynn, 2015). The use of more or less updated versions of Weick's sensemaking (Weick, 1993; Weick & Roberts, 1993) to characterize aspects of situated cognition is prevalent among many authors (Akgün et al., 2003; Guiette & Vandenbempt, 2013; Narayanan et al., 2011; Neill & Rose, 2006). Some interpret "situated" as a cognitive process that is located in an organizational space and characterized by social interactions (Thomas et al., 2019). Overall, there seems to be a diffused understanding of cognition *qua* learning (at least, this is my reading of Campbell & Armstrong, 2013) or as involved in some process that involves learning (Akgün et al., 2003; Grewatsch & Kleindienst, 2018; Nooteboom, 2008; Salaman, 2001; Thomas et al., 2019; Yu & Glynn, 2015) and/or knowledge handling (Borghini, 2005; Gnyawali, Stewart, & Grant, 2005).

A trend that is very much entrenched in many of these publications is the reference to strategic management, especially in relation to cognitive frames and tools for decision making (Manral, 2011; Narayanan et al., 2011; Thomas et al., 2019), team mental models (Guiette & Vandenbempt, 2013), dynamic capabilities (Grewatsch & Kleindienst, 2018; Nobre & Walker, 2011; Weiss & Wittmann, 2018; Yu & Glynn, 2015), learning (Nooteboom, 2008; Salaman, 2001), or complexity (Neill & Rose, 2006).

The above are all standard views on cognition that recall the analyses of the previous pages. Together with these, there are also a few openings on streams that refer to versions of distributed cognition. Apart from Secchi and Adamsen (2017) and Busby & Hibberd (2006) that position distributed cognition at the center of their analyses, others (Borghini, 2005) use a weak interpretation of it (Salomon, 1993) that puts the individual back in central position. In another case, Hodgkinson (2015) recognizes that "the 'taken-for-granted' notion that cognition resides exclusively in people's heads (as implied by stage-based human information processing models of decision making and skilled performance) is increasingly less tenable" (p. 480). In their chapter, Healey, Hodgkinson, and Massaro (2018) answer the question whether "brains can manage" by applying a Turing-like test and presenting literature that is connected to a distributed view.

All the above confirms the general trends as outlined in the previous pages, with some more specific information that can be used to draw implications and conclude this chapter.

2.4 Reflections on OC Trends

While presenting the analyses above, I have also sketched the findings. Given that the analysis has been divided in three parts, it is probably a good idea to summarize them here again, in a way to keep them all in one place.

One of the aspects that becomes apparent very early in the analysis is that the literature is probably less cross-disciplinary than scholars may think (e.g., Hodgkinson, 2015). In fact, publications mainly appear in management and applied psychology journals. In sporadic cases there is a reference to fields outside of the two above, but it is either in passing or to recognize a trend so vast in cognitive science that it has become difficult to ignore. This is the case of the distributed cognition literature, when one excludes those who dedicate their attention to it in full (e.g., Busby & Hibberd, 2006; Healey et al., 2018).

To circumstantiate what stated above, the analysis of keywords co-occurrence indicates that the main areas of research fall within domains that are typical of a management scholar's interests. Topics such as learning, change, decision-making, sensemaking, and leadership (Table 2.2) are all central to this area of research. This is circumstantiated further by the analysis of the most recurrent references. Many are from traditional management research (e.g., Cyert & March, 1963; March, 1991), others from psychology theories that are popular in management (e.g., Ajzen, 1991; Kahneman & Tversky, 1979), and others are still traditional but more tied to specific areas such as strategy (e.g., Adner & Helfat, 2003; Tripsas & Gavetti, 2000), sensemaking (e.g., Weick, 1995; Gioia & Chittipeddi, 1991), or organizational behavior (e.g., Levitt & March, 1988; Walsh & Ungson, 1991).

The overwhelming presence of management research in an area such as OC is expected. Not only these scholars were among the first to reserve a space to the area back in the Nineties (Ilgen, Major, & Spencer, 1994; Walsh, 1995), but they have also massively built on it by relentlessly applying mental models, frames, schemas, and other concepts typical of information processing to management. The 10 areas isolated by Hodgkinson & Healey (2008b) in their literature review are a testament to this dedication. From the analysis carried over in this chapter, I can only point at a few minor but relevant changes.

Before I can do that, I would like to stress this point once again. The literature on OC is dominated by publications in the area of *managerial and organizational cognition*. This is the way in which scholars associated with the US-based Academy of Management officially call this area of research. And this professional association of management scholars is – to date – the largest in the world, hence it is probably representative of the way in which most management scholars conceptualize it. Judging from the literature reviewed here, this exercise has been quite successful in that topics, areas, and methods are clearly the most widely diffused. In other words, it is fair to assume that a large portion of what I have called OC could have been labeled MOC. However, doing something like that I would have probably excluded or failed to emphasize the slight shift that has started to happen.

I am referring to the fact that this literature has started to acknowledge the presence of paradigms other than the classic information processing (coming mainly from the vast influence of Newell & Simon, 1972). This is a very positive finding, indeed. Even scholars whose names have been almost synonym to the traditional OC approach in management (e.g., Healey and Hodgkinson) have started to recognize that there is a broader view of cognition.

Let me be clear about this "gentle" turn in MOC. For reasons I explain in the next chapters of this book, the shift is coming when it is almost too late. By acknowledging that there is a view other than the classic in-the-scull perspective, some advocate a weak form of distribution (Borkar, 2005; Salomon, 1993) while others (e.g., Healey et al., 2018; Hodgkinson, 2015) seem to bridge philosophically distant views together such as those of Walsh and Ungson (1991) and Hutchins (1995a). In general, the most advanced view these scholars cite is that of Hutchins' *Cognition in the Wild*, that appeared in 1995. That is 25 years ago. The views on cognition – even Hutchins' own views – have evolved since then. The risk is that MOC scholars would pick views that are, once again, the past for cognitive science.

A reflection on the side – probably a digression – is that the word "information" does not feature anywhere, nor it seems to be discussed by OC scholars. Given that the exchange of data or information is one of the core tenants of cognitive processes, asking *what* it is exactly that is exchanged should be at least briefly discussed. Instead, most refer to knowledge, learning, memory, and other processes that imply the presence of some information. Even when they discuss information, as in applying Huber's (1991) model, there is little disclosure about what this actually is. I ask the question here, and come back to it in Part III as well as in Secchi (2020b).

The title of this Chapter 2 asks a question that is used to try and capture the attention of the (probably few) readers that come from MOC. Clearly, there is much to like about the attention that MOC scholars have put on cognition over the decades. As a result of those efforts, this area is now an established part of the management discipline. At the same time, the excessive strength with which most defend and attach themselves to traditional views is problematic. Each and every field is relatively rigid and impermeable to change. Yet, especially in science, too much methodological rigidity leads to sclerosis. This book is not an attack to MOC, it is a contribution to support the 'gentle' shift that has already started to appear in the research of some of its most prominent scholars.

Finally, I started the chapter with a reference to my work on ways to theoretically isolate trends in OC (Secchi & Adamsen, 2017). Most of what reviewed in that publication happened to be confirmed by the analysis here. However, back then we failed to see the shift toward more modern conceptualizations that I have been discussing in these pages. At the same time, we kind of hit the right places since the co-citation analysis posits that chapter among the top 5%, meaning that the literature we had been reading is the same used by MOC scholars.

2.5   Summary

The chapter has presented a review of the literature on OC that outlines that (a) most of it is still focused on a classic information processing view of cognition, (b) some take a more advanced stance (e.g., sensemaking), and, along these, (c) there are openings toward other views of cognition. The rest of this book builds on this latter trend and it starts in Chapter 3, with a quick refresher of what embodied/distributed/extended cognition is about.

3

Cognition Outside the Skull

"I seem to have a body which stretches into infinity."
– Spock, *Star Trek*, Season 3, Ep. 1: Spock's Brain

This chapter is an attempt to sketch the basic elements of distributed cognition. This is not an easy task, because there are many versions and they do not necessarily fall in line with each other. Instead of taking a historical perspective that would take us very far from the objectives of this book, it is probably more effective to briefly consider three of the most influential views. These are the *embodied* perspective by Varela, Thompson, and Rosch (1991), *distributed* cognition by Hutchins (1995a), and the *extended* cognition view by Clark and Chalmers (1998).

These three views on cognition are slightly different, mainly in their tone and in the audience they target. They ended up being read by a far wider audience than the authors intended but, originally, from the perspective of the authors, these publications were aimed at specific groups of academics. The book *The Embodied Mind* (Varela et al., 1991) was written for the then emergent community of cognitive scientists, to shake it by pointing at a relatively unexplored direction. The work *Cognition in the Wild* (Hutchins, 1995a) is an ethnographic work and it was aimed at those interested in cognitive anthropology. Finally, *The extended mind* (Clark & Chalmers, 1998) is an article published in a journal, but *Natural-Born Cyborgs* (Clark, 2003) and *Being there* (Clark, 1998) were directed to a wider audience, probably beyond academia.

Computational Organizational Cognition:
A Study on Thinking and Action in Organizations, 37–55
Copyright © 2021 by Emerald Publishing Limited
All rights of reproduction in any form reserved
doi: 10.1108/978-1-83867-511-020211003

The admirable crisp and engaging style with which Clark has written his books makes this intent very clear (to me, at least).

I will not indulge in explaining the differences between these three views in this introduction, and move that to the next chapters. It can be succinctly noted though that only Hutchins makes explicit reference to organizations, teams, and other social aspects of cognition while the other authors remain anchored to a more traditional perspective that includes interactions with artifacts. One aspect probably needs to be mentioned here already. In fact, these three views are grouped here because they all present ways in which cognition is (or can be) distributed across material objects and/or people. This also explains the title for this Chapter 3. The usual summary ends the chapter.

3.1   The Embodiment Proposition

The quote at the beginning of this chapter refers to the (once) popular science fiction TV show called *Star Trek*. Since I assume there is no person reading this book who does not know what Star Trek is about, I focus only on the matter of the episode. The particular circumstances of space exploration brought Spock, the science officer of the spaceship *Enterprise*, in a situation where his brain gets out of his body, it is a *disembodied* brain. The impossible task that is presented to Captain Kirk and the crew is to embody Spock's brain again. Although very entertaining, this re-embodiment task is not what is of interest here.

The circumstances of this episode suggest that it is possible to think of taking the brain off one's body. It is possible, as a thought experiment, to hypothesize the working of a brain that does not need the physiological functioning of the biological body to exist. At first, this does not seem plausible at all. And yet, this is what most of the work on cognition that is based on a computer metaphor of the brain assumes (Newell & Simon, 1972). In other words, they assume that it is possible to maintain that cognitive activities can be separated from their physical–biological container. The hypothesis is not so wild after all.

Even within the conditions of science fiction where almost everything is possible, if there is a tiny link to seemingly scientific grounds, this disembodiment does not seem to work as such. In fact, as the words pronounced by Spock tell us, his brain has moved out of his own body such that Dr McCoy labels it as "a disembodied brain" but it is not nowhere. The brain still needs a location to function and here is what Spock "feels" when he states that his body "stretches into infinity." This is, again, strange, because one may assume that the brain could stay out of the body in some sort of abstract immaterial form. Instead, Spock's brain *needs* another location to function, and it picks anything that suits, any object in the room where the crew is performing their explorations.

So, rather than a disembodiment, this looks like a *different embodiment*, signaling that the brain still needs a medium to work. As a result of this *different embodiment*, since this new medium has now stretched to any object in the room, Spock's cognition has now expanded, its functions are broader.

To try and point at the reflections from this short story, even in the wild imaginative world of science fiction, a brain still needs some "body" to function properly. A disembodied brain can only work as long as it has an alternative location that allows it to perform its activities. But, if this is the case, where does cognition ends to be *just* in a brain and it starts to be elsewhere?

3.1.1 Cognitivism...

In their seminal book on *The Embodied Mind*, Varela et al. (1991) present a series of compelling arguments to indicate that cognitive science does not need to postulate that cognitive processes are *abstract symbolic representations that happen in a brain*. The underlying assumptions that support such a claim are too restrictive and some of them cannot be fully demonstrated. Let me review these assumptions quickly so that the proposal of Varela et al., (1991) becomes more apparent as it is built in opposition to them.

In the following pages, I do not pretend to give a full account of cognitivism nor to present the entire agenda set by Varela et al.'s (1991) seminal work. The purpose of these pages is to sketch some of their contributions, especially the ones that are relevant to the objectives of this book.

The first assumption is *abstraction*. This can be framed as detachment of the cognitive processes from experienced life, more than abstraction in the classic sense (i.e. dealing with ideas). In fact, cognitivism postulates that the essence is in the way in which information is processed by a computational system – the brain. And these processes work as input–output mechanisms such that both the environment and the executing system are non-central, in some cases irrelevant. This also means that the process exists independent of the environment and the system that performs its operations. Imagine you are walking to reach a shop in a part of town you have never been before. You are using your smart phone to guide you. At one point, the software suggests to turn right at the next intersection but that seems counterintuitive because the shop is on the left (according to the map). You are wondering whether to still follow the navigator or to follow your instincts instead. In a cognitivist perspective, the entire situation I just describe is irrelevant. All it matters is the information that is needed to solve the problem. Hence, the input is the information coming from your mobile that is processed by the neurons in a brain, where the counter-intuition works as part of the processing. The decision is the output of this processing mechanism, such that

$$D_i = f(I_j | P) \tag{3.1}$$

where D_i is the decision (output) that is a function of the information one receives I_j, given a cognitive process P. The expression is abstract enough to be applied independent of the context. When I wrote that the situation is irrelevant, I meant that, for example, the information could come from a friend who is walking with you, from the navigator in a car, from a bystander, or a sign on the street. All these can well be represented by Equation 3.1. Also, whether you are making a decision or the mobile is making it for you, it does not matter. In both cases, you have a very similar processing P.

The second assumption that cognitivism makes relates to the use of symbols. Processing is dependent upon the combination of entities that follow specific rules, just like it happens in a computer software. The difference here is that the symbols *are* what they represent. The letter "a" is a, the number "7" is 7, and so on. This correspondence allows for manipulations of symbols that can be studied as one could study Equation 3.1 because they follow specific rules. The idea is that cognitive choices can be thought of as problems looking for solutions (Newell & Simon, 1972). This is very useful when it comes at modeling cognition as symbol computations because it basically overlaps with it. As Varela et al., (1991) suggest, one important aspect to notice is the split between semantic and syntax. In fact, the cognitivist makes no assumption on the content of symbols and their meanings (semantic). They only make sense as they are processed according to a rule (syntax). This is why, in the example above, the context from which the information is generated (a mobile phone) is irrelevant as well as who (or what) is processing that information. It is the computational rule of processing the input that matters, not the history or the context from which it comes from. This is, as the reader may realize, a very strong claim. Another implication of the symbol-bound assumption is that these rules are universal and can be generalized to any input–output relation that represents a cognitive process. Just like the previous aspect, this can be extremely powerful in that it may help find solutions to problems that are indeed generalizable. The paradigmatic example of a cognitivist perspective is the chess player and the decisions made on the board. When the context is limited and rules are fixed then there is some potential for generalizations. In other words, in a world where uncertainty surrounding the conditions of operation and ambiguity of interpretation of the inputs are limited, the cognitivist perspective may be able to reach some generalizability.

However, one needs to ask, how many of these conditions do we find in our world? How many do we find in organizational behaviors?

The third assumption is about representations. Cognitive processing needs that parts of reality find a way to be mirrored within one's computational organ. This means that, in the case of humans, the brain replicates what it sees in order to be able to process it. How does it accomplish this task? This is through symbolic computations of the nature seen above. There are two interesting considerations here, one on the meaning of representations, the other on its meaning for cognitivism.

There is a broad debate on what representation means to cognition and why it should be considered, in which form, or it should be completely discarded. The ways in which cognitivism interprets representations is radical. The assumption is that there is an exact match between the input and the way in which the processor (the brain) considers it. Once again, the representation *is* the represented, to some extent. To hold the image of a dog in one's brain is the image of the dog itself, processed through symbols that make it possible to reconstruct it. As far as I understand it, it is the same as storing a picture of a dog in your computer. The processing units are a file that is made of 01 codings. This is how strong the mapping of "reality" is for cognitivists.

But, by discussing representation, we have hit a crucial point, especially for the *embodiment* proposition.

3.1.2   ...and Its Opposite

The idea of mental representations runs deep in Western philosophy, with key references in Descartes, Locke, Kant, and Leibniz. This is to state that it is not something that was introduced by cognitivism, nor that it is "modern." It is so entrenched in our philosophical traditions that it is difficult to think otherwise, that is to say, to question the centrality and the meaning of mental representations. This is the starting point of the *embodiment proposition*.

The Nature of Mental Representations

Before moving on, let us consider two aspects of the idea that our cognition works through mental representations. The first is that there is an activity that is entirely *internal* to the brain, something happens within the processing system that mirrors essential aspects of what is presented in front of it. In other words, there is a divide between what is inside one's head and what is outside, the environment. The workings of what is inside are separate and independent from what seen outside. There are inputs and stimuli, but the processes leading to a representation and to cognition are different than the processes that govern the outside world. In order to process a dog that passes by next to you, for example, your brain uses the inputs (e.g., what you see) and reproduces the salient points of the dog in the brain. This happens inside and it is separate from the actual dog that is seen outside. In this process, there is a necessary simplification process since, on average, the number of details that accompany even the simple event of 'seeing a dog' are very many. This internal process needs to simplify, probably retrieve additional information from what is stored in the memory, and assemble the representation.[1]

The second aspect of the idea of mental representations that is absolutely essential to make sense of it and to understand the challenge that came from Varela et al. (1991) is that of *objectivity*. In order to represent something that is outside, it is required that this exists independent of the observer and is "real," to use a controversial word. This means that "reality" – the environment, the world out there – is objectively definable and independent from the observer. This is someone who captures essential features of it and represents them in his or her own brain. The information attached to any element of the outside world is defined a priori by the mere existence of the element. The dog of the example above has features that can be described objectively and independently of the observer. This allows for anyone to see it and represent it as a dog in a cognitive process.

In short, representations are *internal* to one's brain and they need an *objective* world to be performed. These two aspects are relatively uncontroversial among cognitivist scholars. But, are they? This is where the *embodiment proposition* starts from.

Embodied Action

The philosophical grounds on which Varela et al. (1991) move their steps are different from the ones above. They are inspired mainly by Merleau-Ponty (1982), Merleau-Ponty and Fisher (1963) and oriental philosophies such as Buddhism. This reference is essential in that it clarifies the perspective with which these authors have started to look at cognition. The first statement that is attributable to an embodiment proposition is that the world is *experienced*. By using the study of color as an example, Varela et al. (1991) demonstrate that even a seemingly objective feature of an item – its color – depends on the perception of the observer. In fact, the classification of colors through, for example, tones of red, green, and blue is dependent upon an agreement on what the

---

[1]A note in passing, this is exactly the same concern I raised with the work of Simon in Secchi (2011).

proportion of the three base colors define (e.g., orange, yellow, purple) rather than on the actual perception of red, green, and blue.

As mentioned above, the cognitivist paradigm scores a relative success when the system of reference has a set number of rules and is relatively unambiguous. This is the case of a game such as chess. To use a vivid expression, the idea to beat the cognitivists on their own ground by using the study of color as a way to open up the discourse is certainly effective. However, it is probably within the social sciences that Varela et al. (1991) could have gained much more from their argument. In fact, by observing the way in which people work in an organization, it is relatively easy to come at the conclusion that objectivity is something evanescent. Think of a group of people that is conveyed in a room (or online) for a meeting. It is not unusual that the first minutes are spent either discussing the agenda or clarifying what the meeting is actually about. In extreme cases, an entire meeting may be spent discussing why people are there and what it is exactly that they are supposed to be doing (this a the case discussed in Jensen, Secchi, & Jensen, 2019). The information on the meeting, likely to be found on an email, is written down and should be something "out there." Yet, in many cases, recipients wonder about its meaning. If the information is objective then, through cognitivist postulates, it becomes difficult to explain that each recipient got a different mental representation of it.

A way to try and solve the problem above would be to apply a shared approach. Yes, the information is not perceived similarly from each of the recipients and yes, they all hold different representations in their mind, the cognitivist would say. Still, there is something out there: the words written in the email. If one were to map these representations, the truth (the objectivity) will lie in the elements that are *shared* by all the recipients. After all, if all recipients got a similar understanding of some of the aspects in the email, this should be the true essence of that information. Hence, it is objective. This is a problem similar to what Cowley and Harvey (2016) write about the illusion of a *common ground* in language studies. The definition of these shared (or common) aspects in the email cannot be objectively defined. To reach a common understanding of a line of text is dependent upon contingent and structural aspects that are incumbent upon the recipient. In other words, we cannot – simply put, there is no way to – detach the context from the email. There are banal elements (contingent) such as who wrote the email, at what time of the day it was received, whether the meeting was one-shot or in a line of other meetings, whether one sits along in a cubical to read or in an office where it is easy to share opinions and to ask for advice. There are less banal aspects (structural) such as one's professional identity, organizational identity, perception of role

(responsibilities, duties, expertise), personal history with the organization, and conventions, norms, rules of the organization. All these, and
much more, contribute to determine a shared or common understanding
of the email. In other words, we cannot detach subjectivity from the way
in which humans access information.

En passant, allow me to notice that at one point in the paragraph
above I have started to use the verb "understand" rather than discussing
about shared mental representation and that I have not commented
on the process of mapping the mental representation such that the
overlaps can be seen. The first case is a call to what Varela et al.
(1991) define "common sense," because humans give meaning to content
such as a line in an email, and that is to say that they *understand* the
email. The exercise above becomes to observe common understanding
rather than to map overlaps in mental representations. Is understanding
the same as mapping mental representations? I think this is a good
question and deserves to be addressed appropriately; I try to do so
later in Chapter 4 and can anticipate the answer is negative. While
understanding is a complex activity, mapping is a relatively unequivocal
rule-bound process. The second case is about the process of producing
a map of recipients' mental representations. I have treated this as a
simple process but, to perform such an act in a cognitivist frame implies
that one makes explicit, hence projects outside, what is only internal.
Whether this is possible and whether it is an activity that is neutral to
cognition is discussed further below in Section 3.3. At the same time,
this consideration introduces the other critical ground on which the
embodiment proposition is based.

The internal nature of representations also comes to be questioned.
Let us continue with the example of the email that calls in for a meeting
in an organization. Recipients have a mental representation of what they
read and this is something that happens in their brains. The information
is coded through a series of symbols typical of a natural language. This
information is imported as input on a brain that represents it capturing
its essential features, and processing it. The information can materialize
if triggered by an external stimulus, probably during the meeting or
before, for example, if a recipient decides to share this information with
someone else. The important point here is that the brain processes inputs
as they come from the outside world. An orderly sequence of letters
composing a word and this word, together with others, make a sentence.
Meaning is attached to these words individually and together according
to the rules of the language in which the sentence is written. This process
happens inside the brain. Does this process hold in general?

When my great-grandfather's family was forced to leave the delta
of River Po by the fascist regime in Italy and to re-settle in Cagliari,

Sardinia, my grandfather was 18 years old.[2] They found a home on a cohort where a family of farmers lived. Back then, Italy was made of wide cultural differences, exacerbated by the use of languages that were fairly diverse. Sardinian is, to some, a neo-Latin language such as Spanish or Italian, and different from them. The language spoken by my great-grandfather's family was a dialect of the Italian and it was easy enough for them to switch to proper Italian. Private school also helped. My grandfather was eager to help the community of farmers, as a way to thank them for their hospitality. So, when the time for *vendemmia* came, he made himself available. He asked the one who seemed in charge when to meet at the vineyard. The old man replied "spanighendi spanighendi." Definitely not Italian. Definitely gibberish to my grandfather's ears. He asked again. Same reply. Couldn't he speak Italian? Not at all.

What is the mental representation of "spanighendi spanighendi?" To an untrained ear, probably there is none. It may be something that is categorized as misunderstanding or an interpretation of a strange language, filtered by the ears of an untrained brain (untrained to hear and understand Sardinian). This is an impasse and no action is possible out of such an uncommunicative situation where representation is too loose to work. From a cognitivist perspective, there is nothing to do, because there is a lack of appropriate representation. From a real life – the Varela et al's "common sense" – perspective, this is unacceptable. In this case, as it happens in many situations, an action is still warranted. But how do you make sense of something you clearly cannot understand?

An obvious way to go about it is to ask someone else who can translate for help. However, you do not want to look like a fool, offering your help to someone you cannot understand, hence making it difficult to work with. So, one needs to choose carefully to whom to ask and, given the circumstances of the anecdote, there was no one. Another option would be to think of the typical life of a farmer to try and understand the time. Precision is not something that characterizes a farmer's day, hence the time is unlikely to be something like 8:15 AM. Also, we are in the 1930s. The second hint is the form of the words. In fact, the final "-endi" resembles Italian gerund form of a verb, and indicates action, something that is happening. The third hint is that the indication should be something one could observe independent of the actors involved, because it would be unlikely that my grandfather would be required to spy on the old farmer to understand when it is time to go. The fourth hint is that all work start in the morning, especially when it is that time of the year when it is time to take the grapes off the vines. What is that imprecise time of the morning when something

---

[2]This anecdote is something that happened to my grandfather, only transposed earlier than when it actually happened.

"out there" is happening? Perhaps a natural event that takes some time to actually happen. My grandfather's guess was the dawn. The same word repeated twice indicated that the meeting was at that time of the morning when the first light starts to appear. It is a time that needs to be related to light, because one needs light to perform the job. If it is a cloudy day (very very unlikely at that time of the year in Sardinia), the light comes in with a slight delay. Also, starting this type of work before the heat of the day is good practice.

This long explanation of how to interpret something that has no (or just a loose) mental representation and still act on it well represents the concept of *embodied action*. The idea is that a representation is not a necessary condition for action to happen. The conditions, history, loose connection to one's knowledge, and some imagination (improvisation) is what makes the trick and allows action in circumstances such as this one. In spite of this anecdote, circumstances such as the ones above happen more frequently than one may think. How many times are you in doubt about what someone else said or wrote? How many times are you in doubt about the actual meaning of what you read? Can you be 100% sure of situations you are in as you observe other people's behavior? In other words, uncertainty and ambiguity are two unavoidable parts of the world we live in.

Moreover, the conditions in which the world is in must be perceived by the individual. This condition of subjectivity is not secondary to the experience. In fact, the body through which we experience the world is not detachable by the cognitive process. All the hints I have referred to above are subjective, they come from a human being. And the options and reasoning come with feelings and emotions that, once again, cannot be discarded because they affect cognizing. In other words, when considering cognition we must relate to an action that needs a body to be experienced. We need *embodied action*.

What are the actual mechanisms through which embodiment happens? What are representations replaced by? The work of Hutchins (1995a) helps us shed some light on these two questions.

3.2   The Distribution of Cognition

The above sets the groundwork for additional explorations on cognition that is not anchored to a strict idea of representation. The work of Hutchins (1995a) *de facto* builds on that of Varela et al. (1991) even though he never cites nor refers to their work. In the following pages, I try to explain in which way Hutchins' work continues the embodiment legacy. Once again, this is not a summary of Hutchins' book I am referring to in these pages, but an account of some of its most salient parts in light of this book's objectives.

Let us go back to the case of Spock's disembodied brain for a moment. When he claimed that his body was stretching to infinity he was referring to the fact that all material objects in the room were used as tools in which the brain was *distributed*. It was as if the brain was all of a sudden located any place in the room other than Spock's body. Needless to state that this is very unlikely to happen (or, is it? See Section 3.3 below), and it is a fascinating thought experiment. As the pages above make clear, the body cannot be discarded and, at the same time, tools, people, artifacts, and natural objects constitute a non-secondary part of cognitive activities. This is how Hutchins explains the way in which cognition materializes.

A background note first. Hutchins' *Cognition in the Wild* is an exploration in cognitive anthropology. For an extended period of time he shared the military ship *Palau* with its crew, learned, and observed their actions. Through the description of the various tasks that the crew performs almost on a daily basis, the book outlines a series of considerations that define cognition in a way that allows it to function for a team. This allows Hutchins to present several propositions on the nature of cognition via the analysis of its manifestations, including, for example, learning, communication, and performance. Two transversal processes that cut across these manifestations are the use of tools or *artifacts* and the understanding of *expectations*.

3.2.1 The Use of Artifacts

One of the most discussed and certainly the most distinctive aspect of Hutchins' work is the description of how cognitive activity happens through the means of artifacts, some of which can be thought of as tools. By describing the various maneuvers that a ship makes as it navigates, Hutchins is interested in cognition applied to task performance. Almost every action he describes in the book is oriented toward a goal, a set of interactions that are set to accomplish something. Everything he considers in the description of cognitive processes is not casual, it somehow serves a function that is useful to operating a task. Of course, this is due to the focus of the narrative, namely that of describing the details of cognitive processes as they happen in an actual environment. Let us take this step by step and describe some of the salient aspects of Hutchins view on cognition. In so doing, I am not going to describe operations on a ship but focus on an example that is set on organizational events instead.

In the pages above, I have used the example of a meeting, in particular of an email that triggered the invitation to describe aspects of the embodied cognition proposition. Continuing with that example, it is easy enough for anyone to think of an actual meeting. To make the example more realistic, we may imagine that the meeting brings together all members of a team for their morning briefing. These team meetings are sometimes conducted on a bi-weekly, weekly, or daily basis, depending on the function of the team and its relevance to the work of the entire organization. In this example, team members are nine, of which one is the manager. The meeting starts and one team member is absent so that there are eight people in a room. They discuss the state of operations and the manager outlines the plan for the day. Each team member is invited to update on anything new that came up and on the work plan for the day. As we have seen above, there has been an email before meeting and it is assumed it sets the agenda. Also, the manager projects a slide with some details of the projects and various other information. The meetings last for approximately 15 minutes, but may go longer if needed.

While navigating a ship into a port has some relatively easy ways to assess whether performance has been satisfactory, the same assessment is rather difficult when it comes at organizational behaviors. The tools that individuals use in a ship have a more or less direct connection to the goal of the entire enterprise and feedback is relatively informative. In an organization, a typical tool is a computer that is used in a variety of ways. If we limit our attention to one of the software that runs on a computer, the assessment may be relatively smooth, still complicated. Take the use of a software that the manager uses to produce the slides for her presentation. The goal of the manager is probably that of presenting information that is concise for an effective explanation of the situation, planning, and organizing. As she is writing the bullet points in the slide, the control tools in the software help her make the typed letters of a certain color, size, font. In a probably strange comparison, these adjustments made through the software substitute an activity that she would have had to perform manually on a piece of paper or in a typewriter, in the old days. The optimization of color, size, and font is outsourced to a machine software that does it for her. Hence, one may claim that these functions have been *distributed* to the tools available in the software. These are no more functions that her brain needs to command the arm to perform on a piece of paper. Of course, the functions of the brain, one may argue, change, because the type of skills needed to instruct a software are different to those needed to draw letters. This is correct, nevertheless the basic drawing functions cannot be claimed to happen inside her brain.

From the above, *distribution* is the continuation of cognition through artifacts external to the brain. In a meeting such as the one rapidly sketched above, each participant has a number of cognitive artifacts. One could start from architecture (e.g., room size, position in the building, shape) and moving to various elements in the room such as tables, chairs, projectors, screens, computers, tools for remote calls, and their layout. On this specific point, Hutchins warns that

> the arrangement of equipment in a workplace might seem to be a topic for traditional, noncognitive ergonomics. However, it has an interpretation in terms of the construction of systems of socially distributed cognition. The interaction of the properties of the senses with the physical layout of the task environment defines possibilities for the distribution of access to information. (p. 197)

The position of all material objects in the room affects, to some extent, the way in which people cognize. To the list above, one should also add personal computers, tablets, paper-and-pencil notebooks, mobiles, and other artifacts that people may bring to the meeting themselves.

The discussion may go in a way such that a slide is projected on a screen and it is visible to all the participants. The slide serves a number of functions. The most immediate is that it works as a repository of information, as some sort of explicit memory tool. By discussing the topic of the meeting, participants do not need to remember some of the details of the project, because they are written on a slide and visible to everyone. They may also listen to what the manager and other team members say in order to interpret the slide and get an idea of the next steps of the project. For now, let us limit our attention to the projected slide. Not only it serves as a way to distribute some cognitive functions, but there needs to be *coordination* between the individual and the artifact. This activity can be highly demanding and it is usually spread over a number of artifacts and other human beings. Think of what you usually do when at a meeting. You listen, watch the slide on the screen, type some notes, eventually organize your thoughts and speak up. To do that, you use the aid of all the tools available in coordination. The notes should support a line of reasoning that is anchored to the slide and, sometimes, to what some other colleagues have just referred to. This, in turn, may be supported by additional information that derives from your own knowledge. All these need coordination to effectively convey into a distributed cognitive process.

The fact that cognition is processed through a number of artifacts does not qualify the process. In fact "the naive notion of these tools as *amplifiers of cognitive activity* was mistaken" (Hutchins, 1995a, p. 170; emphasis added). In other words, the distribution of cognition is a mere description of how it happens while individuals perform a task, it does not imply that the outcome is better when no distribution is assumed. This is a strong point from Hutchins. It basically means that coordination of artifacts and the brain does not add quality to the process, it is just a description of what happens. Operating a calculation "just in your head" or by using a computer may not necessarily affect the end result. The performance may be similar, perhaps time is a resource, together with the type of cognitive process involved.[3]

3.2.2   Managing Expectations

A third set of resources that adds to the components of the room's layout and to the personal tools people may bring with them to the meeting can be identified by the other colleagues at the meeting. This implies a particular climate that pervades the team, but also a general set of norms, values, and expectations that typically accompany any organizational activity.

There are roles tied to the individuals in the room. One may say that even the one person who is absent casts its shadow on the meeting, and is incumbent on how activities are discussed, especially if the project is organized via a set of sequential tasks. The use of the tools and, most importantly, understanding their appropriate use, as well as what people mean when they discuss the topic of the meeting are all subject to organizational bounds. To try and be more precise, understanding how to make artifacts work does not just derive from them being "shared" among team members. It derives from the socially construed actions that the team members build on them, renewed by their continuous use, the habits they create, and their functionality such that they allow operators to accomplish the task at hand. This means that the sense individuals make of the meeting is a function of the social division of labor between them. To this, one should add the organizational constraints that sets a series of goals that are super-ordinate to the ones discussed in the meeting, as well as a set of norms and values that need to be satisfied.

The above makes it such that participants have expectations on what the manager will present and how she will do it during the meeting. At the same time, their professional role is socially co-defined by a mix of repeated interactions with others in the team and in the organization, and by their expertise/knowledge. Unless new to a team, each participant would also have expectations for the self, in terms of goals, performance, and in relation to the others. As Hutchins highlights, the distribution of cognition is very much dependent on the social organization such that, in many cases, it can be referred to as a social distribution of cognitive activities.

---

[3]Whether there is an advantage or not is a point that the simulations presented in this book try to assess. Results are mixed, but generally positive when considering other human beings as external resources; see Part II of this book.

In fact, most of *Cognition in the Wild* is dedicated to the description of team dynamics, performance, and then to learning, and organization learning. This is worth noting because most of the MOC literature focuses on learning (see Chapter 2), and it is surprising that very few have utilized this aspect of Hutchins' work. In his view,

> the proper unit of analysis for talking about cognitive change includes the socio-material environment of thinking. *Learning is adaptive reorganization in a complex system.* (p. 289; emphasis in the original text)

The complex system he refers to here is the one that enables coordination between the various elements in which cognition is distributed. This is a network of connected elements that is always moving in a direction; the interaction between the individual and the tools/artifacts is never static. When a participant decides to speak up at the meeting, by talking about "item 2" in the manager's list, he looks at the slide multiple times, then probably at the notes and he may even find something else to add to what he had in mind as the words come out of his mouth. This is a system that adapts and moves along to accomplish the goal the participant had set in a functional way.

If we soften the bound between the internal and the external, we may realize that learning – as defined above – is more a habit for cognitive systems. This is why we can define the individual as "a very plastic kind of adaptive system" (Hutchins, 1995a, p. 288).

3.2.3   A Concluding Remark on Hutchins (1995)

Many of those who read his work from a MOC perspective (Healey, Hodgkinson, & Massaro, 2018) interpreted Hutchins' work in a way such that he did not reject representations as Varela et al. (1991) did. In fact, these authors claim he just moved the nature of representations by extending them outside of someone's brain. The use of artifacts external to the brain makes it such that they aid the functions already existing in the brain by allowing a better representation of what is a mix of internal and external elements. These authors seldom call this "distributed" but *situated* cognition, and this is probably not a secondary difference in highlighting the role of representations. In this distributed/situated view, there still is an objective "world out there," where artifacts are means to an end, that of cognitively representing this "world out there." The impression is that the goal of cognition remains the same it was for cognitivists – i.e. an abstract symbol-bound representation of the external world – but it is simply carried over differently. This approach only moves representations, it addresses the problem of inside-the-brain-only representations but does not touch the objectivity problem at all. In other words, it avoids ontological and epistemological discussions.

Now, Hutchins' *Cognition in the Wild* is actually very clear in disclosing the ties to cognitivists (especially to Simon) while keeping a distance from the embodied cognition proposition of Varela et al. (1991). Using his words, a task "is accomplished by the *propagation of representational state* across a series of *representational media*" (Hutchins, 1995a, p. 117; emphasis in the original text). Hutchins never challenges directly any of the assumptions around representation or information processing, yet he redefines computation as something that is not necessarily tied to symbols. This way, he includes individual–artifact and individual–individual interactions by assuming that cognition is computation in a broad sense (p.118). Hence, in taking a narrow perspective on Hutchins, Healey et al. (2018) may have inadvertently pointed at one of the possible limitations of the distributed view of cognition.

3.3 Extended Cognition

The end of the 1990s marked a third important contribution in defining this new way to think of cognition. Among the work of the authors involved in this, the article *The extended mind* (Clark & Chalmers, 1998) is probably the most representative.[4] That same year is one when Clark also published the book *Being There* (1998) where similar ideas surface, and a few years later, he produced another book, *Natural-Born Cyborgs* (2003). My personal journey started from this latter book, probably because of the intriguing title. Back then when I read it, I was very curious to see how this idea of human cyborgs was argued for. Still, I believe the best way to introduce the concept is to start from the pioneering article mentioned above.

The perspective with which Clark and Chalmers approach the subject of cognition shares much with the way in which both the embodied and the distributed perspectives came about. Their emphasis is different. They focus on cognitive processes and try to understand how artifacts change the way in which they happen. The claim is that embracing

---

[4]If citations mean anything, it probably is visibility of a particular work. A quick check performed on September 17, 2020 shows the following count: 5690 according to Google Scholar, and 2227 for Scopus.

the hypothesis that cognition propagates on external artifacts has a transformational power on cognition itself.

3.3.1 Active Externalism

The foundation of Clark and Chalmers' (1998) work relies mainly on Hutchins idea of cognitive distribution. They take this as a starting point but they answer differently when prompted the question about the relationship between external artifacts/tools and the individual (i.e. the brain).

The main point is that the effects that external objects exert on cognition are similar to those present in one's brain. Let us go back to the example of the managers who works on a few slides to prepare for the meeting. I have mentioned the interaction with a computer software that allows her to operate on size, color, and font of the text as it appears on the screen. I am sure you have been in that same position in your own experience and performed similar operations on your computer. If so, you intuitively know that the tool you are using – the software – is designed to actively help you perform those actions. In other words, the "external features here are just as causally relevant as typical internal features of the brain" (Clark & Chalmers, 1998, p. 9). Operating on color, for example, is something that gives the idea of what is meant. One could mentally represent (to use the cognitivist point of view) how red text on a black screen looks like, decide it is the way to go, and use the software to implement that choice. This is, for many, a choice that does not play out well. The text will not stand out. To some, this is almost invisible. Once this choice is operated, we can assume that the person does not want to give up the idea of reddish color on a black background. Hence, she starts to adjust the color until she reaches to a tone of orange that looks nicer, more visible, quite all right. Now, the act of modifying the color is not a simple *manipulation* of the tool. Put differently, it is not just an update to the mental representation one builds in her head, it is part of *thinking*.

This is the constitutive element of artifacts that makes them part of an *active* process of thinking. They are instruments of thought and define any cognitive process that engages with them. The thought process we described above with color adjustment cannot be done without the aid of a software.

One may argue that experience, at one point, may surface and anticipate a choice that was once accomplished through manipulation. Yet, the memory would be tied to the software, and the action leading to a choice of color would still need a software to be performed (or thought through).

3.3.2   Couplings

The concept that is used to explain how the individual interacts with artifacts is that of *coupling*. This can be thought of as a mechanism that binds brain and artifact together in mutual interaction or, to put it as Emanuele Bardone and I described it (Bardone & Secchi, 2009), they stand together in "smart interplay."

When the article by these two authors came out, they used the case of Inga and Otto to articulate their argument. They suggested that these two individuals want to go and visit an exhibition at the Museum of Modern Art in New York. Inga remembers that the museum is on 53rd street while Otto cannot and needs a computer to retrieve the information. While Inga is internally coupled with her own brain, Otto is coupled with a computer. Both can retrieve the same information, can find and are able to walk into the museum. The difference between the two is that Inga's process clearly appears to be internal while Otto's is an external coupling mechanism that can be easily de-coupled. This de-coupling is what allows the exploration of differences. But, on the ground of reliability, ease and direct access the two cognitive processes are not that different, after all.

Now, these authors wrote in a time before smart phones. What I think is interesting here is that the pervasiveness of portable tools where information is (almost) always available make the case look very different today. Yes, Inga may have access to her memory and be able to recall the location of the museum. At the same time, it is also very likely that she would consult her mobile phone as she walks there, just in case. This reinforces the memory and may, in the meantime, trigger a couple more options – e.g., an inviting coffee shop may pop up on the map, the app may indicate peak hours at the museum and suggest different times to visit. In this reverse scenario, Otto, who consulted the information on his mobile first, may be in a better position because the options that Inga evaluates later were previously assessed by Otto so that he could plan a better trip to the museum (time, stops, etc.). In the world we live in today, we are dependent upon technology and our tools have entered more literally, perhaps, our cognitive practices. After all, it is almost *unthinkable* to step out of your house without a phone in your hands. These phones are a natural extension of our cognition, and we now rely very much on them.

In other words, the seemingly futuristic perspective that Clark outlined in his (2003) *Natural-Born Cyborgs* is actually here. If anything, this new technological turn has shown our plasticity as human beings, the ease with which we adapt to external artifacts that serve as an extension of our cognitive activities, with possible improvements.

3.4 Summary

In this chapter, I have presented three complementary views on cognition. The *embodiment proposition* belongs to Varela et al. (1991) and directly challenges the internalist and objectivist positions of traditional cognitive science. In so doing, it presents a view of cognition based on experience, where one cannot get rid of the body to make sense of the environment. The *distributed cognition* hypothesis by Hutchins (1995a) is instead more focused on task performance and on how there is a continuity between the individual and the artifacts he/she uses. Finally, Clark and Chalmers (1998) propose a view such that cognition *extends* to the artifacts because these are essential parts of it, instruments of the mind, without which there is no cognition at all.

4

Extensions and Criticism

"The only theory that does not change is a dead theory"
– Personal communication to Marcin Miłkowski[1]

Over the last three decades, the ideas exposed in Chapter 3 flourished, some concepts were extended, some others re-formulated, while others still remained controversial and unexplored. Of the different disciplines that traditionally compose cognitive science, changes were embraced mainly within philosophy and linguistics while the majority of neuroscience, computer science, and cognitive psychology have some stream who turned to this new view, but remain otherwise skeptical. However, the hit wave of work produced as a result of the embodiment "revolution" can hardly go unnoticed.

If one limits the attention solely to the publications covered in Chapter 3, it is easy to understand the depth of their reach. A very quick check on Google Scholar[2] shows that Hutchins' (1995a) *Cognition in the Wild* attracted more than 15,000 citations, Varela, Thompson, and Rosch's (1991) *The Embodied Mind* has more than 10,700 citations, and Clark and Chalmers' (1998) article has around 5,700. It is fair to assume that these ideas have been widely discussed and are now considered a legitimate stream within cognitive science.

---

[1] It was at the social dinner of the 6th Avant Workshop, "Between Computation and Coordination," 23rd May 2019, at the Polish Academy of Sciences in Warsaw.

[2] Performed September 22nd 2020. Google Scholar is not representative of academic work because it does not have an appropriate mechanism to filter out non peer-reviewed publications, working papers, or even slides and student papers. Yet, most of the citations are from academic work; it still gives an idea of the visibility and traction a particular document has been able to generate over the years.

Computational Organizational Cognition:
A Study on Thinking and Action in Organizations, 57–69
Copyright © 2021 by Emerald Publishing Limited
All rights of reproduction in any form reserved
doi: 10.1108/978-1-83867-511-020211004

In this chapter, the focus is on developments of the embodied/distributed/extended cognition paradigm (called EDEC all together). I have categorized them in two perspectives, one that takes an *ecological* stance and another that attempts at providing an *all-encompassing* view. The first category includes, among others, conceptualizations on interactivity (Steffensen, 2013), cultural niches (Hutchins, 2014), and systemic cognition (Cowley & Vallée-Tourangeau, 2017). The second category is instead made of radical embodied cognition (Chemero, 2009), and the so-called 4E cognition approach (e.g., Menary, 2010). The idea of this chapter is to show how the original perspectives evolved since their original introduction in between two and three decades ago. Why these extensions and not others? And what brings them together? There are several reasons that led me to the choice. On the one hand, these contributions are all meant to be either extensions or re-framing of the EDEC views. On the other hand, they all stress a different aspect or build an entire conceptual system on that single aspect. This way, the aspects above can be easily thought to integrate each other. This means that, even though these extensions do not cover the entirety of contributions and may not even be the most influential, they help highlight different facets of EDEC and, at the same time, give an idea of the way in which concepts have evolved. But this is not it.

The extensions introduced below can all be considered building blocks of what is to come in the next Chapter 5, where I outline what is in the *organizational* side of cognitive activities.

After reviewing these extensions, this chapter presents a selection of criticism that has appeared over the years to counter these arguments. I intend to present three views: one that is overtly critical and rejects a non-cognitivist perspective (Adams & Aizawa, 2008), another that is critical but attempts to cover this skepticism (Miłkowski et al., 2018), and the third is a weak view of distributed cognition that is de facto a rejection of it (Salomon, 1993). Once again, these may not be the most representative set of critiques, but they are indeed useful at exploring some of the issues and concerns that these approaches may raise.

4.1   Extensions

The following pages are dedicated to a number of authors who have worked on the premises of the EDEC paradigm and either attempted at building a system around them or working on (and from) a particular aspect. Even though I am treating the three views as part of the same paradigm, they are different, as explained in Chapter 3. The approaches discussed below start from one of them, criticize another, or both.

In the following, I am introducing the *ecological* and the *all-encompassing* perspectives. While the first is a proper extension of the EDEC paradigm, the second is an attempt to systematize the knowledge gained so far.

4.1.1 Ecological Perspectives

One of the aspects that is somehow missing in Clark and Chalmers (1998) as well as in Clark (1998) is, according to some of the authors below, a broader view of the cognitive processes. In fact, the extended cognition tradition has a narrow focus on the individual and the relations that they establish with the artifacts. This is, among others, the view of those who propose to study cognition as *human interactivity* (Kirsh, 1997; Pedersen, 2012; Steffensen, 2011). They claim that the extended cognition perspective is too self-centered and fails to take a true ecological bird-eye view on the process. This is fine but, what exactly is interactivity?

According to one of its proponents, it is "sense-saturated coordination that contributes to human action" (Steffensen, 2013, p. 196). In this definition, there is a direct call to embodiment, when Steffensen refers to "sense-saturated," to distributed cognition, with an appeal to coordination, and to other unspecified external factors that may affect action, indicated by the verb "to contribute." Seen this way, *interactivity* is not necessarily a social process, it includes both animated and unanimated entities. What matters is the mutual dependence of two (or more) entities or their coupling, in other words. If one were to exclude mutual dependence that is typical of coordinated units, the study would focus on 'interaction' rather than interactivity (Kirsh, 1997). The idea is to capture the dynamics of a relation without placing either entity on a central position.

An example that shows the domain of application of the *human interactivity* perspective is that of a case where two company workers struggle to print the registration number of their firm in an invoice they are working on. Steffensen (2013) calls this the "invoice case" and it is interesting because it is a case of problem solving, according to him. Also, the interest lies in the everyday triviality of the banal occurrence: a number is not printed in the invoice. The problem is "found" when the invoice lacks a registration number, essential information, without which the customer cannot process the payment. The solution is found when one of them suggests to print the invoice on a pre-printed paper that has the logo on. The case is very short, lasting only a few minutes. By using a method called *cognitive event analysis* (CEA), Steffensen shows how the two employees in the case couple and decouple with each other and with the artifacts around them, especially with the printed wrong invoice. CEA is a video analysis technique that allows for the study of micro-scales (pico-dynamics), such as bodily movements and various characteristics of spoken language. In the end, it is the reiterated loops of discussions and especially the affordance with the disposition of artifacts in the environment that allows for a solution to be found. In fact, if it was not for the messy desk, the affordance leading to the solution may have not occurred. In summary, the interpretative key of the "invoice case" is specifically the number of couplings that enable and are enabled by what the author refers to as *human interactivity*.

One of the strongest implications of interactivity is the realization that cognition cannot be studied by isolating its single aspects but it needs an idea of the whole to be fully understood. This resonates very closely to what is usually advocated by system theorists (to start with Von Bertalanffy, 1968) and system thinkers (e.g., Forrester, 1994). According to these scholars, the synergies established by the parts of a system are always more than their mere sum. By taking this stance on cognition, the overall concept is more of an *ecosystem* of elements rather than that of a simple *ecology*.

In Cowley and Vallée-Tourangeau (2017), this emphasis is explicitly considered when discussing what they call *systemic* cognition. This view is expressed in the concluding chapter of the edited book *Cognition Beyond the Brain* and, while summarizing what is in the book, it gives its content a theoretical frame. The most striking aspect of this exercise is that the authors start using the verb "to think" to refer to activities that are typically referred to as cognition. Here is their take:

> Thinking arises as people coordinate under physical, biological and cultural constraints. (Cowley & Vallée-Tourangeau, 2013, p. 256)

This sentence establishes continuity with the *interactivity* paradigm and defines "thinking" as, again, coordination. However, from this angle, the environment comes back to a central position. Not only there is a clear reference to embodiment (i.e. the "biological" in the text), but space and spatial configurations (i.e. "physical") and long time-scales (i.e. "cultural") also have a role. These latter two bear the mark of Hutchins. Space architecture is one of the aspects that distributed cognition has helped us reflect upon in the way they enable or disable certain activities, only if one makes "social" sense of them (Hutchins, 1995a). In more recent work, Hutchins (2010, 2014) emphasizes the value of culture for human cognition, by establishing the concept of *cultural niches*, where sense and affordances are made possible. Not only these provide a constraint to our understanding, but they also enable ways in which this understanding could evolve. If my reading is correct, *systemic* cognition is an attempt to bring together all the three perspectives in EDEC.

Back to the quotation above and on the meaning of "thinking." It can be argued that, on the one hand, a proper systemic view emphasizes that these elements all play a role at once, making the job of disentangling their effects particularly hard. On the other hand, they work as "constraints." This implies that coordination is bounded by personal histories, skills, and the configuration of the environment, together with one's own body.

The authors then indicate how this "thinking" materializes:

> Our *systemic* perspective asks *how* thinking self-organises across individuals, dyads and groups. Configurations of control change as brains, persons and artefacts are put to use under shifting supra-personal constraints. Results arise as parts trigger effects in larger systems and, of course, systemic wholes constrain the operations (and modes of organization) of these parts. (Cowley and Vallée-Tourangeau, 2013, p. 257; emphases in the original)

The property that keeps parts of the system together is interactivity. In fact, it is by means of the way in which relations are established that the system assumes its configuration as well as its parts unveil their role. This synergy is important and extends to material and immaterial artifacts, as well as to other human beings.

The idea of cognition that comes out of this is that of a complex system that, when filtered by human interactivity, becomes *simplex* (Berthoz, 2012; Cowley & Vallée-Tourangeau, 2013) – i.e. it can be handled by a simplification of those mechanisms that make it more understandable.

By considering interactivity, the *ecological* perspectives described in the pages above extend the original EDEC by (a) attributing synergies between elements a more active role and (b) attempting to establish a framework on which the three different EDEC views can be made to play together.

4.1.2   All-Encompassing Perspectives

The *ecological* perspectives above are concerned with keeping a common framework that holds positions together and work on a selection of the EDEC features that fit the narrative best. Instead, the perspectives I have labeled *all-encompassing* are concerned with keeping the various EDEC aspects separated. They are attempts to give an overall description of what these concepts explain, but do not care much about homogeneity or building bridges. In other words, one may say that these perspectives set the boundaries rather than unify prospects.

One very popular such views has emerged recently and goes by the name of *e-cognition*, sometimes preceded by a number, depending on how many aspects one is considering. For example, in his editorial to a Special Issue, Menary (2010) specifies these are four. Specifically, one is the tradition of *enactivism* (e.g., Thompson, 2007), then a second is the *extended mind* hypothesis (e.g., Clark & Chalmers, 1998; Wheeler, 2010), third comes *embodiment* (e.g., Chemero, 2009; Hutto, 2008) and, finally, the view of *embeddedness* (e.g., Kiverstein & Clark, 2009). By pointing at differences among authors contributing to the same "e," Menary (2010) indicates that the only aspects keeping these streams together are a fierce criticism of the cognitivist paradigm and methodological individualism.

However, this is not the only way in which one could bring *e-cognition* together. In fact, in a paper with Stephen Cowley, we summarize all the various streams briefly by highlighting that they contribute each a different but fundamental piece of the cognition puzzle. We also consider *ecological* cognition as another "e" to add to the four in Menary's editorial to the Special Issue.

Another perspective that I would like to refer to, even if briefly, is the so-called *radical embodied cognitive science* (RECS) as presented by Chemero (2009). This is an approach that claims its difference from the various other EDEC streams, but it positions itself close to Varela, Thompson, and Rosch (1991). The fundamental proposition of this approach is that it wants to put antirepresentationalism at center stage, by refusing the foundation of cognitivism. In his book, Chemero takes cognitive linguists (Chomsky, 1980; Fodor, 1975) as a negative benchmark for his arguments and, at the same time, many EDEC authors, those who do not abandon computationalism or representationalism (in any form). Hence, distributed (Hutchins, 1995a) or extended (Clark & Chalmers, 1998) cognition are not aligned with RECS. In Chemero's own words, RECS is:

> the scientific study of perception, cognition, and action as necessarily embodied phenomenon, using explanatory tools that do not posit mental representations. It is cognitive science without mental gymnastics. (Chemero, 2009, p. 29)

One very interesting aspect of RECS is that it comes with a specific methodology and that is *dynamical systems theory*. This method is known among computational simulation scientists as System Dynamics and was introduced by Forrester (1958, 1961, 1971) as a way to study the evolving states of a system. It uses systems of differential equations to model stocks and flows of set parameters in a defined environment. This connection to a mathematical (now computational) method as a viable tool to study cognition is a strong tie that unites the work of Chemero and the one presented here. We only differ in that I am not as radical as he is, but await convincing empirical evidence toward representation or its opposite,[3] and I argue for a method that is designed to capture complexity and adaptability of systems – i.e. agent-based modeling. This method is not the only one, nor there is an exclusive match between EDEC research and ABM. As a computational method for the study of complex systems, though, there is nothing like it (more on this in Chapter 6).

4.2 Three Criticisms

EDEC attacks to mainstream cognitive science have not gone unnoticed. Some have defended their position while others have tried to reconcile some of these propositions to a revised cognitivist view. This section is dedicated to three of these reactions. As mentioned above, these are not representative of the entire body of literature produced to counteract those EDEC assumptions that break the core of cognitivism. They express the positions of those who have genuinely engaged with EDEC and rejected, argued against, and/or provided different interpretations.

I have labeled them as the *implausibility clause, le loup déguisé en agneau*, and *misunderstanding*. This section serves the purpose of presenting these criticisms while abstaining as much as possible from comments, unless absolutely necessary. Further discussions of EDEC with suggestions on how to address these criticisms can be found in Chapters 5 and 6, and especially in Chapters 11 and 12.

4.2.1 The Implausibility Clause

I bought the book by Adams and Aizawa (2008) *The Bounds of Cognition* a long time ago, when I was writing *Extendable Rationality*. I bought it together with a bulk of other books that related to the research enquiry of that time. For some reasons, maybe the title, I thought that their critique of EDEC was based on Simonian arguments, hence on bounded rationality. I was plain wrong.

---

[3]From the words in this sentence, it may be assumed that I am basically agnostic over representationalism. To some extent, that is correct however, I am not completely immune from good philosophical arguments and, so far, those produced against representationalism are particularly strong. Even though I await empirical evidence I would test hypotheses on the basis of the strongest theoretical arguments, i.e. those against representationalism. On radicalism, I do think it is a weak position, no matter where one applies it. It may be that some representation happens somewhere in the cognitive process, the actual point here is to understand *what* is represented, *how*, and *where*. For sure, I would agree that there is no such a thing as a "reality" to benchmark against, as the stronghold of the cognitivist position would state.

Adams and Aizawa (2008) take the position of orthodoxy (their word) in cognitive science and defend the traditional claim that cognition happens in the brain. They do so from the perspective of cognitive psychology, hence emphasizing the role of memory and using related research to make their arguments more compelling. Their negative example is especially the work of Clark (2003) and Clark and Chalmers (1998) and of *extended* cognition in general. The thesis is that extended cognition cannot exist, it is an implausible hypothesis that is good in the sense that it strengthens the beliefs that computational representations are the only way to study cognition.

The arguments can be articulated in two main ones: (a) the *problem of content* and (b) the *coupling-constitution fallacy*. The first is extremely interesting in that it posits a question that I have been asking myself and within circles of EDEC scholars for a while now. The starting point, for Adams and Aizawa is the definition of what cognition is not. Only by identifying a clear divide between what is the cognitive and what it is not one can describe the limits of the domain of study. In their view, "cognitive processes involve non-derived, rather than derived, representations" (p. 32). While anything that is anchored to external artifacts or beings is considered derived content, thoughts, feelings, perceptions, experiences are examples of non-derived content. For content to be non-derived it means that they arise

> from conditions that do not require the independent or prior
> existence of other content, representations, or intentional agents.
> (Adams & Aizawa, 2008, p. 32)

These are innate, even though the two authors never call them such. As we know, especially from the work of Fodor (1975, whom they cite), these are conditions that pertain to the isolated individual. Still, they are triggered by external stimuli, but are necessarily internal, as per their definition. Given that neurons fire in specific areas of the brain when one is exposed to stimuli, it is possible to argue in favor of representations. Clearly, something is happening in reaction to this exposure and the authors claim it is very likely it is some form of representation of the outside phenomenon. If there is non-derived content that is represented in and constitutes a cognitive process, then it is also clear that (a) the individual is the core of this process and (b) cognition happens in the brain.

The second of the arguments mentioned above is the *coupling-constitution fallacy*. This is based on a logical error that scholars from the EDEC tradition seem to base their reasoning on. According to Adams and Aizawa's (2008) reconstruction, most EDEC scholars suggest that, since coupling between the brain and an external resource has a causal effect on the cognitive process, then coupling must be part of the cognitive process. In more abstract terms, when a phenomenon X causes Y, then X must be part of Y. The use of paper-and-pencil to perform a mathematical calculation is coupled with the activity that goes on in the brain of the person doing the math. This coupling activity is constitutive of the cognitive process (also called system). This is a fallacy, because it uses causality as a way to expand the domain of the cognitive where it should not be. The fact that the use of paper-and-pencil makes it easier to handle mathematical calculations does not mean that these resources enter cognition, it only means that they have a causal effect on cognition. But the brain remains the brain and the paper cannot cognize anything, nor can the pencil. Whether this interpretation is true to the nature of EDEC is uncertain (see Chapter 5). In their favor, Adams and Aizawa produce quite a good number of quotations to support their view. Whether they all support this reconstruction is for readers to assess.

Adams and Aizawa's arguments are way more convincing and articulated in their articles and in their book. I have attempted to reproduce two of the most interesting and relevant of their critiques, I hope with some precision even if succinctly.

4.2.2 Le loup déguisé en agneau

The main source for this second stream of criticism is an article written by Miłkowski et al. (2018) on what they call "wide accounts of cognition" or, shortly, *wide cognition* to refer to the EDEC approaches (including their extensions). In order to make their arguments, these authors provide their short summary of these "wide" approaches. And here comes the first interesting aspect. They list the enacted, embodied, embedded, and extended traditions to which they add distributed cognition, considered the only one that deals with human–human interactions. This is not a critique, it is just a way to make a distinction between the four Es and Hutchins' perspective on cognition. It is a very important point that aligns well with what is to come from the next Chapter of this book onwards.

There are several elements that these authors indicate to constitute weaknesses of "wide" accounts. Some are not necessarily meant as criticism, yet they sound like it. For example, the statement that none of these approaches are proper theories, because they are very vague and could, at best, be considered traditions in cognitive science. They add that computationalism is one such grand traditions – of a different kind, obviously. So, not a criticism but, still, a possible problem when it comes to postulate testable hypotheses, for example, or predictions.[4] Theory aside, according to Miłkowski et al., concerns for "wide cognition" reside in that (a) it typically asks yes/no questions (to nature), (b) it provides so-called "guiding heuristics," and (c) each perspective does not provide a distinct contribution but can be merged with others. Let me take these criticisms one by one.

The problem with asking yes/no questions is probably too obvious. If a perspective is concerned with establishing whether the environment is constitutive of cognition or not, then it may be difficult to operationalize this claim and test it. Moreover, these yes/no questions remain very abstract and end up losing the grip with practice. The argument is very old, one used by Newell (1973) against cognitive psychologists dealing (better, struggling) with tasks. The point here is that the focus should be on processes, to explain how cognition happens. And these can be expressed *mechanistically*, due to causal relationships between the elements of the system. This is the most important point of the article, the fact that cognitive science should isolate *mechanisms* that help us understand the process better. EDEC does not usually do this but, they claim, remains at a wider philosophical (abstract) level, asking yes/no questions typical of grand traditions.

The second aspect relates to heuristics. These are usually defined as "rules of thumb" and provide a generic indication of what can be done in certain circumstances. Miłkowski et al. (2018) suggest that EDEC traditions are *guiding* heuristics, because they inform the direction in which a line of research should move but, as such, they cannot provide specific indications to, for example, a research agenda. This aspect is related to the one above. Actually, asking yes/no questions is a result of these traditions being *guiding* heuristics. The proposal that relate to this point is the same as the one above. That is, we should rely to *mechanisms* and, in short,

> A mechanism is an organized spatiotemporal structure responsible for the occurrence of at least one phenomenon to be explained. The orchestrated causal interaction of the mechanism's

---

[4]Prediction is something that comes from Miłkowski et al. (2018) and it reveals that these authors (many are philosophers) have natural sciences as a benchmark for cognitive science. The claim is probably correct for neuroscience and artificial intelligence, two of the "fab5" disciplines that compose cognitive science – i.e. philosophy, cognitive psychology, linguistics, artificial intelligence, and neurosciences – but it is hard to identify an easy path to prediction for the other four. Disciplines with strong ties to the social typically struggle in light of this benchmark. Therefore, to use "lack of prediction" as a fallacy or criticism for EDEC is a bit peculiar, given other theories in philosophy, psychology, and linguistics do not, on average, predict much.

component parts and operations explains the phenomenon at hand. (pp. 4–5)

In light of this definition, a mechanism has a structure that shows an internal consistency (i.e. it is organized) dependent on both spatial and temporal conditions. This seems, to me at least, a definition that becomes closer enough to that of a system however, the authors indicate this would not be recommended. And this is confusing because, if one keeps reading the quote above, it becomes clear that a mechanism has interacting parts. Not the mechanism as such, but its sub-systemic components are responsible for a causal relation with the phenomenon to be explained. A mechanism is tied to the phenomenon it explains. Those mechanisms that explain how a phenomenon occurs by use of internal parts and functionality are said to provide *constitutive* explanations. In this view, the system is the phenomenon and the mechanism provides its explanans.

The third aspect on the overlap between EDEC research also points at the emergence of mechanisms. In fact, if the boundary between each tradition is blurry, there is no clear mechanism stemming out from one or the other. Hence, it becomes very difficult to identify the actual contribution of one or the other. However, the mechanistic approach is probably a criticism only to those authors in the EDEC tradition who are not already using it. The turn in the argument by Miłkowski et al. (2018) comes later on in the article, where they claim that mechanisms are already used in "wide cognition." They go on with an example where they apply "wide" accounts to mindshaping (something I knew under the label "theory of mind"; see Premack & Woodruff 1978; Schaafsma, Pfaff, Spunt, & Adolphs 2015) and is the study of how individuals read (guess) what another person is thinking. The field uses a typical model-based approach that, as the name suggests, is grounded on mechanisms.

Overall, these authors remain skeptical over the actual contribution of EDEC research traditions and, at the same time, propose a way in which these can be re-aligned to a more orthodox perspective. In other words, I have the impression that the authors are trying to put a computational straight jacket on EDEC perspectives.[5] This is the "wolf in lamb's clothes" of the title, because there is a superficial embracement of EDEC while, in reality, the representationalist and computationalist component is alive and kicking.

4.2.3 Misunderstanding

This part of the chapter is dedicated to the position of Salomon (1993). He is very much concerned about the role of the individual and his

---

[5]This is, at least, what is found in other publications by some of these authors (e.g., Miłkowski, 2017; Miłkowski & Nowakowski, 2019).

criticism pertains to the fact that a distributed cognitive system may diminish the role of individual's cognition. I have to come clean and disclose my position on this work since the beginning. I do not think Salomon's chapter is of the same standing as the other two criticisms above, not in terms of the quality of the arguments nor in regards to their depth. The only reason why I am dedicating some space to Salomon (1993) is because it is used often by MOC scholars (e.g., Borghini, 2005; Healey, Hodgkinson, & Massaro, 2018).

The *misunderstanding* I mention in the title is not attributable to Salomon. In fact, I do think that he did a pioneering job in discussing distributed cognition before its time, namely two years before Hutchins published his *Cognition in the Wild*. And the literature that Salomon refers to when making his points about distribution and the role of the individual are preliminary (at best) attempts to sketch distributed cognition and various aspect of EDEC. The misunderstanding I refer to is that of MOC scholars who use Salomon's work as a reference to distributed cognition, ignoring the fact that, for cognitive science, that is mainly after Hutchins. Hence, by using Salomon's work, these MOC scholars are misinterpreting the nature of the concept. What Salomon describes as distributed cognition is not what I have introduced in Chapter 3, but a preliminary (tentative) version of it.

In his book chapter, Salomon describes distributed cognition as "stretched over" over individuals and artifacts. This implies, as he clearly explains, that distribution is a concept close to a *system*, i.e. one where the interrelations between parts make it function properly. His focus is on the role of the individual within such distributed systems or networks. Maybe his concern derives from the tradition in cognitive psychology or from organizational studies, where methodological individualism has been rampant for many decades. To use his own words, his concerns are around three questions:

> can we afford *not* to include the individual in such theorizing? [. . .] are distributed and individuals' solo cognitions interrelated? If so, how? [. . .] what educational implications can be derived in terms of goals and practices? (Salomon, 1993, p. 113; emphasis in the original)

I will disregard the third question, because this book is not interested in education. The question on the exclusion of the individual is handled in four steps. The first is that of asking how much of cognition is actually distributed. He makes the example of a person sitting at a desk thinking of the arguments to include in a book chapter to claim that no distribution of "notable quality" probably happens. And, just like this example, there probably are many more where cognition is not distributed. The second step is to indicate that there is some cognition that may not be distributable. He then continues with the third step that entails representations play some role on action and concludes with a fourth step, where he argues that change in distributed cognitive systems are necessary changes in individual cognitions. I have probably not done a very good job in summarizing Salomon's points, but I have a hard time connecting his position to that of modern distributed cognitive accounts.

The second question on interrelations is based on a logical argument. Salomon claims that distributed cognition is considered as a system and, as such, its interacting parts support each other. From this, he also suggests that, according to this understanding, then the parts of the system cannot be studied. Basically, the idea is that a distributed cognitive system cannot be studied by considering its parts individually, because they cease to be meaningful parts of a system, hence they are different. His concern is that individual cognition could not be analyzed – for distributed cognitive scholars – unless it is part of the distributed cognitive system. He argues this is a limit of the approach and, to assume that parts of a system are only determined by the system itself is a logical fallacy.

In the end, Salomon's position is that the individual is necessary and central to understand the most salient characteristics of distributed cognitive systems. Most of his points are actually addressed by the EDEC literature I reviewed above and this is the cause of the misunderstanding that some MOC scholars have of distributed cognition.

4.3   Summary

This chapter has presented a few relatively recent extensions of the EDEC traditions. Far from being comprehensive, these evolutions of the original paradigms have been classified into two streams, the *ecological* and the *all-encompassing* perspectives. Within the first, I have considered *human interactivity* and *systemic* cognition, while the second includes *e-cognition* and *radical embodied cognition*. The second part of the chapter has been dedicated to criticism of EDEC. Among them, I have considered the *implausibility clause* that sees EDEC as based on unacceptable assumptions, *le loup déguisé en agneau* where a computationalist view is used to reframe (and distort, to some extent) the nature of EDEC, and what I have called the *misunderstanding* of some MOC scholars who lean on a preliminary version of EDEC. Again, what has been presented is probably not representative of the wider literature but it is instrumental for the discourse that starts from Chapter 5 onwards.

5

The Social Distribution of Cognition

"Could my mental states be partly constituted by the states of other thinkers?"

— Clark and Chalmers (1998), p. 17

Much of what happens in an organization relates to its human participants, whether they are employees, managers, executives, members of the board, etc. The expression "human capital" is common in management as well[1] and there is a tendency to consider the actual differential or advantage an organization has on competitors as relying on those who work in it.

This is common sense in many disciplines and I am not going to dispute these statements since I agree with them, in principle, at least. The problem I have with them is that they seem more statements coming from some casual talk rather than specific enough to define what it is exactly that people do within organizations. Moreover, they are not clear on whether the direction is one- or two-way. The former case suggests that people make the organization the way it is, the latter may allow for some loop where also the organization supports workers in what they do. Again, there is nothing to disagree with the statements above, but they sound a bit empty.

This chapter is dedicated to an attempt to substantiate the claim that the human factor is what makes a difference in organizations. In

---

[1] It originated in economics (see, e.g., Becker, Murphy, & Tamura, 1990; Schultz, 1961; Coleman, 1988).

Computational Organizational Cognition:
A Study on Thinking and Action in Organizations, 71–84
Copyright © 2021 by Emerald Publishing Limited
All rights of reproduction in any form reserved
doi: 10.1108/978-1-83867-511-020211005

particular, in the following pages, I will claim that this difference is substantial when there is an alignment between the organization and the way in which its members cognize. And this cognition is tied to the social milieu that constitutes part of the environment in which people work. In other words, an organization is successful to the extent to which it enables active cognitive distribution processes, mainly among its human members. This outlines the *socially distributed cognition* (SDC) theory and gives a first connection with prosocial organizational behaviors.

The next section describes the concept of *docility*, intended as a behavioral instantiation of EDEC, while the following section is dedicated to its applications to organizations. Most of what comes in the next pages constitutes the theoretical backbone informing the choices for agents in the simulations that make Part II of this book. The last section of this chapter is a bridge to Part II.

5.1   The Concept of *Docility*

After more than 10 years from Secchi and Bardone (2009) and Secchi (2011), the literature on *docility* is still limited although our work has attracted some attention. In this section, I introduce the work from where inspiration for this concept comes from and then elaborate on what Emanuele Bardone and I have thought the relation with EDEC perspectives lies.

5.1.1   Simon's Take

The thesis of Simon's (1993) article is that one characteristic of humans is their sociability, hence they indulge more often in other-oriented behavior (altruism) rather than self-oriented behavior (selfishness). In order for individuals to receive acts of altruism, they need to perceive them as relevant and useful. In this respect, they have to be *docile* or have a disposition toward using information, recommendations, persuasion, and suggestions coming from other individuals and to make decisions. According to Simon, this is an indispensable characteristic of human beings that defines them as a social species as well as a strategy to cope with their *bounded rationality*. This latter point is especially interesting.

Most of the readers may recall that bounded rationality is a concept that defines our ability to reason – i.e. cognize – as being shaped by two sets of limitations (e.g., Simon, 1955, 1978, 1979). There is an *external* limitation that concerns the extent to which decision makers access information and the quantity of information that is available. The other limitation is *internal* to the brain and it refers to the bounds of intracranial information processing; even if decision makers had access to the entirety of information, they would not be able to process it in full. Now, Simon (1993) claims that *docility* is a way to cope with these limitations. In the passage below, he explains why bounded rationality serves as an enabler of docility in human beings. A disclaimer before you read the excerpt below. Simon refers to "fitness" because he suggested that docility is a feature that has evolutionary repercussions. In order to successfully live a social life, human beings have developed prosocial dispositions to cope with threats and challenges that the environment (and other humans) would present them. The word fitness is to be intended as a better fit to society.

> Because of bounded rationality, docility contributes to the fitness of human beings in evolutionary competition. [. . .] In large measure, we do what we do because we have learned from those who surround us, not from our own experience, what is good for us and what is not. Behaving in this fashion contributes heavily to our fitness because (a) social influences will generally give us advice that is 'for our own good' and (b) the information on which this advice is based is far better than the information we could gather independently. As a consequence, *people exhibit a very large measure of docility.* [. . .] Since docile persons depend heavily on socially provided advice and orders, they often make choices that reduce their own fitness under social advice to do so. They are often unable to judge independently that a recommended choice is actually disadvantageous to them as individuals. This inability is a necessary consequence of their bounded rationality, the same bounded rationality that makes docility, on average, enhance their fitness. (Simon, 1993, pp. 156–157; emphasis in the original)

There are many parts of the text above that are worth a comment or two but, in this section of the chapter, we are interested the arguments connecting bounded rationality to docility. The mechanism is relatively simple in that bounded rationality triggers docility. In fact, the use of advice that is socially supplied derives from the limited access to information. In other words, since some knowledge cannot be experienced directly, decision makers do not have much choice but to trust information that is coming from social sources (e.g., doctors, articles, government, others). In some cases, this is detrimental and leads to a poor decision (see Chapters 6 and 7 on this specific point).

5.1.2   Secchi and Bardone's Take

When Emanuele Bardone and I first encountered the idea of docility in Simon's (1993) paper, it took us by surprise. The context in which this concept was introduced was that of explaining altruistic behavior. Simon was not interested in expanding the cognitive domain of individuals, nor in refining the concept of bounded rationality. His benchmark was, once again, the *homo oeconomicus* and, this time, he was concerned with selfishness. This is hardly surprising, since fighting against economic neo-classic rationality has been Simon's life-long fixation. What is surprising is that a hard-core cognitivist such as Simon, one who spent a good part of his career to advocate that the brain works on symbol processing like a computing machine and who never took his focus off the individual decision maker, had finally opened up to *the social*.

The way he did it is, indeed, a very peculiar way to give in to the realization that sociality has a weight in rational choice and decision making. Still it is a relevant find. As shown in the excerpt above, the idea of docility that Simon presented is wired with that of bounded rationality and, more precisely, to the limits of information processing. The fact that there are internal limitations is something that shapes the choice of which source to trust. Clearly, at least from the 1993 article and from the text reproduced above, this is taken as yet another limitation, as if first-hand experience is, after all, better.

Passive Versus Active Docility

Emanuele Bardone and I were very much in doubt about the ties of this concept to bounded rationality. It actually did not need bounded rationality, it needed an EDEC perspective to work and be understood properly. The first thing we noticed was that Simon's concept was *passive*. The emphasis was on being dependent on information coming from so-called *social channels* – e.g., colleagues, family, strangers, but also institutions, organizations, governments. However, the process of getting information is almost never one-way, especially for an employee of an organization, our case in point. Think of one of the most common ways of receiving information nowadays: emails. Most of them, especially those coming from people you work with require a reply, are triggered by a previous email, or by a conversation. There are countless occasions where there is an exchange more than a one-way feed of information from a source. But there is more to it. In fact, from a cognitive perspective, we do manipulate information to the point that making sense of it can easily require action of some sort. Take the case of the email and imagine the message directed to you is somehow cryptic. When you start answering the email, you notice something you have not noticed before and, all of a sudden, that's how you interpret the message. You understand it now. In other words, it is the action of replying – i.e. writing as an aid to further thinking – that enables a more appropriate interpretation. This is something that calls directly in an EDEC perspective and can be called cognition *through doing* (Magnani, 2007). Hence, in order to properly consider docility, one has to allow for both passive and *active* exchanges. Someone passively taking information, recommendations, suggestions, or being persuaded by someone else is probably in a vulnerable position. On the one hand, others may stop sharing information with this person, given that he/she does not reciprocate. On the other hand, the person may not be too different from a selfish individual, who only takes and never gives. We cannot exclude that these individuals exist, but they are part of a spectrum.

It is possible to map various docility types by comparing active and passive features. Fig. 5.1 is an attempt to map various types by varying levels of active and passive behaviors. A person showing only passive features is categorized as a complete selfish individual, vice versa, one showing only active features is fully altruistic. Both extremes are rare to find in an actual organization because, on average, they are both behaviors that are looked upon suspiciously by others. The fully selfish would never share anything with anybody and may only be concerned about his/her own knowledge gains, but never give advice. The fully altruistic may only be concerned about passing what he/she knows on to others, but never take any advice. Both behaviors fail to establish proper social connections with others over time and are atypical.

Fig. 5.1. A Map of Possible Docility-Induced Characters.

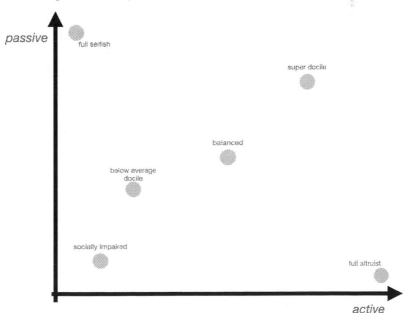

A balanced individual, located at the center of Fig. 5.1, typically operates on a variety of mixed behaviors, sometimes leaning more toward the passive, sometimes more toward the active. An individual who shows higher rates of information sharing can be categorized as a super-docile, as we suggest in our work (Secchi & Bardone, 2009). This type builds on hyper activity and usually functions as a connector within a team or an organization. The final two types represented in Fig. 5.1 are the individual showing below average docility and appearing to perform at lower rates of information sharing, both active and passive, and a person who does not share almost any information at all. I am proposing to label this one a "socially impaired" individual here because of the inability to function properly in a social environment.

Another way to interpret what presented in Fig. 5.1 is that of a range of possible behaviors that a single individual may practice. This depends on a mix of personal and environmental constraints and enablers. For any given situation, a person may have a starting point – i.e. one of the six positions on the map – and move up-down-left-right in a range of positions around one's own average. To fully understand the conditions that lead to a range docile behaviors, we need to explore the cognitive backbone of the concept and its environmental settings.

Cognitive Backbone

As mentioned above, while working on docility we took it as a behavioral manifestation of distributed cognition. In this book, due to what presented in Chapter 3 and Chapter 4, it is probably easier to connect docility to parts of the EDEC perspectives.

At one point in the previous subsection, I have mentioned Magnani's (2007) idea of cognizing *through doing* as a manifestation of embeddedness, embodiment, and enaction. Manipulation – of ideas, artifacts, resources of various kinds – requires an understanding of the context in which this is happening. Building on the example above, making sense of an advice while replying to an email is undetachable from the computational means, the organizational context, the sender's position and relation to the recipient, as well as the design of the software used. These are only a few circumstances that make email writing embedded in a context, the list can be extended depending on the specific case. The important element here is that, in order to act upon the email, there needs to be a contextualized understanding of it.

The second aspect that makes manipulation tied to an EDEC perspective is that it can only happen through a personal involvement in writing. It is by channeling the self onto the act of writing that interpretation happens. The sense of puzzlement felt upon reading the advice, the urge to ask for clarifications, and the personal way in which each one of us approaches text indicate that the action is embodied, i.e. it cannot be separated by the human being who is actually performing it without losing its sense and becoming something else. Of course, one should then consider how actual manipulation of text works while writing an email. It may happen by quoting the original text, by rephrasing it, by expressing it differently still using the same words used by the sender, or by using other strategies. Independent of how it is done, what matters is that it is done *by someone* because the way in which this act is performed depends on the mix of subjective operations on the text.

Embodiment is essential, because it means that it cannot be separated by both contexts (or situations) and the meaning of the specific action that is performed. If one takes the above as a paradigmatic example it becomes apparent that cognizing *through doing* is more common than one may think, not just in relation with docile-based behaviors. At the same time, docility does not always require action. On the one hand, dealing with exchange of information is action-bound, on the other hand, it may not be either immediately prone to action nor ever. Especially in its passive form, that of receiving advice, for example, docility may not trigger any action at all simply because the advice is taken but not acted upon. Again, this is just a possibility and it is part of the spectrum (Fig. 5.1).

According to EDEC perspectives, especially to advocates of distributed cognition, individuals use a variety of resources that are to be found externally. In an organization there are plenty – e.g., computers, desks, colleagues, texts, routines, norms. These are all existing as part of an environment and interpreted, used, or exploited by an interacting person. The fact that the use of external cognitive resources is widespread has a fundamental implication. To support cognitive activities, we create external resources (as in, e.g., Norman, 1993). This is embedded enaction, as Varela, Thompson, and Rosch (1991) would put it and it is one of the most common ways in which we operate. Think of one of the most basic human activities: language or, better, languaging (Cowley, 2011). While language serves a rather functional role in our lives by satisfying the need to communicate with others, at the same time it helps us make clarity on what we mean. In many instances we use language as a way to put forth a concept, to clarify what we mean to say to ourselves at first, then to others. In other words, there is a process of *externalization* that is constantly in the making. If one thinks about it, this is not only true for language (spoken, written, body), but also for tools, artifacts and other things we make (examples of these are in Magnani, 2007; Secchi, 2011; Bardone, 2011). But, let us stick with language.

When you step into a pastry shop and see all the choices you have as beautifully displayed in front of you, suddenly you cannot decide. When your turn comes, you have to make a choice but have not decided yet. So, you start saying a few words and realize, that way, what you really want. Not only this represents an externalization process but it also signals that something else has happened soon after that. In fact, after creating these external resources in the form of words, you have made sense of them as they appear out there. Your words are both yours and, at the same time, different from you, they are "out there." They have become part of a distributed cognitive system that now includes those who listen, the context in which the words are pronounced, and you, as a sender-receiver of them. By pronouncing the words, you have started another process that has been called *re-projecting* (Magnani, 2007; Secchi, 2011). The words are used as external tools by you and others and this use changes the way in which you go about them. Naming one pastry or asking about its ingredients may trigger other thoughts and make you remember how some of them taste, whether you have liked them before or whether you are up to a new experience, if you have not.

Docility is a behavioral manifestation of EDEC perspectives because *it requires reasoning about external resources by using them to perform one or more actions.* This is particularly relevant to an organization because the external cognitive resources the docile individual uses are *social* resources. This is what makes it different from standard EDEC and it is the foundation of a theory of *SDC* in organizations.

Setting

If docility is particularly useful to describe how individuals cognize and behave in organizations, what are the conditions that enable or disable it? Even though one may agree with Simon and consider that, on average, humans exhibit docility as a social characteristic, there are instances in which this is not the case. There are organizations in which employees are encouraged to show competitive behavior and act as selfishly as possible to avoid being ranked in the lower 10% and face the risk of being fired. This is the notorious case of Jack Welch's General Electric, and it is not an isolated one, unfortunately. In organizations such as these ones, prosocial behaviors of any kind are discouraged and probably seen as a weakness. So, the question stands: what are the conditions for docility to flourish?

In other work (Secchi, 2011; Secchi & Bardone, 2009), I have discussed these conditions as something that should be in place before docility can actually manifest itself. Hence, it is probably more accurate to refer to them as *preconditions* rather than simply conditions. They are three, listed here in no particular order: (a) *community* part-taking, (b) existence of information *sharing channels*, and (c) public *availability of information*.

The first precondition is probably the most important. In order for prosocial behavior to be the norm in a given organization, individuals should feel as if they belong to the same community. This feeling of belongingness triggers trust in others and the conviction to be in a safe haven, where exchanges happen fairly, as much as possible. In Magnani, Secchi, and Bardone (2007), we make the example of the community of open source software developers to exemplify docile behaviors. These people (we call them "hackers") have to trust that their code inputs to the software fall in the "good" hands of others in the community who will delete parts of them to make room for improvements, will provide comments where necessary, and use them as a basis to add their own. They typically feel that they belong to a community with shared goals and ideals. This is a necessary precondition for a "hacker" to start working on code development and feed it into the public domain. Similar settings are those of teams, work groups or organizations as a whole, where employees need to feel this sense of belongingness in order for them to perform prosocial docile behaviors.

The second precondition is that of the existence of appropriate channels to allow for the exchange of recommendations, advice, sugges tions and, more generally, information. Organizations are very rich environments in which exchange of information happens widely. However, they are also places where bottleneck effects may happen and where information is sometimes lost in procedures, especially in large stateowned organizations (Bozeman & Feeney, 2011; Kaufmann, Taggart, & Bozeman, 2019). In general, these channels are intertwined with the sense of community because they guarantee that sharing processes are fair and information is safely exchanged. They may vary significantly depending on the organization, the team or the group in which they are needed. Some teams use daily briefings or meetings, while others prefer constant communication updates via a company chat, yet others use emails. No matter how, transparency and fairness (or organizational justice, using a more appropriate terminology; Colquitt, Lepine, Piccolo, Zapata, & Rich, 2002) is a key element here.

Finally, the third precondition is the public availability of the information shared. This is probably not as immediately understood as the other two. In Secchi and Bardone (2009) we used the community of mathematicians to exemplify what this means. In such an academic community, mathematicians share their work using blogs, web-based repositories, books, and mainly journal articles – let us assume that we are discussing those operating in a particular domain of mathematics such that we can actually talk about a community. In order for them to progress in their work, they need access to what others have been working in the past and are currently working on. There is one condition for this to work: the information must be coded right. In other words, it must become available to the public – i.e. within the community – and it has to be understood by community members properly. The notations, equations, formulas, algorithms, language and formats of the specific domain of mathematics the community is used to are part of this precondition. Without appropriate code for communication and without it being publicly available, there is no community and there is obviously no docility. These conditions are also applicable to, for example, a team in an organization. Information shared must become available to the others if it solves a problem or if it is used to perform a task. Others in the team need that information to move on in their work. In order for this to work, the solution or performance need to become available through a language that everyone in the community (team) can understand. Think of an IT team, an accounting and finance team, or a team in operations. They typically make these solutions available and code them in a way that others in the community can understand. On some occasions, others in the organization may need it as well. And this requires a process of de-coding the internal (community-oriented) information to make it available to others outside. This is because the information for the team is docility-enhanced (see Chapter 8) and needs decoding to become available to others externally.

If one reflects broadly on the meaning of the three preconditions, it becomes apparent that they meet also requirements for the distribution of cognition. The existence of a community is pointing at the macro-structural element that both constraints and enables meaning making, in line with the ecological/systemic view presented in Chapter 4 (Cowley & Vallée-Tourangeau, 2013). And, of course, when I mentioned the *feelings* of belongingness, I was implicitly referring to embodiment and structural conditions for enaction. The existence of channels that allow for external resources to become available to cognition is also relevant for cognition to be properly extended. While the third precondition may seem far away from EDEC, it is actually not. In fact, for information to be available in a public (community) space it means that it becomes local or situated in time and space, hence cannot be acted upon unless this local meaning is actually interpreted.

5.2   Operationalization of the Concept

The conceptualizations built around the idea of *docility* are enough to call in for a theory specifically aimed at explaining the working mechanisms of the *social* distributions of cognition. Although I never dare to call it this way in my previous works, this is probably the most appropriate denomination for the body of knowledge around it. An organization that embraces this disposition and actively promotes exchanges of information among their members is benefiting from a *docility effect* (Secchi, 2011; Secchi & Bardone, 2009) and has been indicated elsewhere as a *docile organization* (Secchi, 2011, Chapter 9). If we want to talk about a theory around the concepts presented in this chapter, then we shall refer to it by the name of SDC theory (further details on this in Part III of this book).

To study this theory, the likelihood of its assumptions as well as its workings within organizations, I have produced a number of studies targeted at exploring the robustness and consistency of the theoretical implant. The most obvious starting point was that of continuing within the same tradition outlined by Simon (1993) and work on the three fitness equations he introduced.

In the same article that has been repeatedly mentioned early on in this chapter, Simon presented a system of three equations that studied the effects of being docile and intelligent, I, docile and unintelligent, U, and non-docile and selfish, S. The first two types have to deal with the costs of altruistic behavior, according to a general interpretation of altruism in economics, while the third type has not any, just benefits deriving from others being altruistic. To compensate with the cost, the first two docile types have a fitness surplus deriving from being docile, hence fully integrated in a social environment. The difference between the two is that the intelligent is able to discriminate against information being processed while the unintelligent cannot. Here are the original equations (p. 157):

$$fI = fn + fd \cdot dI + faI \cdot qI \cdot cI + faU \cdot qU \cdot cU - c \cdot cI \qquad (5.1)$$

$$fS = fn + faI \cdot qI \cdot cI + faU \cdot qU \cdot cU \qquad (5.2)$$

$$fU = fn + fd \cdot dU + faI \cdot qI \cdot cI + faU \cdot qU \cdot cU - c \cdot cU \qquad (5.3)$$

where f is fitness, fn is the natural fitness that every individual has, d is the increment to fitness due to being docile, q and the letter next to it identifies the quantity of individual type in the population, fa are increment to fitness due to altruistic behavior, and c is the cost of being altruist while cI and cU are the extent to which I and U are altruists. Simon then attributed the following values to the parameters in the equations: $fn = 1.01, fd = 0.02, c = 0.005, faI = 0.01, faU = 0.005, q_0I = 1/3, q_0S = 1/3, q_0U = 1/3, dI = 2, cI = 0.8, cU = 1, dU = 1$ (p. 158).

From Equation 5.1 to 5.3 and parameter values, it is apparent that the non-docile almost disappears from the system while the intelligent docile multiply. Simon was interested in evolution, hence the movements in the values he attributed to the parameters in the equations represented changes in the different generations.

The first approach I took with the operationalization of docility was that of continuing along the lines of Simon, hence using the same equations he presented and exploring their meaning further as well as their implications. I have discussed these at length in various other work (Secchi, 2007, 2009, 2011; Secchi & Bardone, 2009). For a more in-depth discussion of the findings I invite to consult those publications, while their discussion here serves a slightly different purpose. The aim with which I studied these equations was twofold. On the one hand, I wanted to explore whether the findings Simon presented were accurate. On the other hand, I thought the system needed to become more dynamic if one were to apply it to an organization. By exploring the first part of the aim, I developed a *theory of docile society* (Secchi, 2007) through which it became clear that the selfish does not disappear (as Simon argued) but takes a "back seat," so to speak, in a social system. While applying the equations to an organization, Emanuele Bardone and I implemented the equations in a hawks-and-doves game (Secchi & Bardone, 2009) where fitness led to a switch such that the employee may change docility type, when more convenient. In other words, we made the system of equations more dynamic by allowing change of behavior (represented by the intelligent–unintelligent, and selfish types). We did not like the intelligent-unintelligent dichotomy and re-labeled them as docile behavior that could be average or above average (i.e. super-docile). Findings of that study show that the vast majority of individuals in an organization are average docile, a very limited percentage are selfish non-docile, and about 18% are super-docile. This is the equilibrium we found.

This operationalization was somehow poor. There was something missing in the way in which equations represented actual interaction between individuals in an organization. The issue was specifically that the equations provided an overview of population dynamics in an organization (or in society). In the game we implemented in Secchi and Bardone (2009), payoffs and fitness are calculated on the likelihood that one individual meets one of its own or another type. But this happens at the aggregate level, such that, for example, $qI = 1/3$ in the population means that the likelihood to gain from I is exactly $1/3$. This is a bird-eye view that does not tell much about what is happening at the individual level, nor it tells much about finer differences between individuals.

The other slight discomfort I had with the equations above and as implemented in the various studies related to the assumption that each one of the actors in an organization would know exactly what the situation in the entire organization was. The exchanges were based on a pure probabilistic rule. In other words, the idea that each organizational member holds an idea of what is happening in the organization as a whole is a very strong assumption. More than that, it is an assumption that goes against the dictates of bounded rationality. It was as if, by using these simple equations, Simon had forgotten about the bounds he so strongly advocated in his work (and early on even in the paper on docility and altruism!).

The numerical analysis that derives from assigning Simon's or other values to the equations leads to set solutions. In Secchi and Bardone (2009) and Secchi (2007) we found an equilibrium. Nothing wrong with that, but these results were set. In other words, given the inputs, the solution could only be one and always the same. Now, given the nature of organizational interactions and exchanges, this is hardly the case. Of course, one could interpret the set results as an average, what would happen in that particular situation, on average, but not necessarily. Yet, the solution is deterministic and leaves no room for understanding what is the possible dispersion around the mean.

While the dissatisfaction above was mounting, I tried to see whether I could work on refining the theory a bit more. This is where I expanded the behavioral outcomes of docility to include not just altruism but also cooperation, volunteering, philanthropy, and social responsibility (Secchi, 2009). The theory of the docile organization was becoming something that had to do more with a wider range of prosocial behaviors rather than simply with altruism. In another effort with Emanuele Bardone (Secchi & Bardone, 2013), we wrote equations to study how docility would favor or hinder the rapid diffusion of practices, ideas, behaviors within an organization (bandwagon). While I was satisfied with the heuristic use of the results coming from these equations and from the way in which theory was developing, something was still missing to reach more accuracy.

After all this reasoning, I was left looking for a different way to operationalize the concept. Since I had given much importance to the idea of docility, it was also important that the method with which the related theory of *SDC* was explored was appropriate. In the end, I wanted individuals in the organization to have partial and imperfect knowledge of the entire organization, to know those with which they were at close contact better than others, to show variants of docility instead of the same average number, and to be mistaken about the other person's "type." These simple consideration imply that I was looking for a truly dynamic system, where equilibria could emerge as well as non-equilibria. At the same time, this meant that the system needed to reflect some aspects of complexity, such that results may fall in a range of possibilities rather than indicate one fixed and stable point. In other words, I did not know it back then but I was looking for *agent-based modeling*.

5.3   Summary

In this chapter, I have taken you to the journey that led me to discover the concept of docility from Herbert Simon's work. After a succinct summary of his work, I have moved to show how docility has been re-interpreted by Emanuele Bardone and I, by attaching an active side to it. This active/passive concept presents a closer link with EDEC perspectives, in particular when looking at cognition *through doing*, and at the various processes of *externalizing* and *re-projecting*. By outlining the preconditions for docility to exist and be promoted, I have sketched a *SDC* theory. The chapter ends with a description of how the concept was operationalized in Simon's and in my work. This led to dissatisfaction with the mathematics used to analyze this theory and opened up the opportunity for me to find another, a better, method. I accepted this challenge. Part II of the book is the story of how I dealt with the challenge.

Part II
Agent-based Computational Organizational Cognition

6

Agent-based Modeling and Cognition

"Socially situated autonomous agents evolve a capacity to filter external (social) inputs and adapt to and take advantage of them ('social responsiveness', as distinct from reactivity)."
                                        – Rosaria Conte (1999, p. 204)

As I write this chapter and set myself to introducing agent-based computational simulation modeling, I realize that I have done so several times already in a number of publications (Herath, Homberg, & Secchi, 2021; Homberg, Secchi, & Herath, 2020; Secchi, 2015, 2021; Secchi & Neumann, 2016). Nevertheless, this introduction is necessary here because one of the aims of this book is to establish agent-based computational organizational cognition as a research area. In line with that, what follows is tied to this method and it would make it difficult for readers to understand the implications of these models without a general overview. At the same time, I have a theoretical objective in this book and the method is a means to that end. Hence, while presenting the rudiments of agent-based modeling (ABM), I am keeping it short and ask readers to kindly refer to Secchi (2015), Fioretti (2013), and especially to my recent Secchi (2021), a book entirely dedicated to introducing ABM for management and organization research.

Computational Organizational Cognition:
A Study on Thinking and Action in Organizations, 87–94
Copyright © 2021 by Emerald Publishing Limited
All rights of reproduction in any form reserved
doi: 10.1108/978-1-83867-511-020211006

6.1   What Is an Agent-based Model?

ABM is an advanced computational simulation technique that is
employed to study complex systems (Edmonds & Meyer, 2017b). Given
the complex features of social systems, these models are used widely
in sociology (Squazzoni, 2012), economics (Tesfatsion & Judd, 2006),
social ecology (Grimm & Railsback, 2013), while they are still in their
infantry in psychology (Smaldino, Calanchini, & Pickett, 2015), social
psychology (Eberlen, Scholz, & Gagliolo, 2017; Jackson, Rand, Lewis,
Norton, & Gray, 2017) and organization research (Davis, Eisenhardt,
& Bingham, 2007; Fioretti, 2013).

For some, computational simulation is a type of mathematical modeling (Carley, 2009; Knudsen, Levinthal, & Puranam, 2019), for others
it is a different kind of modeling (Conte, Hegselmann, & Terna, 1997;
Edmonds & Meyer, 2017b; Gilbert, 2008; Gilbert & Troitzsch, 2005;
Secchi, 2021). Some computational simulations are tied to mathematics,
because they remain very much connected to the formal structure of
mathematics. For example, System Dynamics is based on sets of differential equations (Forrester, 1961), and NK models are based on a set
of fitness equations that requires operations on matrices (Kauffman &
Weinberger, 1989). In these cases one may argue that the computational
part is a supplement to the mathematical formulation and allows for
analytical solutions that would be very difficult to find without the
power of a computer. When looking at ABM, the prospect is rather
different. Indeed, one can implement various mathematics-based algorithms and do it at various stages of the modeling process however, the
mathematics is never the central point of an agent-based model. This
is because, unlike other computational simulations, the core of ABM is
in its programming, in the code that drives it. And, again, this code
may include mathematics but it is fundamentally based on objects and
logics. The code is a language that mixes instructions to a computer
with mathematics, statistics, and other types of logical commands.

The fact that ABM follows an object-based logic simply means that
the way in which the modeler approaches a problem is different than
mathematical modeling. The interest is on the *what* is going to be modeled in a particular simulation, its characteristics, locations, behavior,
processing abilities, and interactions or, more broadly, its settings. The
what of ABM is the *agent*. *How* it operates depends on its settings, on
the settings of other agents in the simulation and on the settings of the
environment in which it is located and behaves.

Of course, one may object, a modeler may not think math when
locating an agent on the environment and still, there is an underlying
formula that allows that agent to appear right there. This is not far from

the truth but there is a difference between coding to instruct a computer and writing an equation. The location of an agent in an environment is the same as programming a computer such that a dot appears in a particular position on the screen. In all the years of coding, it never happened to me to write an equation for that. I did write a code in one of the programming languages. And a programming language is a formal type of language but it is of a kind different from mathematics. Programming follows logics and bits of natural languages that make that logic operational. Moreover, if software programming and mathematics are two of the same kind, then I am wondering why computer scientist do not usually come from math departments of universities. So, I maintain there is a difference, and quite a significant one.

Having cleared that the difference between mathematical and computational modeling is both *substantive* – i.e. related to the approach required – and *procedural* – in that it pertains to the way in which it is practiced – I can move to describe general characteristics of ABM. The following subsection is dedicated to the functions of a model while the section after the next addresses the scope of applications.

6.2   The Dynamics of ABM

A standard way to describe ABM (also followed in Secchi, 2015) is that of considering its three main components: (a) *agents*, (b) *environment*, and (c) *mechanisms* (or rules). Briefly, an *agent* can be anything a modeler wants it to be, from individuals to entire organizations or countries, as well as tasks, ideas, and other immaterial or material artifacts. The *environment* is tightly connected to the agents and is usually designed accordingly. Here too, the extent to which an environment is defined depends on the purpose of the model and what agents are set to do. *Mechanisms* are the processes that allow agents to function in an environment and in relation to other agents. They are instructions on what they are supposed to do when a set of conditions materialize.

Instead of indulging on a detailed description of these three main components, I think it is more appropriate to focus on some of the general characteristics of ABM. The model presented the following chapters of Part II serve the purpose of detailing these three main components. For the sake of this introduction, the rest of this subsection is organized around a discussion of the level of specificity an agent-based model can get, on its treatment of non-systematic events, on the role of time and space as well as on the emergent properties of the agent-based system.

6.2.1   Descriptive Versus Simple Models

Every modeler who observes a system to represent via the means of scientific enquiry (traditionally, mathematics) faces the pragmatic need to be parsimonious with characterizations and dynamics. In other words, in using traditional tools the modeler needs to make sure the phenomenon is formalized in a way that is manageable. This approach is described by the warning "Keep it simple, stupid!" And simplicity has always been the golden standard, a general aim to which a modeler should aspire. As Edmonds and Moss (2005) explain, ABM puts this aspiration upside down.

With ABM one does not need to be parsimonious in either the number of parameters considered or the way in which they are specified. In fact, these models can be – according to some (Edmonds & Moss, 2005) they must be – descriptive. Of course, there is a level to which description needs to be functional, i.e. relevant to the purpose of the model. However, the message is that ABM can handle complex agents, environments, and articulated mechanisms of interaction. As Edmonds & Moss (2005) put it, the new warning to the agent-based modeler is "Keep it descriptive, stupid!"

6.2.2   Stochastic Processes

Another crucial feature of ABM is that they usually include several random elements. These are, as one may imagine, *pseudo*-random because generated by a computer and not coming from natural events. Still, as we explain in Seri, Secchi, and Martinoli (2020), the state of random numbers generation is at a very advanced stage today such that it is difficult to distinguish natural from pseudo random.

Since agent-based models are used to study social phenomena, they can be made to include random elements at every step of their settings and procedures. This is important because the model will then generate alternative possible scenarios, given the variability as inputed by the modeler. Social systems, especially organizations, are unpredictable and allow for varieties of configurations, results, solutions to problems, executions, performance, functionalities, etc. For a simulation model to keep these features of the modeled system alive is, again, crucial.

Random elements can be included as one sets the agents, for example, by assigning characteristic C to the population following a specific distribution. Parameters are, in this text and from now on, indicated with the `courier` font, so that they are always visible. In an agent-based model, parameters are those elements that are used to manipulate the conditions under which the simulation is performed. A parameter can be fixed, in which case it is better called a constant, or it can take a set of values. Let us imagine that we have a workforce of 100 and that one parameter is age. We assume that the average age, $\bar{a} = 43$, and can model that as a normal curve such that, with a standard deviation, $s_a = 10$, 68% of the agents will have between 33 and 53 years of age. So, a random-normal attribution may work just fine, we would only make sure to avoid that an agent has $a < 18$ (school age) or $a > 70$ (retirement age). With such a procedure we would not know which agent has specifically what age, but have an organization that on average reflects the characteristics we want it to have. A similar approach can be applied to other parameters, either linking them to this one (e.g., seniority) or not (e.g., competence).

Parametrization procedures such as the one described above can also be attributed to the environment or to the mechanisms. The location in which an agent moves in the environment can change as, for example, the understanding of a topic also changes (i.e. in case the environment is not physical but a psycho-cognitive space; see below). Most interestingly, mechanisms can update themselves and change with the agents, with the environment, or with both at once. Mechanisms can be interpreted (actioned) differently by agents, depending on location, interaction, and/or their characteristics.

These are only a limited number of examples, to show how easy it is for ABM to embed random components in each and every single aspect of modeling.

6.2.3   Time and Space

While having a space in which to operate is probably a natural feature for an agent to have, time is probably not as immediate as space. As mentioned cursorily above, an environment does not necessarily need to be a representation of physical space, for example, office layout, streets, territory. Space can also be a state of mind where agents find themselves close or distant from others in the system. This is particularly interesting from an EDEC perspective because ABM makes it easy to study the contingencies of situatedness. In other words, the proximity of agents typically drives their actions in a way such that this is contingent to the situation in which they find themselves. Again, this proximity can be cognitive or psychological, not necessarily physical. The COVID-19 crisis the world is living as I write this is an example of what I mean. Many workers today are close to others in their organization, because they meet, perform tasks, communicate, solve problems and perform other organizational chores. This is even though they are far away from each other, because the pandemic has forced many to work from home.

Almost all agent-based models I can think of have a time element. This is another very useful feature of these types of models. The way in which agents behave in the system is simulated dynamically over time. Most traditional modeling techniques struggle with representing the passing of time. This is, after all, a fairly complex aspect of life and work. The average agent-based model handles this relatively easily, instead.

6.2.4   Emergence

All the elements above make agent-based models complex systems. The outcome of a moderately complex model usually comes in the form of a series of alternative directions in which the system can move. These alternative directions (or patterns Grimm & Railsback, 2013) can vary quite significantly when the configurations of parameters change, although variation is observed also when parameter values are kept constant. This means that the system is relatively unpredictable, given its initial conditions (i.e. the setting of the parameters) and, as seen in Chapter 1, this is a characteristic of complex systems.

The patterns or directions in which results from the model move toward are so-called *emergent properties* of the system. For a more in-depth discussion of emergence in ABM I can recommend Chapter 2 of Secchi (2021). For the purpose of the current presentation, "emergence" can be defined simply as observed characteristics of an agent-based model that cannot be directly predicted by simply looking at the initial parameter settings.

6.3   ABM for Science

Now that I have provided a brief introduction to ABM, one may start wondering what kind of scientific problems they are more suitable to answer. This is a very relevant question that all modeler needs to answer, one time or another. There obviously are limits to what a computational simulation model can accomplish and it may be good to quickly review some of the options one has.

A group of modelers (Edmonds et al., 2019) teamed up together to list and explain the various purposes to which agent-based models can be used for. By looking into purposes we can, at the same time, have an idea of what type of scientific enquiry these models may help with. Here is the list they provide: "prediction, explanation, description, theoretical exploration, illustration, analogy, and social learning" (Edmonds et al., 2019, para. 1.7). The first one listed is *prediction* and it refers to the willingness of the modeler to anticipate future events, patterns, trends, or behaviors. This is a very traditional purpose for science and it has very deep roots in the natural sciences. On the contrary and in spite of

the multiple attempts, the social sciences have not been very successful in this respect. Nevertheless, due to their potential descriptiveness,
agent-based models can serve the purpose of producing forecasts. ABM
examples that fit this category are scarce, as far as my knowledge is
concerned. Yet, this possibility remains open.

The second purpose is *explanation* and relates to models that are
designed to show features of a particular system or phenomenon. This
is specifically directed toward uncovering the mechanisms that lie under
a given phenomenon. Many models fit this purpose. For example, Miller
and Lin (2010) attempt to explain how organizational learning depends
on agents' beliefs (that they call "epistemologies") and environmental
constraints (that they call "contingencies").

The purpose of *description* is slightly different from the previous
one because the model of the observed is such that it provides a fair
representation of it. To some extent, all models present some descriptive features, to be meaningful in respect to their aims, the difference
here is that description as an ultimate purpose leans heavily on data
availability. Examples of this kind are Moss et al. (1998) on critical
incident management systems, or Heckbert (2013) that simulates the
ancient Mayan socio-ecological system.

Theoretical exploration is something that have been advocated many
times for ABM (Davis, Eisenhardt, & Bingham, 2007; Harrison, Lin,
Carroll, & Carley, 2007; Smaldino et al., 2015). This is probably one
of the most interesting features because it puts ABM right where other
mathematical modeling techniques are used for in science, that is, tools
to develop theory. This is what is done by Muelder and Filatova (2018)
with Ajzen's (1991) theory of planned behavior, where authors explore
different versions of code that variously apply to the theory.

The two purposes of *illustration* and *analogy* are different but they
both refer to a somehow broader use of ABM. The former is about
making a particular point, showing that an idea, a theory, or a specific
conjecture is possible. This way of using ABM is sometimes more for
the self than for others, as a way to clarify alternatives in modeling. The
latter is, instead used to make a point on a system by using abstract
characteristics from some other systems. It is the case of using the
concept of fitness from biology, while modeling how organizations adapt
to their socio economic systems.

The definition for the purpose of *social learning* is "A simulation is
a tool for social learning when it encapsulates a shared understanding
(or set of understandings) of a group of people" (Edmonds et al., 2019,
para. 8.3). This does not happen too often because community modeling
(the activity of developing models through a shared understanding of the
observed phenomenon) is time consuming. Together with participants

of the Agent-Based Modeling of Organizational Behavior Workshop Series No.4, sponsored by the European Academy of Management (OB Strategic Interest Group), and hosted by the University of Huddersfield in 2018, we have engaged in one such community modeling activities by following Siebers and Klügl (2017). This effort was directed to reflect on and model organizational plasticity and it has now been published (Siebers et al., 2020).

Besides the above, it is worth writing about two more reasons to engage with ABM. One has been mentioned at the beginning of this chapter and it refers to the unfeasibility or unpracticality of using mathematical or other traditional formal modeling approaches. Whenever the solution of a system of equations cannot be found, the mathematical algorithms are too complex, or the particular mathematical form one is looking for is not easy to find, then computational simulation is a good alternative.

The other point is about policy making. Occasionally, organizations need to change their structure, re-organize their activities, resize, change locations, re-allocate responsibilities, flatten their structure, move online, or perform major changes. Confronted with these decisions, management is usually ready to reason on the basis of theoretical arguments, past experience, information coming from competitors, role models, and speculative scenarios. The option of trying one alternative and then move back to where the organization was before is not available because of the immense economic and social repercussions. In these cases, ABM can gather data and create a simulation that presents management with alternative what/if scenarios and counterfactuals.

In a recent Special Issue for the *Journal of Simulation*, Vol. 15, Nos. 1-2, Stefano Armenia, Federico Bernabè and I have collected and present a number of articles that illustrate the use of computational simulation for policy making, with a focus on sustainability.

6.4   Summary

This chapter, the first of Part II, has presented a concise introduction to the main method of the book: agent-based computational simulation. Chapter 6 has been concerned with discussing the benefits of ABM in terms of dynamics and how they constitute a significant advancement over other simulation techniques, if one is interested in understanding and analyzing complex social systems.

7

An Unusual Diffusion Model

My first ABM ended up being a disappointment and, at the same time, an invigorating scientific challenge. The disappointment was not in terms of the model per se or the modeling activity, but because of its findings. In fact, I did not find what I thought I was expecting to find. This was, among other things, an application of the socially distributed cognition theory of docility (SDC) in an organization. The agents were designed to reflect various aspects of this disposition while facing an increasingly popular trend that was materializing among co-workers. I expected that docility would make employees more mindful and make it more difficult for a trend of diffusion to materialize. Before digging into the results, it is important to understand how the model is structured, what its purpose is, and what are its principal mechanisms.

Due to the challenge to my pre-judicial theoretical frames, I am no more disappointed by results of this model. On the contrary, and with an ex post view, I am very much excited by the fact that the model triggered a series of other models, bounced back to theory, and, overall, it improved my understanding of organizational social processes. The model generated a long streak of questions that I am still answering today.

7.1   A Model of Diffusion

The literature on the diffusion of innovation is quite extensive and has a very strong tradition that cuts across disciplines in the social

Computational Organizational Cognition:
A Study on Thinking and Action in Organizations, 95–111
Copyright © 2021 by Emerald Publishing Limited
All rights of reproduction in any form reserved
doi: 10.1108/978-1-83867-511-020211007

sciences (e.g., economics, sociology, management; Rohlfs, 2003; Strang
and Tuma, 1993; Rosenkopf & Abrahamson, 1999). When I started
reasoning on diffusion with Nicole Gullekson, then my colleague at
the University of Wisconsin (USA), we asked what would happen to a
diffusion process if we were to locate it within instead of between organizations. The result is the article Secchi and Gullekson (2016), published
in the journal *Computational and Mathematical Organization Theory*.
We assumed that some elements typical of diffusion outside would still
operate inside (e.g., uncertainty, ambiguity, imitation). Some others
would be peculiar to organizations instead, and that would include
making an assumption on the cognitive attitudes of workers. Another
element we included was a two-level hierarchy.

The idea was to consider a diffusion process that was fast and mindless. In the literature, this goes under the name *bandwagon* to recall
everyone's attitude of following the band on a wagon during a parade.
This indicates that the diffusion of such a behavior is usually mindless,
because one does not really reflect or rationalize on why he or she is
adopting it. A bandwagon is also defined by the sheer number of people
who adopt. In other words, the driver of a bandwagon effect is precisely
given by the numbers involved. According to some (Abrahamson &
Rosenkopf, 1997), bandwagons emerge due to the popularity of the idea,
process, behavior, product that is involved in the diffusion process. In a
graphical representation where adopters are on the y and time is on the
x, the graph takes the form of an S-shaped curve (see Fig. 7.1). This

Fig. 7.1. A Very Simple S-shaped Bandwagon Curve.

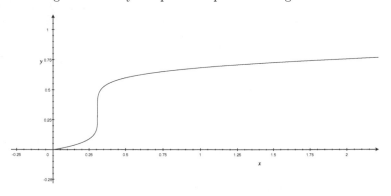

Note. The curve is generated using Apple software `Grapher` and equation $y = x \geq$
$0 \ ? \ a + \left(\frac{x-b}{N}\right)^{q}$, $N = \{100\}$, $q = \{0.2\}$, $b = \{0.308\}$, $a = 20^4 b^{5+20b}$, where y is
the probability to adopt, x is the number of individual who actually adopt, N is the total
number of individuals, and q is a parameter that represents the distribution of thresholds.
The remaining a and b are optimization parameters.

is because bandwagons are fast, and the number of adopters typically passes from few to many very quickly.

There are many ways to understand how individuals join a bandwagon. Independent of the specific reasons (some are outlined below), an effective way to represent the process is that of considering the individual trigger, a threshold (originally explained by Granovetter, 1978). This is a limit of tolerance before acting or adopting and it can be thought of as the number of individuals who have already adopted before you. Imagine you are a member of a tennis club. At one point, you notice that many of your fellow club members use a specific model of a racket. At first, you may not give it too much of a thought. However, at one point, probably after noticing that eight out of ten people you meet use that racket, you start considering buying it yourself. When you do, you have probably met your threshold and joined a bandwagon. According to this way of representing the trend, individuals have different thresholds, because of their motivations, beliefs, values, and other characteristics. In spite of its simplicity,[1] this assumption on individual "triggers" is able to represent a wide range of bandwagons and it has been used quite often in the literature (e.g., Chiang, 2007; Strang & Meyer, 1993; Strang & Soule, 1998; Abrahamson & Rosenkopf, 1997).

When Nicole Gullekson and I started our reasoning on diffusion, we could not find a model that would consider what happens within an organization. Back then, we thought this was extremely relevant, both for "positive" and "negative" effects of bandwagon (similar to the reasoning for Secchi and Bardone, 2013). For example, when implementing new policies on sustainability, an organization's hope is that it would be adopted as soon as possible by employees and managers, so that its benefits could come into effect without too much delay between deliberation and implementation. A similar case is that of legislative implementations, where the risk of a fine is sometimes associated to the lack of alignment with the law. Yet another example, not available back then but timely and relevant today, is that of an organization urging employees to work from home as much as possible because of the risk of COVID-19 contagion within the workspace. This latter case is also interesting in that it may exemplify both positive and negative instances. The sheer number of workers who either participate in a work-from-home initiative may influence what others will do. At the same time, if the number of

---

[1]The use of models that rely on thresholds have been criticized exactly because of simplicity. In fact, the assumption is based on generic triggers with little or no interest as of what they exactly are; typically, these models only care that there is such a trigger. Another criticism is that the threshold is inaccessible and it only materializes through behavior. As such, there is the risk to fall back to behaviorism, because all it matters is the actual doing.

work-from-home individuals is a minority, there is a likelihood that the others continue to show up at work.

An actual example of a COVID-19 related instance is that of a university implementing a 1/3 rule for its teaching. Due to the limited number of seats in a classroom, the university decided to implement a rule such that students are divided into three equally sized groups so that 1/3 sits in the physical space preserving social distancing while 2/3 attend the same class that is also streamed online. Besides considerations of the pedagogy involved into such a mixed approach, the important fact was that students decided not to comply. Knowing that a class was taking place in an actual classroom in one of the university buildings, some students decided to show up, independent of the group they were assigned to.[2] At the beginning, only a couple of students showed up, then they became a few more, and more, until the lecturer could notice that more than 50% of the students were in the classroom making social distancing impossible. The class was then suspended and the university was forced to rethink about this strategy.

The example we used as a basis for the study was taken by stories about the mindless use of ratios and indicators by bankers responsible for the recession starting in 2008. It seems that a bandwagon effect started by imitation, when a new reading of some of the financial solvability ratios of the mortgage applicant surfaced. In this way, the risk appeared to be bearable by the bank. This would increase the number of mortgage loans and, thus, become appealing in general short-term business. At the same time, the banks were exposing themselves to a massive number of possible insolvent clients. They realized it when it was too late, as we all know and have learned through the harsh economic conditions that span off that behavior.

So, the question is what triggers fast and (relatively) mindless bandwagons within an organization? Some of the considerations above led us to develop the agent-based model of intra-organizational diffusion processes that features in this chapter. Among the factors that could possibly either slow down or kill this diffusion process is that of actually exchanging information with others in the workplace, to make a more socially mindful decision. Stated differently, this means bringing in a *docility effect*. As I will show below, findings show that a model of organizational cognition based on docility mechanisms facilitates diffusion, especially in large organizations. Docility is intended as a cognitive

---

[2]It is probably necessary to notice that this happened in Denmark, where the average person is strictly law abiding. The government has been playing down the pandemic and, as a result, people were not scared enough such that most dismissed social distancing, did not wear face masks, and partook at meetings with up to 50 others. The rest of Europe had implemented different more stringent rules while Denmark's policies looked at Sweden more than at Continental Europe.

mechanism for workers to gain awareness and mindfulness in the face of a bandwagon-like (fast and mindless) diffusion process. But the simulation shows that this is not the case. Quite the contrary, docility helps mindless diffusion. Why? What have we missed?

The ABM introduced here will be referred to as `OrgBand2.0` to indicate it is about intra-organizational bandwagons (the "OrgBand" part) and that it is an improved version (the "2.0" part), slightly different from the one in Secchi and Gullekson (2016).

7.1.1 Parameters

Agent-based models have been widely used to simulate diffusion dynamics (see Kiesling, Günther, Stummer, & Wakolbinger, 2012), mainly concerned with innovation. The adoption of practices, products, behaviors, ideas or something else within an organization have not been considered (still today, after we published our models; Secchi & Gullekson, 2016; Secchi & Bardone, 2013). The particular conditions that shape behavior in an organization are different – this is the claim of the model – than those that generally apply outside of it, in the general society or in the marketplace. The choice of the parameters and, most importantly, the mechanisms of operation (see the next subsection) capture only some of these conditions.

In the following only parameters[3] that take different values will be considered. Table 7.1 presents a summary of the parameters, their notations, their values and description.

All the parameters in Table 7.1 are specified at the beginning of the simulation and work as initial conditions on which each agent operates in relation to the environment. At the beginning, each agent occupies a random position in the organizational environment that is represented by a three-dimensional space. The three dimensions do not represent any particular characteristic, only serve as a way to spread agents around, making it more or less likely to get in touch with others. The environment is to be thought of as a socio-cognitive space (Secchi, 2015) where agents that are close either share a task, may be members of the same team, and share some other work-related responsibilities.

The simulation has the opportunity to set the number of employees working in an organization, N. The original simulation (version 1.0) compared four types: 100, 200, 500, and 1,000. Using that as a calibration round, in this set I have only considered two types, namely 200 and 1,000 since, from the previous study (Secchi & Gullekson, 2016), it seems that results from $N = 100$ are similar to those for $N = 200$ and

---

[3]Remember that parameters are indicated with the `courier` font, so that they are always easily recognizable.

Table 7.1. Parameter Notations, Values, and Descriptions for OrgBand2.0.

Parameter	Notation	Values	Description
Agents	N	$\{200, 1000\}$	The initial number of agents that are set at the beginning of the simulation.
Move	M	ON/OFF	The organization makes agents take fixed positions (OFF) in the environment or move slightly toward each other, when a link is established (ON) to represent *ambiguity*.
Range	r	$\{4, 6\}$	The vision range of each agent that determines with whom they can interact.
Hierarchy	H	ON/OFF	When turned ON, this parameter allows for a two-level hierarchy where agents are divided into agent-workers and agent-managers.
Management[a]	P_N	$\{0.1, 0.2\}$	The proportion of agent-managers on the total number of agents N is determined by this parameter, when H = ON.
Conformity	K	$\{0, 0.1, 0.5, 1\}$	This is organizational *cultural conformity* and it defines the extent to which an agent imitates what seems the general trend in an organization.
Threshold[a]	t_i	$\sim \mathcal{N}(\bar{t}_i, 0.15)$	The tolerance to which every agent is bound before taking the action of adoption. The threshold is distributed normally at random among the agents and it is to be intended as a percentage of other adopters within range. The mean takes two values: $\bar{t}_i = \{0.25, 0.5\}$
Docility enabler	d_e	ON/OFF	This makes agents lean on docility rather than on a conformity norm; when d_e = OFF then only K is active.
Docility	d_i	$\sim \mathcal{N}(0.5, 0.25)$	This is an attribute of each agent and it is distributed normally at random in the population; the distribution is constrained to vary such that $0 \leq d_i \leq 1$.

Note. [a] Parameter specification added for OrgBand2.0.

the case of $N = 1,000$ appears to push results to the extreme of the case when $N = 500$.

The agents can move in the simulation environment, move (M = ON), or statically occupy their initial position (M = OFF). Movement, m, happens as a function of the connections (links) that each agent establishes with those in range, r, based on reciprocal attraction a, a spring constant, b, and a repulsion constant, c, such that $m = f(a, b, c)$ where $a = 0.02, b = 0.5 \cdot \gamma, c = 0.1 \cdot \gamma$ and $\gamma = r/4$.[4] There is the possibility for agents to be split into two categories, agent-workers and agent-managers, when hierarchy H = ON. The proportion of

---

[4]This is to reduce the likelihood that all agents converge to the center of the space as range increases.

managers in the agent population is dependent upon what is set in the parameter management, P_N, and have been made to take two values, $P_N = \{0.1, 02\}$. Diffusion works on the basis of a threshold, t, that is distributed at random in the population such that every agent has a slightly different attitude toward adoption. The mean of this random-normal distribution can take two values, $m = \{0.25, 0.50\}$. These values are attributed at the beginning of the simulation and the threshold is adjusted as the simulation progresses, depending on docility, d_i, and organizational conformity, K (see the next subsection). The first is distributed normally at random with $d_i \sim \mathcal{N}(0.50, 0.25)$ and the second is the same for every agent in the space with $K = \{0, 0.1, 0.5, 1\}$. There is a switch, the docility enabler, d_e that activates d_i.

7.1.2   Procedures

The procedures in this diffusion model are simple and work on the basis of three loops. Fig. 7.2 shows the basic procedures in a flow chart. After defining the general settings as explained above, the simulation starts with a comparison of each agent's threshold with the number of agents who adopted around them. The simulation works on a *local* basis, and this means that it does not assume that each agent knows (neither has access to) the status of other agents in the entire system. This is particularly important because it makes this computational simulation different from the equation-based approach taken by Simon (1993) and by Secchi and Bardone (2009, 2013). So, again, each agent acts locally, it has a limited range of action, defined by the homonymous parameter, represented by letter r.

Given this limited range, adoption is then triggered by comparing the agent's threshold, t_i with the number of adopters in range r.[5] If $t_i \leq n_a$, then the agent becomes an adopter, given n_a is the number of neighboring agents that have already adopted. The simulation automatically stops when the number of adopters reaches 90% of the total number of agents N.

Once this first step is completed, the simulation runs a few other checks. If the docility enabler is ON, then agents adjust their threshold on the basis of the neighboring agents, in a way such that

$$t_{i,1} = t_{i,0} - \frac{d_i}{2} \cdot (t_{i,0} - \bar{t}_{n,0}) \tag{7.1}$$

where $t_{i,1}$ and $t_{i,0}$ are the thresholds of agent i at time 1 and 0, d_i is the docility level of agent i, and $\bar{t}_{n,0}$ is the mean threshold of neighboring

---

[5]The subset of agents who are in the vicinity r of another agent are defined neighbors.

Fig. 7.2. OrgBand2.0 Flow Chart.

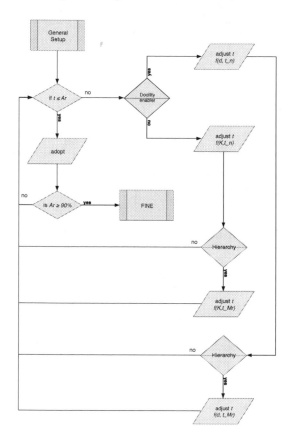

Note. t = threshold, Ar = adopters in range r, K = conformity, d = docility, n = neighboring agents in range r, Mr = managers in range r (Flowchart Designer version 3.3.5).

agents n at time 0. This means that docility functions as a way to conform one's own attitude toward the innovation as a function of what happens among those other agents that are close to it. When `docility enabler` is OFF, Equation 7.1 becomes:

$$t_{i,1} = t_{i,0} - \frac{K}{2} \cdot (t_{i,0} - \bar{t}_{n,0}) \tag{7.2}$$

where K is the parameter `organizational conformity` that is not agent-specific but it is the same for every agent in the system.

When `hierarchy` is turned ON then, to Equations 7.1 and 7.2, a second set of equations is added

$$t_{i,1} = t_{i,0} - d_i \cdot (t_{i,0} - \bar{t}_{m,0})$$
$$t_{i,1} = t_{i,0} - K \cdot (t_{i,0} - \bar{t}_{m,0})$$

$$(7.3)$$

where $\bar{t}_{m,0}$ is the average threshold level of the neighboring agent-managers connected to the agent-worker. The two equations are activated depending on whether `docility enabler` is ON or OFF, and they indicate that the effect that a manager has on the average worker is much higher compared to that of a fellow worker.

7.2 Results

Version `OrgBand2.0` has been transferred and modified to work on `NetLogo 6.1`, a software specifically designed for agent-based simulation modeling (Wilensky, 1999).

As I was approaching this simulation again, and since this was a project that started nearly 10 years ago,[6] I decided to perform a new set of runs and gather some additional data. This becomes necessary every time the original code is modified and even if, such as in this case, it has been to a very minor extent. Nevertheless, it is better to make sure that the findings are robust enough so that I can build on this simulation.

As anticipated above, I have used the work done in Secchi and Gullekson (2016) as input for calibration. This means that this new set of results is based on those parameter configurations that appear to show stronger effects on the outcome variable. The choices made can be deducted from reading Table 7.1 and lead to a factorial design of $2 \times 2 \times 2 \times 2 \times 2 \times 4 \times 2 \times 2 = 512$. By following the work Raffaello Seri and I have been doing on the way to determine the number of times a simulation should be performed (Secchi & Seri, 2017; Seri & Secchi, 2017), I have applied statistical power analysis to this factorial design. An ANOVA reverse F-test where $\alpha = 0.01$, $1 - \beta = 0.95$, effect size is small $f = 0.1$, and group number $= 512$ leads to a number of runs that

---

[6]The publication that features what can be called the simulation `OrgBand1.0` appeared only in 2016, but the work on this simulation started in 2011. Publication is, at times, not very straightforward. In this case, even though the journal *Computational and Mathematical Organization Theory* was my first choice, my coauthor and I decided to submit the article to a number of highly ranked management journals. These all rejected the article after at least one round of revisions. By the time we decided to follow our first choice, the article was accepted in 2015 and appeared in a journal issue in 2016. The original model is available on OpenABM, an online repository for agent-based simulation models: https://www.comses.net/codebases/4716/releases/1.0.0/

is ≈ 28. Taking this as a reference, I have performed each configuration of parameters 30 times, for a total of 15,360 simulations.

To be able to obtain the results at a reasonable time, the total number was split into four chunks, each ran on two nodes of the supercomputer Abacus 2.0, the fastest Danish computational infrastructure, available at the University of Southern Denmark. The computation lasted approximately 10 hours per each chunk, for a total of 40 hours, 47 minutes, and 19 seconds.

In the following pages, I will only review a partial section of the findings, mainly related to the role of docility, d_i. Given that this new data is very close to the one in Secchi and Gullekson (2016), readers interested in a wider discussion can refer to that article.[7]

One of the findings from the simulation published earlier was that docility was not a factor that could limit the spread of bandwagon. While this is confirmed in this new set of results, the concern goes over the type of support to bandwagon that docility is capable of providing. In other words, it could be interesting to *qualify* the contribution of this factor to the spread of a thought, process, product, or behavior in an organization.

The simulation makes a distinction between the workings of docility – that is, the way in which agents can be open to use information coming from their team to make a decision on adoption – and a general conformity rule that is something that every agent in the system follows. It is important to be reminded that both conditions are still *local*, meaning that the agent has no information about other teams or the organization as a whole, but can only observe its own neighbors (other agents to which it is connected). As per the procedures above, the adjustment operates on the threshold levels that increase or decrease depending on the average observation of what is happening around the agent at that point in time.

7.2.1   Docility Versus Conformity

When the conditions for interaction are static and do not change over time – i.e. when move, $M = \text{OFF}$ – the evolution of diffusion is similar, independent of the various conditions. Instead, when the environment is much more fluid (ambiguous) and connections evolve over time, there are varying effects of conformity, K, and of docility, d_i. It is under this condition that agents are set to move (albeit slowly) in the organizational environment and establish new connections as they do so. As one may imagine, larger organizations offer more such opportunities for interaction. Fig. 7.3 presents the proportion of adopters on the

---

[7]It was published under an Open Access license and it is available at https://link.springer.com/article/10.1007/s10588-015-9199-4.

number of agents in the organization, N, when ambiguous conditions are triggered by $M = \text{ON}$. Given the way in which d_i has been distributed among agents $(\bar{d_i} = 0.5)$, it comes at no surprise that it is roughly similar to a rule of `conformity` that is $K = 0.5$. Even though there is quite a sizable variation in the distribution of d_i, with a standard deviation $s = 0.25$, this does not seem to have an impact on adoptions. Let us see what is in this Fig. 7.3 in more details.

Fig. 7.3. Proportion of Adopters Over Time, Split by Organization Size (N), `Hierarchy` (H), and `docility enabler` (d_e) and visualized by `range` (r) with `move`, $M = \text{ON}$, `management`, $P_N = 0.1$, and mean `threshold`, $\bar{t_i} = 0.25$.

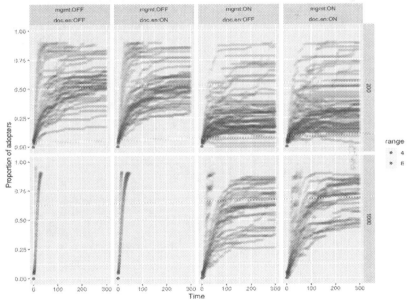

Fig. 7.3 presents observations split into two sets of four panes, each by organization size N. Persistence of color depends on recurrent trends in the data. The four panes are then divided by the presence $(H = \text{ON})$ or absence $(H = \text{OFF})$ of management and, within these two, by conformity $(K = 0.5)$ or docility $(d_e = \text{ON})$. Results by size are different but they both confirm a general trend for this simulation and that is that the presence of even a single line of hierarchy (at $P_N = 0.1$) is an essential factor – probably the most powerful one – in decreasing the chances of a rapid spread of something in an organization. The two bottom left panes for $N = 1{,}000$ and $H = \text{OFF}$ compared to the two bottom right panes where $H = \text{ON}$ provide a very clear example of how

strong H can be. It is worth noting that doubling the proportion of management at $P_N = 0.2$ does not produce a decreased spread. In fact, it seems that results are very similar to the ones produced in Fig. 7.3 (more on this below). By observing the way in which docility enters the simulation and comparing it to its absence, it is difficult to ascertain a difference. In both cases, when $d_e = \text{ON/OFF}$ there is a clear effect of range r on the data indicating that more connected agents are also more likely to contribute to the spread of this idea, process, behavior, or else. The case in which $r = 6$ and $N = 1{,}000$ is particularly interesting because there the presence of management is only capable of delaying the spread for a while, but nothing can do against reaching 90% of adopters, given the appropriate time span. The case in which $r = 6$ ends up in a bandwagon-type diffusion in six out of eight of the panes in Fig. 7.3 (the two top right panes are excluded). A small difference in docility can be seen for $N = 200$ and $H = \text{ON/OFF}$ (the two upper right panes). These two panes show that when $d_e = \text{OFF}$ some diffusion patterns for $r = 6$ overlap while others are even lower than for $r = 4$. Instead, when $d_e = \text{ON}$ there is a clearer demarcation between the two levels of r. This is interesting and it may be due to the fact that a "team effect" is probably more visible when docility is at play as opposed to K. This means that the agent is more tied to what is happening *locally*, within their teams.

7.2.2   Zooming in on Thresholds

There are a few questions that the above discussion raises. One is the actual role of management (H) in relation to the diffusion process. In general, Fig. 7.3 shows that there is a negative effect of H on how fast the spread grows. The question is whether the decrease in speed (spreading rate) is due to the fact that managers are less likely to adopt. Given their effect on agent-workers, this may explain the effect.

Fig. 7.4 shows adoption numbers in relation to adoptions among management (x axis), both in a static ($M = \text{OFF}$, Fig. 7.4(a)) and in a dynamic environment ($M = \text{ON}$, Fig. 7.4(b)). The difference between this figure and the one presented above is that Fig. 7.4 only shows the end point of the simulation, that is the final step. Be reminded that a simulation can end before step 300, if the number of adopters $N_a \geq 90\%$.

The other information that is added in these graphs relates to a change in parameter mean threshold, with $\bar{t}_i = \{0.25, 0.50\}$. When the environment is static, a higher $\bar{t}_i$ does not lead to any diffusion at all, independent of range r. It is also worth noting that the absence of conformity ($K = 0$) does not lead to any diffusion at all. Stated differently, the sole initial conditions do not allow for diffusion processes to start. The only difference is the case of a large organization with

Fig. 7.4. Proportion of Adopters over the Proportion of Adopters Among Management, Split by Organization Size (N) and conformity (K) and Visualized by range (r) and mean threshold ($\bar{t}_i$) with move, $M = \text{OFF/ON}$, management, $P_N = 0.1$.

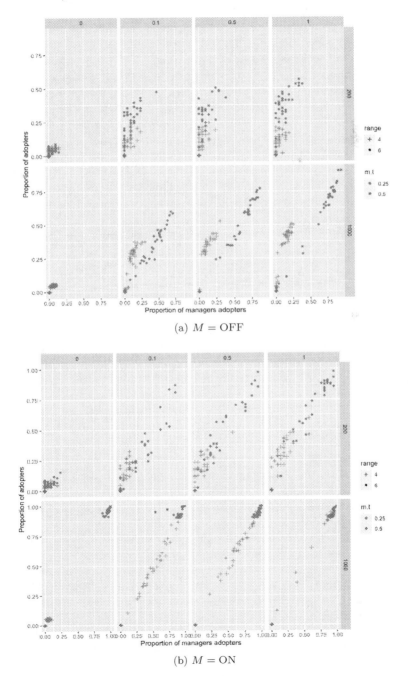

(a) $M = \text{OFF}$

(b) $M = \text{ON}$

$N = 1,000$ and $r = 6$. In this case, all agents, including management, end the simulation with a proportion of adoptions between 0.85 and 1.0. A focus on $\bar{t}_i = 0.25$, that is on the green observations in the plot, allows further understanding of these processes. The panes under $M = $ OFF and $K > 0$ show a split in the effect of range r. A lower range always sees points mainly located at the left of the diagonal, and that indicates that agent-workers show higher adoption rates than agent-managers. The higher range of $r = 6$ shows that the proportion is, on average, higher for agent-workers when $N = 200$ and it is more distributed around the diagonal when $N = 1,000$. Only the bottom right pane shows most simulations that end up with more than 50% of adopters when $r = 6$.

The case seem to vary with ambiguity, i.e. when $M = $ ON. Fig. 7.4(b) shows that most of the observations lie on the diagonal, especially for $N = 1,000$ and, most importantly, when $r = 6$, diffusion is almost always approaching either 90% or 100% of agents. These results confirm what seen in the previous simulations, i.e. that larger organizations are more likely to give way to diffusion processes, especially bandwagon effects.

Fig. 7.5 helps to appreciate what docility brings in, when conformity K is not considered. This figure has been created in a way similar to the one above to increase comparability. The trends shown are in line with what seen above, probably showing a trend that is in between $0.5 \leq K \leq 1$, that is on the high end of conformity.

The overall message of both Figs. 7.4 and 7.5 is that management behaves as an integrated part of the organization, showing trends similar to those of agent-workers and affecting them as well as being affected by them. The increase in the threshold mean $\bar{t}_i$ in the system is particularly effective in making diffusion much less likely to occur. However, this bound on diffusion is still affected by range $r = 6$ and either $K = 1$ or $d_e = $ ON, under conditions of ambiguity (i.e. $M = $ ON).

If the above is correct, then it makes sense to ask whether the dispersion of thresholds within the population of agents has any effect on the way in which docility operates. Fig. 7.6 explores this aspect by plotting the proportion of adopters on the standard deviation of the thresholds in the organization. These standard deviations have been harmonized by the number of total agents in the organization, so that they can be compared to each other in the two sets of panes, the top, with $N = 200$, and the bottom, with $N = 1,000$.

In general, one may think that the larger organization may lead to wider dispersion rates, given its size. However, large organizations are also allowing for larger teams to gather together and this means that Equations 7.1 and 7.3 operate on wider numbers, hence bringing thresholds closer for larger numbers of agents at once. Smaller organizations also have smaller teams, hence there may be a wider spread, since there

Fig. 7.5. Proportion of Adopters over the Proportion of Adopters Among Management, Split by Organization Size (N) and move (M) and Visualized by range (r) and mean threshold ($\bar{t}_i$) with management, $P_N = 0.1$.

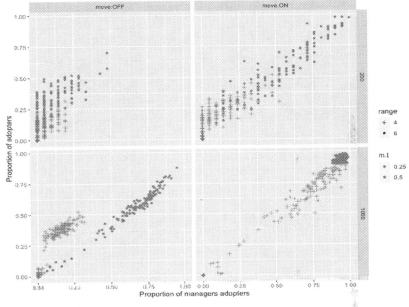

are probably not more but possibly wider variations from the grand mean. This is, if one thinks about it, an implication of the Central Limit Theorem.

Given the above, one should not be surprised when observing wider dispersion rates for $N = 200$. The observations that reflect $\bar{t}_i = 0.50$ are mainly found at the bottom of all the four panes, and this means that they are mainly diffusion-less except when the standard deviation becomes wide enough (ca. $s_t > 0.15$) to allow for some diffusion to happen.[8] Still, that is not enough for the effect to become widespread in the organization. In general, a small standard deviation on a small enough average threshold level is enough to allow for diffusion processes to successfully enter organizations. In summary, one can assume that there is an effect of docility that goes against the diversification of thresholds (i.e. attitudes) in an organization.

---

[8] A few exceptions are found for $N = 1,000$, $M =$ ON, and $r = 6$.

Fig. 7.6. Proportion of Adopters over the Standard Deviation of Thresholds, Split by Organization Size (N) and move (M) and Visualized by range (r) and mean threshold $(\bar{t}_i)$ with management, $P_N = 0.1$.

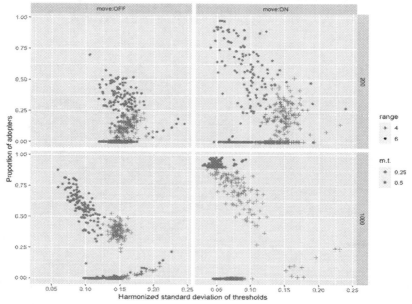

7.2.3   The Ugly Truth About Docility

From the results shown above, I have been able to confirm the effect of docility in support of diffusion processes and eventually bandwagons in organizations. This is something that was already apparent from previous work. What has emerged in this chapter is that (a) docility seem to work as a conformity mechanism, and (b) it makes it such that there is an alignment between the management and the rest of the organizational members. In addition to these two effects, the last part of the analysis has indicated that (c) docility operates mainly by reducing variability within the organization. These processes increase with organizational size.

7.3   Summary

This chapter has been dedicated to an actual model that simulates diffusion processes inside an organization. Called the OrgBand2.0 model and based on the concept of docility (as outlined in Part I), results show that there is a small difference between how the application of a conformity rule is experienced as opposed to individuals showing docility. So, is docility *just* a disposition toward conformity or imitation? And what are its boundaries? These and other questions are covered by another simulation, presented in Chapter 8.

8

The Operational Boundaries of Docility

"Bounded rationality may be seen as a universal primordial feature characterising every being, whereas docility is a capacity that may evolve, given the right conditions."
— Thorbjørn Knudsen (2003, p. 234)

The quote with which this chapter opens is taken from one of the very few articles completely dedicated to Simon's concept of docility. The reading that Knudsen (2003) gives is in line with Simon's evolutionary (biology-related) concerns oriented toward explaining the existence of altruistic behavior in spite of its cost for the person who practices it. This concern is resolved by theorizing that individuals lean on altruistic acts coming from others (docility) because of their bounded rationality, hence are encouraged to behave altruistically themselves. While bounded rationality, Knudsen writes, is something that comes within the nature of human beings, docility can be thought of as an evolutionary feature, subject to certain conditions.

The central theme of this chapter reverts around these conditions, although they are discussed within the domain of organizations. I am not disputing the general tenet that docile behavior is widespread in our societies, as both Knudsen and Simon claim. It is apparent that we all use information coming from social channels as a basis for our short- and long-term choices (just think of how many times you check your phone for information of any sort). What I am interested in is how this general disposition enters an organization and becomes a feature

Computational Organizational Cognition:
A Study on Thinking and Action in Organizations, 113–122
Copyright © 2021 by Emerald Publishing Limited
All rights of reproduction in any form reserved
doi: 10.1108/978-1-83867-511-020211008

of effective work. As mentioned in Chapter 5, Simon's view (1993) is that there is an individual fitness enhancement that comes from being docile. This was also confirmed by other studies (Knudsen, 2003; Secchi, 2007; Secchi & Bardone, 2009) and led me to think that this enhanced individual fitness had some repercussions on the organization as a whole. That is how the discussion around a *docility effect* started (Secchi & Bardone, 2009; Secchi, 2011). This effect was supposed to improve the overall performance of the organization, for example, by preventing ideas, behaviors, processes, or else to spread mindlessly. By relying on individual "local" resources, it would have given the organization the ability to react and define a different pattern for diffusion processes.

Findings of the `OrgBand2.0` model (Chapter 7) do not align with the assumptions above. In other words, the enhanced fitness that each individual gains from being docile does not transfer to the organization as a whole. Or, to be more precise, it does transfer but it generalizes a relatively mindless attitude. The assumption made in the model was that the object of diffusion was damaging to organizational performance, hence it needed more cognizant (or mindful) appreciation to limit its adoption. This is a typical concern with diffusion processes that are fast and mindless (i.e. bandwagons), triggered by popularity rather than rational decision-making. Docility, when modeled as an individual characteristic, transfers to the organization by mimicking a conformity norm, hence helping the spread of a mindless idea, process, product, behavior, or else. In other words, the simulation presented in Chapter 7 left us with the possibility that docility can be dysfunctional to organizations. How does this happen? When does docility become a disposition to be mindless?

While the previous chapter has attempted to explore the mechanisms of why this is the case, this chapter presents another simulation model that focuses exclusively on docility in organizations with the sole purpose of exploring its limits. The agent-based simulation was first presented in a book chapter (Secchi, 2016) but, due to the restrictions back then, all the implications could not be fully explored. This chapter offers the optimal outlet to do so and can be read as a companion of previously published findings.

Before We Step into the Model

The quote I have used at the beginning has been instrumental to introduce the overall theme of this chapter but I think it is controversial. This is for two main reasons. One is that Knudsen assumes that there is a clear divide between bounded rationality and docile behaviors and the other is that, as a consequence, the latter does not affect the former. As I explain elsewhere (Secchi, 2011), bounded rationality is a way to describe cognition (see Newell & Simon, 1972). Drawing from the enacted and embodied components of the EDEC perspective, it is impossible to draw a clear line between cognition and the actions that support it. Hence, behavior that is socially grounded such as altruistic or other prosocial behaviors are connected to the way in which our cognitive functions are shaped. In other words, not only the cognition of bounded rationality is intertwined with the way in which humans socialize, but it is very much the latter that shapes the former. To demonstrate how this works in an organizational context is the overall goal of *Extendable Rationality* (Secchi, 2011).

8.1   The Model

The `OrgBand2.0` model reviewed in Chapter 7 only summarizes docility dispositions by attaching a value through a parameter and allowing for a more or less open consideration of others' inputs (information, advice, etc.). The model featured in this chapter serves a different purpose and has been built to check the assumptions as well as the workings of docile behavior in organizations. This model was originally programmed in 2013 and, in spite of the push that every modeler feels when approaching an old model of his/her, I have resisted touching the code nor have I run additional experiments. This is because what appeared in Secchi (2016) only presented partial results, as stated explicitly in that work. In this chapter, I am summarizing those results and move to present what was left out of the previous study. For simplicity, I call this the "docility in organizations," or `DIO1.0` model.[1]

The model starts from the original assumptions as they have been presented earlier (Secchi, 2007, 2011; Secchi & Bardone, 2009; Simon, 1993, and Chapter 5) and discusses docility as an organizational fitness mechanism. This means that higher fitness corresponds to an agent that is successful in the organization. This may be intended as good performance, motivation, and overall satisfaction with the work done. In other words, the word "fit" is intended as a good match between the organization's settings and what is required from its participants. `DIO1.0` features agent-employees and an environment that represents the settings of an organization.

The model was implemented through the software `NetLogo`, version 5.2 and updated to version 6.1 for this book.[2]

---

[1] I have not called this model in the chapter where I have introduced it first, but I think that giving specific names to the models makes it easier when comparing them to explain the differences or simply their results.

[2] A version of this model is available on `Github`: https://github.com/dsecchi/ABMOsimulations/blob/master/simon93model_2020.nlogo3d.

8.1.1   Parameters

Table 8.1 presents the selection of parameters that have been used to program the simulation and launch computational experiments. The model strictly follows Simon's fitness Equations 5.1–5.3 (Chapter 5). Every element in those equations is parametrized in the model and it appears with a range of value options in the DIO1.0 model. However, not all these parameters have been used to produce computational experiments because they are either irrelevant to the questions asked or because their impact is negligible.

Table 8.1. Parameter Notations, Values, and Descriptions for DIO1.0.

Parameter	Notation	Values	Description
Agents	N_i, N_u, N_n	60	The number of intelligent docile agents, N_i, unintelligent docile agents, N_u, and non-docile agents, N_n that are set at the beginning of the simulation. Each of these types is assigned 60 agents for a total of $N = 180$ agents in the simulation.
Fitness	f_n	1.01	The "natural" or normal fitness assigned equally to each agent.
Docility fitness	f_d	$\{-0.1, -0.2, 0, 0.1, 0.2\}$	This is the fitness increment (or decrement) due to the agent being docile.
Altruism fitness	f_i, f_u	2, 1	Incremental fitness deriving from being altruistic; it is $f_i = 2$ for A_i and $f_u = 1$ for A_u.
Altruistic extent	e_i, e_u	0.8, 1.0	The extent to which docile agents are altruistic; it is $e_i = 0.80$ and $e_u = 1.0$.
Altruism gains	g_i, g_u	0.01, 0.005	Increment in fitness due to the action of docile agents behaving altruistically – i.e. giving advice or sharing information. It takes different values and it is $g_i = 0.01$ for A_i and $g_u = 0.005$ for A_u
Cost	c	$\{0.005, 0.05, 0.5\}$	The cost of being altruistic and sharing information with other agents.
Range	r	$\{3, 6, 9, 12\}$	The vision range of each agent that determines with whom they can interact.
Expand/Adapt	E	ON/OFF	When ON, this parameter sets the expand condition, when OFF it sets the adapt.

There are three types of docile individuals, the intelligent, A_i, the unintelligent, A_u, and the non-docile, A_n. The main difference between A_i and A_u is that the first discriminates against the information received by others while the second cannot (or does not want to). Agents of the A_n type only take information but do not give away any. Consistent with previous operationalizations of the concept (e.g., Simon, 1993; Secchi, 2007; Secchi & Bardone, 2009), the starting number of agents is the same for each type, such that initial conditions are the same.

All the settings are described in Table 8.1 in a way that is more analytical than the description offered when introducing Equations 5.1–5.3.

Some of the notation is the same as before, while some other has changed. Most importantly, what changed the most from Chapter 5 is the operationalization. These equations are in fact applied with a local `range`, meaning that each agent can only exchange information and benefit from interacting with neighboring agents in a defined `range`, r. This changes the dynamic of the exploration because agents in `DIO1.0` are truly bounded by their surroundings and the way it impacts their cognition.

Since the notations are different, by using what is in Table 8.1 we can rewrite the equations with these new specifications:

$$P_i = fn + f_d \cdot g_i + f_i \cdot \frac{n_i}{n} \cdot e_i + f_u \cdot \frac{n_u}{n} \cdot e_u - c \cdot cI \qquad (8.1)$$

$$P_n = fn + f_i \cdot \frac{n_i}{n} \cdot e_i + f_u \cdot \frac{n_u}{n} \cdot e_u \qquad (8.2)$$

$$P_u = fn + f_d \cdot g_u + f_i \cdot \frac{n_i}{n} \cdot e_i + f_u \cdot \frac{n_u}{n} \cdot e_u - c \cdot cU \qquad (8.3)$$

where the notation n_i, n_u, and n indicates, respectively, the number of A_i, A_u and the total number of agents that can be found in the specified `range`, r. P_i, P_n, and P_u are the payoffs of the three types (called fitness above).

8.1.2 Procedures

At the beginning, all agents appear on a 3D organizational space at random. They also move slightly around their initial position depending on the links they establish with their neighbors (in `range`, r), on the basis of a mechanism similar to what described in the `OrgBand2.0` model, such that three constants are used to attract agents as a function of the connection they establish with each other.

There are two general procedures in this simulation, exemplified by two conditions, one is called adapt, the other expand. In the former condition, agents screen the most successful strategy around them and switch to a different type if that is the case. In other words, they adopt the most successful strategy around them, according to

$$\text{IF } P_i < \frac{\sum_{j=1}^{n} P_j}{n} \qquad (8.4)$$
$$\text{THEN } A_i \text{ becomes } A_j$$

where j is any of the three types, and this means that the agent may remain as it was or change depending on the average level of local payoffs. Hence, this condition is very close to the traditional setting because individuals change by adopting the most successful *local* strategy. This means that a local assimilation strategy may not be the prevalent strategy occurring at the system's (or organizational) level.

The other condition, called **expand**, works on agents as they multiply or disappear from the organization, depending on a mechanism opposite to the one above, such that

$$\text{IF } P_i > \frac{\sum_{j=1}^{n} P_j}{n}$$
$$\text{THEN } N_{i,1} = N_{i,0} + 1 \tag{8.5}$$
$$\text{OTHERWISE } A_i \text{ disappears}$$

where $N_{i,0}$ is the number of A_i at time $t = 0$ and $N_{i,1}$ is the number of A_i at time $t = 1$. The procedure works equally for all the agent types. This creates a different situation in the environment because all agents are bound to multiply or disappear due to their *local* understanding of successful behavior in the organization, represented by the payoff functions P_i, P_n, and P_u (respectively Equations 8.1–8.3).

8.2   Findings

The simulation explores the parameter space around the two conditions above by letting only three parameters vary. As Table 8.1 shows, these are `docility fitness` (f_d), `cost` (c), `range` (r), and the two conditions `expand/adapt` (E). These define a parameter space that can be exemplified by a factorial design of $5 \times 3 \times 4 \times 2$ equal to 120 configurations of parameters.

The data for this simulation were generated at the time when I wrote Secchi (2016), and the determination of the number of runs followed a slightly different logic than the one in the previous chapter. Back then, I was presenting results for the **adapt** condition and I estimated an effect size of 0.2, with 60 configurations, $\alpha = 0.05$ and $1 - \beta = 0.99$. These were used as inputs to a reverse F-test in an ANOVA calculated using the package `pwr` in `R` (a computational statistical software). The number that I reported in the other study was ≈ 25, and the number used was 30 runs. Studies on this method developed later with Raffaello Seri (Secchi & Seri, 2017; Seri & Secchi, 2017) show that the most appropriate balance for α and β in ABM research is $\alpha = 0.01$ and $\beta = 0.05$. This is because, on the one hand, there needs to be a proportion between the two and, on the other hand, a computational simulation should try to aim at more accurate results than empirical research (where $\beta = 0.20$). By updating these results with the two new values for α and β, I obtain 24.57 that is very close to the previous result. The problem is that I am now comparing the two conditions, hence need to calculate statistical power for 120 configurations of parameters. The new calculation gives 16.40 runs and this means that I am likely to overpower the simulation if I keep the 30 runs used previously. To avoid this problem, I have only kept the first 18 simulations per each configuration of parameters. In short, the data are made of $120 \times 18 = 2,160$ simulations, each performed per 100 steps (the internal time of each simulation run).

The results can be analyzed by looking at the final state of the simulation run and as a trend, to understand when and how each one of the three types gained or lost positions (fitness) in relation to each others. The last observation is probably a good starting point because it allows to determine the general end states, given the parameters considered. The two plots in Fig. 8.1 are an attempt to do just that. In fact, they plot the proportion of agents in the simulation for one type in relation to another type. The benchmark for both A_i and A_u is their antonym A_n; as the proportion of this last type increases, the two other types are likely to decrease. The question is what makes these types modify their relative weight in the organization, i.e. which parameters are responsible and how much effect do they have.

Results can be read in relation to the main diagonal (i.e. $y = x$). When points fall below that diagonal, then the proportion of A_n is higher than that of A_i or A_u; when the points are located in the upper left part of the quadrant, i.e. above the diagonal, then A_i or A_u have a higher proportion than A_n. The first aspect to consider is that when $r = 3$ there is no discernible difference between the two conditions defined by parameter E, adapt/expand. As docility fitness f_d increases the observations start to split, so that A_i and A_u increase, especially in the expand condition ($E = \text{ON}$) and reduced cost, ≤ 0.05.

For range $r = 6$ the split discussed above becomes more and more apparent when $f_d > 0$, in that the effect of cost, $c \geq 0.05$ is positive for A_i and negative for the other two types. The effect of the expand condition ($E = \text{ON}$) is more visible and seems to make results more extreme. In fact, while the enhanced fitness of $f_d = 0.1$ leaves some room for both A_i and A_u, this is not the case in the expand condition, where almost all agents are A_n. This result is very consistent as $r > 6$.

Overall, there is prevalence of A_n in the expand condition when $f_d < 0$, independent of r and c. This points at the need that an organization institutionalizes the benefits of prosocial behaviors that come out of docility. In absence of this support, it becomes very difficult for A_i to emerge. The interesting part of this is that four of these bottom left quadrants are actually the perfect ground for A_u to become the most successful type. While A_u reach between 0.6 and 0.8 of the total number of agents, the other two occupy the remaining positions. This happens when both docile behavior leaves negative marks on one's payoff (i.e. $f_d < 0$), interactions are rather frequent and wide (i.e. $r > 6$), and the cost is relatively low (i.e. $c \leq 0.05$). Under these circumstances agents are better off if they do not discriminate in their

Fig. 8.1. Proportion of A_i and A_u in Relation to the Proportion of An in the Organization, Last Observations, Split by r and f_d, and Visualized by E and c.

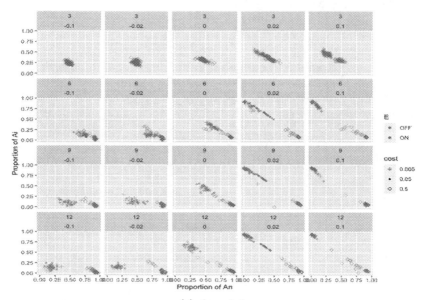

(a) A_i and A_n

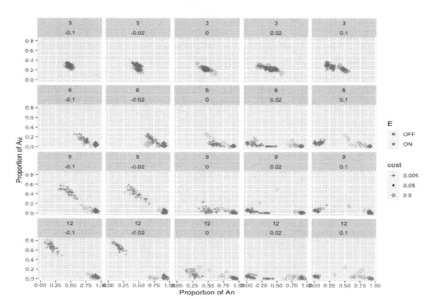

(b) A_u and A_n

altruistic efforts. However, this strategy only works when agents do not have the opportunity to leave. When that is the case, then A_n is always the strategy that seems to increase the payoff the most. The exact opposite situation is there for A_n when the expand condition is ON and the cost of prosocial behavior is at its lowest, with $c = 0.005$. To this, one matches the higher range of interactions $r > 6$ and the number of A_n in the system collapses. A similar result is also visible for $E = $ OFF but results are less robust.

8.2.1 Understanding the Limits

In general, cost is the one parameters with the most effective negative effect on the success of A_i and A_u. The range of interactions is another with a positive effect only when costs are low. The docility fitness parameter seems to have different effects depending on its sign. When negative, there is a positive effect for A_u when both $c \leq 0.05$ and $r > 6$, when positive, then A_i increase when, again $c \leq 0.05$ and $r > 3$, even though there are limited effect when $r = 3$ (see the comments above).

The simulation DIO1.0 showed that the type more likely to have emerged in OrgBand2.0 is the A_u type, giving way to the conditions under which bandwagons could emerge. In fact, one could re-interpret the threshold as well as the conformity rules of the simulation presented in Chapter 7 as affecting both cost (c) and docility fitness (f_d) as discussed in the above. In other words, according to results from DIO1.0, the organizational bandwagon simulation was the case of an inappropriate organizational incentive to docility and, at the same time, of the prevalence of lower costs for its behavior. The increase of interactions allows this effect to spread.

8.3 Summary

This chapter was dedicated to the test of boundary conditions for docility. Results from the previous chapter ended up not in line with the theory, as outlined in Part I. This triggered questions on the *when* and *why* docility may become a useful strategy in an organization. The simulation DIO1.0 explores exactly these aspects. By going back to its equation-based roots, this computational model has looked into the factors that make a mindful docile disposition, represented by agents A_i and payoff P_i in the simulation, a mindless docile disposition, represented by A_u and P_u, or a non docile disposition, A_n with payoff P_n, more likely.

The DIO1.0 Model is in line with previous studies and it allows to make a more precise interpretation of the bandwagon results. At the same time, it opens up a few question marks. For example, it is not clear what is it exactly that organizations should do to encourage mindfulness. At the same time, it is not easy to understand the difference between the fitness mechanisms and what we have labeled costs here. The next two chapters are an attempt to answer these (and a few other) open questions.

9

Relaxing the Assumptions

While Chapter 8 is dedicated to an analysis of the conditions under which docility may end up to be detrimental for organizations, it does not directly cover what was missing in the study on diffusion presented previously. In fact, `DIO1.0` is a general study of the aspects that may or may not lead to the prevalence of one or another type of docile behavior in a social system such as an organization. As seen before, this has pointed at various combinations of cost, docility enhancement mechanisms at the organizational level (what was called *fitness* improvements), and how widely people interact with each other in the organization (this was *range*). By comparing the behavior that emerged in `OrgBand2.0` and at the prevalence of one or the other "type" of docile individual in `DIO1.0`, it was possible to deduce that the mindless type (unintelligent, for Simon) featured in the former simulation by allowing bandwagons to become widespread.

One of the implications of the combination of the two studies in Chapters 7 and 8 is that small communities may cause individuals to behave too restrictively on others, and lead to what is usually referred to as "groupthink" (Moorhead & Montanari, 1986). That being the case, one could ask questions such as: What if some workers do not take team comradeship so seriously? What if some take the problem more seriously than any commitment or conformity to their team? What if the organization encourages communication across teams (divisions, departments) in order for employees to try and solve a problem? From a more

Computational Organizational Cognition:
A Study on Thinking and Action in Organizations, 123–140
Copyright © 2021 by Emerald Publishing Limited
All rights of reproduction in any form reserved
doi: 10.1108/978-1-83867-511-020211009

theoretical perspective, this would mean a relaxation of the community precondition (see Chapter 5) for some agents in the simulation.

Working with Emanuele Bardone, this is what we did in an agent-based simulation (Bardone & Secchi, 2017). We introduced a variation on the cognitive attitudes of some individuals, by allowing them to be more *inquisitive* than others. Not only this improved the number of problem solved, it also allowed teams to operate by using less competencies. In other words, inquisitive individuals – those loyal to the problem and not exclusively to their team – are still docile, but extend this quality to produce more awareness and mindfulness in the organization.

This chapter is dedicated to the *inquisitiveness* model, called INQ1.0.1, that featured in a series of publications so far (Bardone & Secchi, 2017; Seri, Secchi, & Martinoli, 2020; Secchi, 2021). Before zooming in on this model, I believe there is the need to specify one of the core assumptions of this and the other models covered in this book.

9.1 *Social* Beings

The previous two chapters have sketched a view on cognition in organizations based mainly on a socialized view of the individual. Throughout this book and as an underlying factor inspiring the two models in Chapters 7 and 8, the most important assumption has been that organizations are *social* systems. This is almost common sense, and does not add much to the interpretation of what has been done so far in this book. The relevant aspect here is what is meant by *social*.

The way in which I have intended it is very much (and not surprisingly) in line with an EDEC perspective, although it departs from it quite substantially because it emphasizes that the social element has a constitutive role for cognition. It is by means of a dynamic set of adaptive mechanisms[1] that cognitive processes come to life, especially through the activities that are typically performed by many in organizations. These dynamic adaptive (cognitive) mechanisms (DAM or DACM) are defined and define what I mean with the word *social* as it refers to organizations. Clearly, there is no "center" in this interpretation of cognition in a social system, because processes are distributed among people, artifacts, and other immaterial understandings (e.g., ideas, thoughts, interpretations). I have dedicated an entire section of this book (Part III) to define the social and to reflect on its implications for cognition and MOR. However, after the work presented so far, I believe it has become necessary to specify such a fundamental assumption further.

---

[1]By now, it should be clear that a mechanism is not necessarily a deterministic rule or an automatic trigger for action, thinking, behavior, or else. It is simply the formalization through computational or mathematics means of a given process.

The view of the *social* domain as outlined above does not mean that we can disregard the individual nor that we can construct it as a simple sum of individual actions and/or thinking. By simplifying the debate a bit, it can be written that to engage in the former one embraces *holism* – a view of the system that considers its components to serve the function of providing an understanding of the whole (e.g., Luhmann, 1995). By taking the second seriously, one is applying a version of *reductionism* – the assumption that everything can be understood (hence studied) by dissecting it in its sub-components and re-assembling it together at a later stage (e.g., Hayek, 1980). When organizations are the subject of study from a *holistic* perspective, cognition becomes visible in its culture, routines, procedures, norms, and other macro-structural aspects. The way in which these elements have been formed over the years is relevant and it has been studied for quite some time (e.g., Nelson & Winter, 1982), but the contribution of organization participants and of other resources is somehow lost in the narrative (with some exceptions; e.g., Breslin, Romano, & Percival, 2016). More precisely, that is not the purpose of the narrative because scholars are interested in the general patterns that emerge from an entire organization's behavior. Cognition is, upon this view, visible in its crystallized manifestations that constitute an organization's heritage and endowment, available to its participants.

A *reductionist* point of view on organizations takes the opposite side and looks at individuals – the unit of analysis – as the exclusive source of information. This means that the *social* element of the system is the result of the combination of these basic units. This combination can be more or less simple. For example, what is done by MOR scholars when analyzing the perceptions of organizational justice (Colquitt, Lepine, Piccolo, Zapata, & Rich, 2012; Colquitt & Rodell, 2011) is a rather simple combination of self-assessments measures. The extent to which justice becomes "organizational" depends on how close individual ratings are. The social element is a simple combination of what individuals share. The assumption here is that, when many experience similarly, then there must be something common in the middle. This is just a single example, but many concepts work similarly in MOR – e.g., organizational citizenship behavior (Podsakoff, MacKenzie, Paine, & Bachrach, 2000), shared cognition (Cannon-Bowers and Salas, 2001; Langan-Fox, Wirth, Code, Langfield-Smith, & Wirth, 2001), organizational commitment (Meyer & Allen, 1988), person-environment fit (Edwards, 2008). An example of less simple aggregation of individual outcomes is given by those using multilevel statistical procedures (Bliese, 2002; Klein & Kozlowski, 2000; Raudenbush & Bryk, 2002). These procedures are very much used in team research and start from the assumption that the observations cannot be independent from each other. On the contrary, they influence each other by means of sharing the same environment (being it a team, group, department or organization). For this reason, part of the variability of the dependent variable is explained by individuals sharing a common ground, hence the statistical procedure splits and factors these effects out explicitly. This is a fairly more advanced procedure although it still requires individual input and still determines what is shared by means of individual ratings. In summary, social cognition is based on combinations of individual-centric cognitions.

By giving such a short summary of the two views above – holism and reductionism – I have highlighted some aspects and neglected others. Hence, I realize that the picture is incomplete, at best. Yet, at the same time I think there is a way to which the EDEC approach and especially the *socially distributed cognition* (SDC) theory I have sketched in Part I are very different. In fact, the social is not visible only at the macro nor only at the micro domain of interactions. Instead, it is probably located in-between these two, as a way to connect the reaching out efforts of individuals as enhanced and conditioned by the macro super-structure of an organization. Stephen Cowley and I (2018, 2019, 2020) have called this the *meso domain* or, better, the meso domain*s* (because there are many working at the same time). The actions that happen in these large connectors of micro and macro elements have been named *social organizing* (more on this in Chapter 12).

The INQ1.0.1 model presented in this chapter as well as all the models presented in this book share this understanding of what is meant by *social*. ABM can be thought of as a way to make this interpretation transparent, given they rely heavily on DAM and, in the models featured here, on DACM.

9.2   The Inquisitiveness Model

The inquisitiveness model, or INQ1.0.1, has been developed to put forward what learned by the DIO1.0 model. This is that there are different organizational conditions that affect the way in which mindful attitudes are enabled. The reasoning around the model has both a theoretical backbone as well as it is based on previous findings.

From Chapter 5, we have learned that one of the preconditions for docility is the existence of a *community* of reference, to which members feel they belong. It is by feeling part of a system of interactions that individuals may start the exchange process that has been labeled "docility." The question is how strict this community boundary really is. If it is too strict such that an individual may feel like it is impossible to gain something by engaging in exchanges with non-members then opportunities and relevant information may never be found. If it is too relaxed, then there is no actual community and docility may disappear or it may not develop at all. The solution stays somewhere in the middle between these two extremes. Fig. 9.1 reports a range where the community precondition varies from being strict to being relaxed, and describes how docile behavior may vary under those conditions. I assume that the other two preconditions – i.e. a common code and public availability of information – are met.

Fig. 9.1. Applications of the Community Precondition to Docile Behaviors.

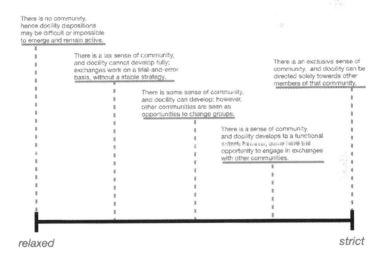

The two extremes have been already presented in the text above, although I have not provided organizational exemplifications of what these may mean. From now on and in the rest of this explanation, I will mainly draw examples from the organizational work life. The case where there is an exclusive sense of community is a case where team members only feel loyal to their own team and perceive other teams as threats to their own team's uniqueness or even existence. This extreme case is difficult to find in practice, although it is mainly visible when professional identities mix with productive work. The IT department of an online banking business may dislike dealing with the HR department, with sales, or with other teams within operations. Some dislike is natural and almost unavoidable, but here we are discussing about an exclusive sense of community at the expense of organizational cooperation that manifests in the IT department's failure to communicate their achievements/advancements on product development, for example, or failure to listen to the requirements and indications coming from sales, for example. Such an IT department is a very good environment to work in, but completely counterproductive to the real meaning of working in (and as) an organization.

If one relaxes the assumptions completely, we have the case of a flat and open organization that is either *plastic* (Siebers et al., 2020) or practices *disorganization* management (Herath, 2019; Herath, Secchi, & Homberg, 2016). The idea is that the community is the organization and everyone is docile independent of interactions in a small team, group or department. This is the case where the most trivial problems can be addressed by the CEO of the company and the most crucial strategic decisions can become available to a janitor. The exchanges are random so that there are no teams, other than eventual get together occasions where solutions are worked by individuals. If we have teams, then results can vary in that there is a consolidation of the relationships (Herath, Costello, & Homberg, 2017). The bottom line is that docile behaviors are not encouraged and they may appear as a functional feature, something that is needed to perform a task or solve a problem.

In between the two extremes mentioned above, Fig. 9.1 shows three alternative cases. The alternative in the middle is one where group identity is not as strong and exchanges can happen across teams/groups. Given there is not enough grip to hold people to one group, the situation is fluid and allows for group members to leave and join a different team. In a university where departments have changed their head very frequently over the last five years, faculty do not feel they have a grip on their group. Those whose research spans across disciplines (or can be seen as contributing to other disciplines) may see interaction with colleagues outside of their department as an opportunity to move to a department that is relatively more stable and hence has a stronger identity.

From the situation above, one can move to an even more relaxed situation or to a stricter presence of communities (teams, groups, and departments in the organizational world). A more relaxed situation is one where teams allow for in-and-out configurations. It is not the case where there are no boundaries, but it is an intermediate case where the teams are formed on an ad hoc basis. In other words, the organization works as a coordinator of a multitude of task forces, set to confront a problem when it happens. These task forces are temporary and may or may not form again in the future, because their constitution is relatively arbitrary. A small start-up business may be organized this way. There are persons who have competence and responsibility to deal with a specific area, but problems can be of such a gravity and urgency that others need to contribute. The situation described on the right of the center in Fig. 9.1 – where there is a stricter identification with a community – is the one where the teams, groups, or departments are set and work relatively smoothly but exchanges across them are possible and sometimes encouraged. This is left to those individuals with higher dispositions to perform such activities. After all, it takes some competence (and skills) for a salesperson to talk to IT personnel – he or she must know what they are talking about. Other than that, it is mainly a point of how many team members perform this cross-departmental exchange. If it is widespread, then team identity may soon collapse and we may be into the situation in the center of the diagram or into that at the immediate left of the center. This is to say that some members of a team may be willing and able to set communication bridges with colleagues in other teams.

This latter case is one where some individuals may show a disposition toward problem solving that is prevalent to the disposition toward the team (or community) to which they belong. This latter is the disposition of the average docile individual. Imagine the software developer who suddenly finds a serious bug in the program that is the blockbuster sell for the company she/he works for. The problem is brought to the attention of this person's department and they start to work on it. As they do, they realize that the way in which the problem can be solved is not irrelevant for the customer experience. In other words, by fixing this, they may influence behavior of their users. These solutions need a decision. An input from marketing and sales, and probably from the execs is necessary. This is not just to put in place appropriate behavior, but it is also a concern for responsibility. By implementing a solution, the team (or the person who made the decision) also becomes responsible for possible failures or misunderstandings. A bridge is necessary. However, these discussions across departments also face the potential to be time wasters. On many occasions the software development team has been confronted with attempts to re-set their priorities, redo much work already done, and compromise on code efficiency. The person who takes the problem at heart and wants to see it solved is probably the one to go and talk to colleagues from the other teams/departments. Emanuele Bardone and I have labeled this individual *inquisitive* and "use the word 'inquisitiveness' to refer to an agent who mostly relies on *learning by inquiry* and *open explorations* of his or her own environment, including social channels" (Bardone & Secchi, 2017, p. 68; emphases in the original).

9.2.1 Parameters

There are two types of agents in this simulation model: (a) agent-employees working in a company with their activity limited to problem solving, and (b) agent-problems, distributed over the organization's space and varying in difficulty. The simulation has a number of parameters that deal with general settings for the organization and other specific settings that relate to the agents. Table 9.1 specifies all the parameters, their notations, values, and offers a short description for each one of them.

The simulation starts with setting the number of decision makers or employees (A_{dm}) and problems (A_p) that appear at random in the environment. Just like seen in the other simulations above, the environment is to be intended as socio-cognitive context where the agents interact. Closeness, defined by the parameter range (r) means proximity in terms of access to problems and to other agent's competencies.

The organization can be set as one that offers the opportunity to its members to practice inquisitiveness or not, through a binomial parameter. When this opportunity is promoted by the organization, it is only available to those A_{dm} with appropriate levels of docility and enquiry. Also cooperation (C) is something that is part of the organization's environment, since it can be supported as a general way to work on problems $(C = \text{ON})$ as opposed to working separate from each other $(C = \text{OFF})$.

Another general setting called shortly LFP (see Table 9.1) is to give A_{dm} a proactive role such that they find their own problem to engage with, or to make them engage only with problems that are close to them, i.e. within r. When an agent A_{dm} or a team of agents deal with an agent-problem A_p, the organization may discourage waste of competence when there is a disproportion between them and the problem's difficulty. This proportion is given by the parameter tolerance (T) that works as a threshold and affects competence negatively as a result of an agent-decision maker applying over-competence to a seemingly easy problem.

Finally, the simulation controls the number of problems that can be generated at every simulation step, especially by those A_p that are among the most difficult in the organization space. Some problems are so difficult that they spin off (ϕ_p) other problems, typically easier and connected to them. The value the parameter takes is to be intended as the possible maximum number of new problems generated, the actual number being a random integer up to the value.

9.2.2   Procedures

What follows here is also described very similarly in the Supplementary Materials of the model, available online on the platform OpenABM.[2]

---

[2]At the webpage: https://www.comses.net/codebases/4749/releases/1.0.1/

Table 9.1. Parameter Notations, Values, and Descriptions for INQ1.0.1.

Parameter	Notation	Values	Description
General settings			
Steps	s	500	The opportunity that each agent-employee has to interact with others, move, and solve a problem.
Inquisitiveness	I	ON/OFF	When ON, this parameter enables A_{dm} to exercise their enquiry abilities, if conditions allow for them to.
Range	r	$\{3, 6\}$	The vision range of each agent that determines with whom they can interact, both in relation to other A_{dm} and A_p.
Looking for problems	LFP	ON/OFF	When ON, A_{dm} move purposively toward a random available A_p.
Cooperation	C	ON/OFF	This switch allows for A_{dm} to form teams around the A_p they are trying to solve.
Tolerance	T	3	This is a general threshold that determines the extent to which competence decreases because of over-competence exercised by A_{dm} on a problem A_p.
Characteristics of agent-employees (A_{dm})			
Number of employees	N_{dm}	$\{100, 200\}$	The number of decision makers, A_{dm}, also referred to as agent-employees, that appear in the environment at the beginning of the simulation.
Competence	c_{dm}	$\sim \mathcal{N}(\bar{c}, s_c)$	The parameter is distributed normally at random with mean $\bar{c} = \{1, 2, 3\}$ and standard deviation $s_c = 1.5$.
Delta competence	Δ_{c+}, Δ_{c-}	$[0, 1]$	Depending on problem solving, each A_{dm} has an increase or decrease in their level of C_{dm}; in this simulation, the range of increase is $\Delta_{c+} = \{0.15, 0.3\}$, that for decrease is $\Delta_{c-} = \{0.1, 0.05, 0\}$.
Docility	d_{dm}	$\sim \mathcal{N}(\bar{d}, s_d)$	This is the disposition to which A_{dm} use information coming from others; it is distributed normally at random with mean $\bar{d} = 0$ and standard deviation $s_c = 1$.
Enquiry	e_{dm}	$\sim \mathcal{N}(\bar{e}, s_c)$	This is the attitude each A_{dm} has to relax the community precondition; it is distributed normally at random with mean $\bar{e} = \{0, 1, 2\}$ and standard deviation $s_c = 1$.
Characteristics of agent-problems (A_p)			
Number of problems	N_p	$\{100, 200\}$	The number of decision makers, A_{dm}, that appear in the environment at the beginning of the simulation.
Difficulty	δ_p	$\sim \mathcal{N}(\bar{\delta}, s_\delta)$	This is the level of complexity that is attached to each A_p; it is distributed normally at random with mean $\bar{\delta} = \{0, 1, 2\}$ and standard deviation $s_\delta = 1$.
Evolve	ϵ	ON/OFF	When ON, it allows problems to multiply by a rate that is a random number between 0 and spin off.
Spin off	ϕ_p	$\{2, 4\}$	This is the rate with which problems multiply in the organization.

The model stops when the interactions count, step, reaches $s = 500$. There are other two ways in which the simulation could end, one relative to the activity of A_{dm}, that is when 90% of the initial number of A_p are solved. The other is relative to A_p and it happens when the situation is out of control and problems are 3 times more than their initial level.

The general rule for movement in the environment is that A_{dm} get closer to a problem when a link is established and when LFP is turned OFF. When this switch is ON instead, it is possible to move forward one position at a time to reach a problem – this is, of course, if the agent-employee A_{dm} is not involved with any problem at that moment. Problems do not move, but their size increases as their difficulty evolves. This feature is not reflected in the flow chart below (Fig. 9.2) but it is important. Problem difficulty is not a static quality. In fact, a problem's difficulty increases as time passes by and as it remains

Fig. 9.2. Flow Chart of the INQ1.0.1 Model.

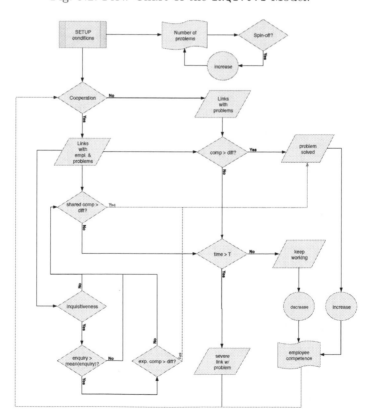

unsolved. However, this is not done for easy problems. At every round, a random selection of two of the most difficult problems are set to increase their difficulty by 2%.

Each agent scrutinizes the area around `range` looking for problems. When it finds one, a link with a problem is established while links with other agent-decision makers A_{dm} are only established when `cooperation`, C = ON. Once connections with problems are established, their thickness grows 0.1 at every step (tick), as a reference for the continued efforts exercised by A_{dm}. After 20 steps, the link is severed. This is to indicate that an agent cannot keep working on a problem forever; in an organization, there are always new tasks and new problems to solve. One needs to move on.

The solution of a problem is a rather simple matter, when the `competence` (c_i) of A_{dm} is higher than the `difficulty` (δ_p) of A_p, then it is solved. When solved, a problem disappears from the system.

A flow chart of the main processes in the model is presented in Fig. 9.2. This takes some of the options described above for granted, and part of a general setup, while other procedures that affect the end result more promptly are shown. A few disclaimers to be able to read the chart are necessary. As a starter, all basic functions are performed given a certain value for `range` that does not change during a simulation's run.

Shared competences ("shared comp" in Fig. 9.2) is a measure calculated by taking the mean of `docility` × `competence` as in $d_i \cdot c_i$ for all A_{dm} in range of proximity, and connected by a link to the decision maker. The agent making the decision is the one connected to A_p.

$$S_i = \frac{\sum_{i=1}^{n}(c_i \cdot d_i)}{n} \tag{9.1}$$

where S_i is the value for shared competences, n is the number of A_{dm} in range, r, c_i and d_i are competence and docility (also called, in the paper, socially oriented decision-making) of A_{dm}.

Under `cooperation` there are two possibilities for A_{dm}. One is to use the sharing option just described that works for the average individual, with $d_i < \bar{d} - 0.75 \cdot s(d)$, where d_i is the docility level for the agent-employee, $\bar{d}$ is the mean and $s(d)$ is the standard deviation of d in the system.

For highly docile individuals, with $d_i < \bar{d} + 0.75 \cdot s(d)$, the system works differently, because these individuals are supposed (according to the theory) to deal more efficiently with information coming from others. Agents also use `enquiry` e_i if the switch `inquisitiveness` is ON, such that those agent-employees with $e_i > \bar{e}$ can use competence from outside of their teams. This implies an increase in the `range` parameter that, for these highly inquisitive agents, is defined as $\Delta r = r \cdot 1.5$.

For highly inquisitive agents, the shared information is re-coded as:

$$S_e = S_i + S_i \cdot \left(1 + \frac{e_i}{max(e)}\right) \tag{9.2}$$

where S_e is the shared competence for highly inquisitive agents, the shared competence is S_i (Equation 9.1), e_i is the level of the parameter enquiry for the agent, and $max(e)$ is the maximum level of that same parameter in the system. Then, the competence of the inquisitive agent becomes

$$E_i = c_i + \frac{1}{|c_i|^{ln(S_i+1)}} \tag{9.3}$$

where E_i is benchmarked with the difficulty of a problem δ_p and, if

$$E_i > \delta_p \tag{9.4}$$

then a problem is solved. Equations 9.3 and 9.4 are also the same used for highly docile individuals, with S_i defined as explained above (Equation 9.1).

At the end of every procedure, when a problem is solved or abandoned, each agent-employee resets its shared competencies, but keeps some trace in its competence levels that increase or decrease according to the two parameters described above.

9.3 Findings

The original INQ1.0 model had a factorial design of $2 \times 2 \times 2 \times 2 \times 3 \times 3 \times 2 = 288$ configurations of parameters. It took $N_{dm} = \{100, 200\}, N_p = \{100, 200\}, I = \text{ON/OFF}, \Delta_{c+} = \{0.15, 0.30\}, \Delta_{c-} = \{0, 0.05, 0.1\}, c_{dm} = \{1, 2, 3\}, \phi = \{2, 4\}$, with $r = 6$ and $\bar{e} = 0$. The procedure I use to determine the number of runs and described in Secchi and Seri (2017), Seri and Secchi (2017), is a standard in this book, and it was calculated as 30 runs, for a total of $30 \times 288 = 8{,}640$ simulations.

The simulations run for this chapter include the variation of $\bar{e} = \{0, 1, 2\}$ and of $r = \{3, 6\}$. This multiplies the original configurations times 6, for a total of $288 \times 6 = 1{,}728$. Now, this new number requires a different calculation for estimating the number of runs, since repeating each one of these 30 times may lead to overpower (see Secchi & Seri, 2017). Using the reverse F-test from ANOVA – package pwr in R – with a small effect size, $f = 0.1$, $\alpha = 0.01$, and $\beta = 0.05$, I obtain that 14.9 runs are enough. Hence, we can settle on 15.

Fig. 9.3 presents results for the impact of the initial setting of parameter competence, $\bar{c}$, on the number of problems, N_p, in the system as time (better: opportunities to interact) goes by. The curves are an

Fig. 9.3. LOESS Curves per Mean competence ($\bar{c}$) Levels, as They Evolve Through Time (Steps) and Affect the Problems Ratio ($P_t/P_{t=0}$) in the Organization, with $\Delta_{c+} = 0.15, \Delta_{c-} = 0, r = 3, e_{dm} = 0$.

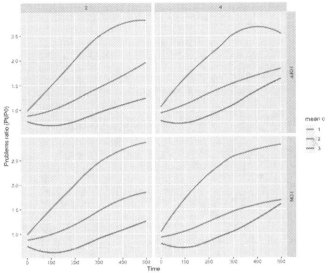

estimate based on a regression method called LOESS (locally estimated scatterplot smoothing), that gives a general idea of the trend in the data. The second important element to notice in Fig. 9.3 and the following ones is that, given that there is a multiplication factor ϕ_p, N_p tends to increase as steps (time) increase. From the plots, it is easy to observe that they can increase up to more than 2.5 times their initial level. As $\bar{c}$ increases, the rate with which problems increase reduces significantly. The LOESS curve for $\bar{c} = 3$ stay under 1.0 to raise and gain the initial number of problems only after half simulation steps. As expected, the increase is less steep when spin off is on the low, i.e. $\phi_p = 2$. From the curves in these graphs, it is apparent that competence plays a very important role in problem solving. The question is whether an increase in the levels of inquisitiveness helps.

From what can be observed in Fig. 9.3, it seems that the effects are minimal, probably more pronounced when $\bar{c} = 3$. However, the effect is not remarkable, at least not when $\bar{e} = 0$. If we increase $\bar{e} = 2$, the effect is still very similar to the one observed in Fig. 9.3 (this plot is not shown here because too similar to the one already in).

The increase in opportunities for interaction r makes for an increased number of problems solved. Fig. 9.4 shows these effects in a similar fashion to what discussed previously. The trends show an increase that is smoother, especially as $\bar{c} > 1$. Cooperation in teamwork seems to be another element that supports problem solving, especially when considered together with a higher average competence. The difference between the two sets of figures with $I = \text{ON}$ and $I = \text{OFF}$ do not show, again, any difference that is worth noting.

Fig. 9.4. LOESS Curves per Mean competence ($\bar{c}$) Levels, as They Evolve Through Time (Steps) and Affect the Problems Ratio ($P_t/P_{t=0}$) in the Organization, with $\phi_p = 4, \Delta_{c+} = 0.15, \Delta_{c-} = 0, r = 6, e_{dm} = 2$.

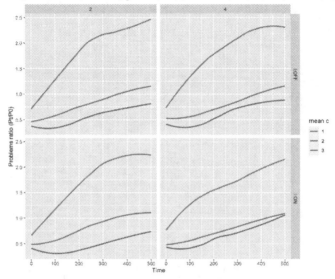

The above requires a different take on the topic, to try and understand if and when inquisitiveness bears any effect on problem solving and the work of teams in organizations. Fig. 9.5 splits the sample by initial number of decision makers N_{dm} and initial number of problems N_p in the organization. The patterns are different depending on whether $N_p = N_{dm}$, $N_p > N_{dm}$ or when $N_p < N_{dm}$. Inquisitiveness is more effective when $N_{dm} = 200$ and $\bar{c} = 3$, although some effects are also visible for $\bar{c} = 2$. There is a remarkable effect of I that is extremely powerful in that it seems to bring the curves to end prematurely, due to a solution brought in for most problems. It is worth noting that these results are more likely when $\phi_p = 4$, the case where problems multiply at a higher rate. In the case where $N_p = N_{dm} = 100$ there is an interesting pattern for $\bar{c} = 1$ as the LOESS curve draws a reverse U. The pane with $I = \text{ON}$ seems to anticipate the curve that is in $I = \text{OFF}$, ending with a lower value of the problem ratio. It is as if low competence takes more interactions to become effective and affects problem solving although it will eventually work better than the mid-level of $\bar{c} = 1$.

Fig. 9.5. LOESS Curves per Mean competence ($\bar{c}$) Levels, as They Evolve Through Time (Steps) and Affect the Problems Ratio ($P_t/P_{t=0}$) in the Organization, with $\Delta_{c+} = 0.15, \Delta_{c-} = 0.05, r = 6, e_{dm} = 2$, Split by N_{dm} and N_p, and $I = $ ON/OFF.

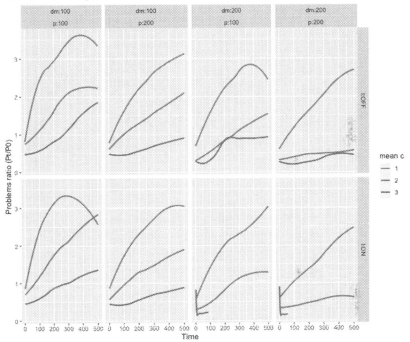

The following step would be to zoom in these agent orientations as they emerge from Fig. 9.5. This is done by looking into observations that reduced the number of problems in the system as the two bottom right panes of Fig. 9.5 show. Fig. 9.6 maps the level of calculated competence, $\hat{c}$, in the organization. From the previous paragraph, we know that the parameter competence only sets the initial level, but c can evolve, depending on problems solved or not (mainly through Δ_{c+} and Δ_{c-}). The purpose of plotting how competence changes with $\hat{c}$ and compare it to those agents that act more inquisitively than others is to understand whether more or less is needed. Another aspect to remember is that agents can adopt the behavior of others, if deemed successful. This is how the numbers of inquisitive agents can increase and an increase is a sign that their *inquisitive* strategy has worked.

The increase is justified in that highly docile and inquisitive agents increase more than other types of agents. In a plot that constitutes a

Fig. 9.6. Mean Calculated Competence ($\hat{c}$) Levels by the Number of Inquisitive Agents in the Organization, with $\Delta_{c+} = 0.15, \Delta_{c-} = 0, r = 6, e_{dm} = 2, N_p = 200, I = \text{ON}$, Split by N_{dm} and $\bar{c}$; Observations Cover the First Three Quartiles of Competence $\hat{c}$.

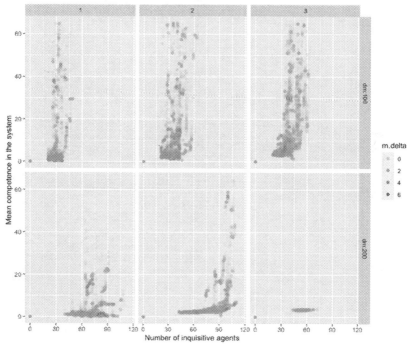

preliminary analysis to Fig. 9.6, it is possible to observe that $I = \text{ON}$ leads to an increase in the number of inquisitive agents over those who are not (under conditions similar to those in the figure reproduced in this book). The findings in the panes at the bottom of Fig. 9.6 with $N_{dm} = 200$ show that there is an increase in the numbers that supports inquisitive behavior, more apparent than that for $N_{dm} = 100$. However, most of the competence needed to solve problems is $\hat{c} < 10$. The bottom right pane shows agents that use very limited competence to solve all of the problems in the organization.

9.4   The Implications of Wide Sociality

The above points at one of the most important results of the INQ1.0.1 model, one already mentioned in Bardone and Secchi (2017). This is that, among other advantages, inquisitiveness seems to require an approach to problem solving that optimizes the use of social resources around the task. In fact, results indicate that there is an *economizing effect*, due to the pulling of competence (resources) across teams to work on a problem. Not only the strategy is successful, but it becomes widely imitated, provided other conditions are met.

These other conditions are not secondary at all. In fact, the findings discussed above in relation to the *economizing effect* can only happen if there is a good ground for social relationships in the organization. This means that the organization needs to establish the channels that employees can exploit to practice inquisitive behavior. This is something that became apparent by comparing results for agent's opportunities to interact, as they are parametrized by range, r. An organization that does create the conditions for employees to meet and work together is very much oriented toward a "silos" (or compartmentalized) mentality. These conditions may vary significantly from organization to organization and do not need to be necessarily expressed through formal means. A cafeteria or a Friday bar are popular initiatives that lead to people from different teams and departments to know each other a bit better. More formal initiatives may include the establishment of "mixed" task forces or committees that represent different professions, typically people from different teams.

Another condition that favors inquisitiveness seem to be the size of an organization. In order for work across teams to be effective, there need to be actual separation between teams, and actual team with specialized knowledge. These are, again, preconditions that emerge from the results above, especially from Fig. 9.5. The idea that has emerged is probably counterintuitive, since smaller organizations ($N_{dm} = 100$) are usually those where there is minimal distance between competences, skills, and professions. In other words, smaller organizations are those where it is more likely that people work across their team's bounds, simply because they can be thought of as one large team, sometimes. This is what we see in the results of this simulation. Smaller organizations do not need inquisitiveness as much as larger organizations do.

Finally, a last condition is that of the number and type of problems that are best handled by inquisitive agents. On the first element – i.e. number of problems (Fig. 9.3) – it seems that inquisitiveness does not mind dealing with increasing numbers. The majority of problems are probably solved by individuals in those cases and an increase of relatively simple problems does not affect the results. The patterns in Fig. 9.3 are, after all, very similar. What makes a difference, though, is what emerges from Fig. 9.6, where it seems that inquisitive agents are particularly effective with more complex problems, probably by using a coping strategy that matches the *economizing effect* of competences with the increasing difficulty of problems.

9.5   Summary

This chapter has started from where Chapter 8 left, by taking the challenge offered by the DIO1.0 simulation in an attempt to understand whether there is a different way to theorize about how the social individual operates in organizations. In the model presented here, the INQ1.0.1, I have modeled agents as they work in teams and cooperate with each others. At the same time, in an attempt to reduce the costs of docility, I have reduced the bound on the team to which they belong, and introduced the *inquisitive* individual. This is someone who is concerned with the problem more than with loyalty to his/her group or team. The findings indicated that inquisitive behavior can be successfully deployed by organizations to use competences more efficiently and solve problems effectively.

Now, organizations may have the need to use more inquisitive and docile behaviors. But organizations experiment, at times, difficult adaptations to a turbulent environment, and the extent to which inquisitive or docile behavior are required may vary depending on these external pressures. This is to write that the organizational "environment" in which employees and management interact is not neutral, but it is always a representation of a mix of internal and external factors. The models presented so far have disregarded external elements. Chapter 10 presents a model that makes explicit reference to these external pressures, especially some where different EDEC strategies are compared.

10

Wild Inquisitiveness: The Plastic Organization

> *"Organized anarchies require a revised theory of management.*
> *[...] Where goals and technology are hazy and participation is*
> *fluid, many of the axioms and standard procedures of manage-*
> *ment collapse."*
>
> – Cohen, March, and Olsen (1972, p. 2)

When inquisitiveness is promoted and practiced at large in an organization it implies that the structure is, more or less, leaning toward a flat hierarchy, such that operations can run smoothly across departments and teams. This approach has a long tradition in MOR, especially when it comes to simulations. In fact, the Garbage Can Model (Cohen et al., 1972; Fioretti & Lomi, 2010) tackles with the effects of an organized anarchy on problem solving, given solutions, opportunities, and decision makers. The opening quote refers to the original study (1972), where the authors highlight that management has always been a study of *organizing* and of *organization* and it may come unprepared to deal with unorganized or disorganized entities. Their consideration is about the theories of management that circulated 50 years ago, when they published the study, but not much has changed. This is understandable, given that organizations and organized aspects of our societal lives depend on such forms. Yet, this declaration of inadequacy is still particularly relevant because, as it has become more apparent recently (Herath, 2019), parts of the way organizations function may be messy,

Computational Organizational Cognition:
A Study on Thinking and Action in Organizations, 141–161
Copyright © 2021 by Emerald Publishing Limited
All rights of reproduction in any form reserved
doi: 10.1108/978-1-83867-511-020211010

disorganized, disordered, and even scattered (Abrahamson & Freeman, 2007).

To put it differently, the search for regularities is a standard norm for management research as well as for many scientific disciplines (e.g., Grimm et al., 2005). This is why scholars have focused much on *organizations*, because they can be defined on the basis of regularities and standards. Most importantly, when these are found, they can be replicated and sometimes generalized. These regularities are, however, equivalent to a mean, an average. In fact, dispersion around this mean can be wide. It can take the form of ambiguous understanding of internal norms as well as uncertainty about pressure from the outside. This dispersion is unavoidable and the quote at the beginning of this chapter makes it explicit. When behaviors in an organization are far away from what prescribed by a (mean) standard management theory, then this theory is not enough to capture the essence of what happens in that organization. Stated differently, when behavior is such that it varies very much (it is dispersed) such that its mean is not representative of this variety, then a standard theory of management may become difficult to apply. This latter situation is represented by what Cohen et al. (1972) called "organized anarchy" and what modern scholars have labeled "disorganization" (Herath, Secchi, & Homberg, 2016) or, lately, *plasticity* (Herath, 2019).[1]

What we have learned from the literature above is that some ambiguity cannot be factored out. In some cases, this ambiguity remains at manageable and controllable levels while in some others it becomes widespread and increasingly difficult to tackle. We have all witnessed (and still are witnessing) the extent to which ambiguity can become a common feature of organizational lives. The impact of the global pandemic related to the coronavirus SARS-CoV-2 is an out-of-proportion effect of ambiguity where almost everything – from human relations to service and product delivery – had to change fast and according to an untested, theory-only, and sometimes non-existent plan. This sudden exercise made a literal mess of most organizations, unveiling how important it is for MOR to find ways to make sense of disorganization and plasticity.

Some of the research recently conducted in this area (Herath et al., 2016) shows that disorganization can be beneficial to work with in social settings. It has been shown to increase motivation and the number of problems solved as well as tasks successfully performed. In light of the task of understanding docility and socially distributed cognition further, I ask whether this is a ground for *inquisitiveness* to flourish, and how

---

[1]As I write this book chapter, a Special Issue on Organizational Plasticity is in the process of being finalized for the types of *Evidence-Based HRM*. It will appear in one of the issues in 2021 although most of its articles are already available online and some of them are cited in this chapter.

far can disorganization/plasticity go. This chapter is an attempt to present the issues around plasticity and suggest a few critical points to be looked at.

10.1 What Is Plasticity?

The simple question in the title of this subsection is only apparently simple. In fact, there is limited literature on *plasticity* and on what it actually means. During the Third Agent-Based Models of Organizational Behavior (ABMO3) Workshop,[2] organized in 2017 by Dinuka Herath and I to discuss issues and topics around organizational plasticity, we suddenly realized that participants came in with different ideas. These differences as well as an attempt to build a common ground for an agent-based model of plasticity are documented in Siebers et al. (2020).

An approach that can be taken to discuss this concept and try to answer the question of this section is to look at concepts that are close to plasticity. The attribute "plastic" is referred to something malleable and flexible and is used to indicate extreme adaptability to given circumstances. The word comes from biology to describe, for example, organisms that adopt strategies of structural changes to adapt to the system in which they live in (e.g., Kurakin, Swistowski, Wu, & Bredeson, 2007). When transferred to organizations, the concept may be similar to *resilience* or to *disorganization*.

10.1.1 Disorganization

As anticipated at the beginning of this chapter, this concept is the antithesis of the core focus of the management discipline. Some have highlighted (Abrahamson, 2002; Abrahamson & Freeman, 2007) that organizations have a natural tendency toward messiness and disorder, in the sense that tendencies such as accumulation, juxtaposition, improvisation, and ambiguity lead to a relaxation of what keeps a workplace organized. Together with these tendencies an organization needs to keep business going and, as such, either makes disorganization work and/or attempts at minimizing its negative side effects. These are particularly visible, especially when disorder reaches a point in which it saturates options for decision making or affects the client (hence the bottom line). Imagine you enter an ice-cream shop and order an ice-cream. As you are there, you notice that there are local sweet pastries and biscuits on

---

[2]From which the *Evidence-Based HRM* Special Issue has taken inspiration. More information on ABMO3 is available here: `https://sites.google.com/view/abmworkshops`.

display as if this was a pastry shop.[3] You then ask for two pastries to take home. The reply you get is that those sweet pastries are only there as samples and that, if you need them, you can order them and come pick them up the day after. How does this make business sense? The explanation is that the shop was originally a pastry shop and the owner decided to sell ice-cream because overwhelmed with the regular business. As a result, things spun out of control, to the point that she/he did not even took leftovers out of display, pretending they were there for you to order. One may conclude that the shop has a short life and the owner needs to seriously think of claiming back control over a disorganized business.

In light of the above, a more interesting perspective is that of "managing" disorganization, as Herath (2019) suggests in his work. In fact, there are *functional* and *structural* effects that need to be considered when looking into the phenomenon. The first is such that keeping things disorganized – or following a path of controlled disorganization (destructuring) – may actually increase effectiveness, because it makes potential solutions closer to problems (this is a classic management topic; see Barnard, 1938; Simon, 1997/1947). Consider a start-up business that is struggling to satisfy their clients and keep up with orders. Finding an efficient way of processing these orders is very important but actually not as important as dealing with the order that is incumbent here and now. So, the former should not be done at the expenses of the latter or the company is out of business. The former may eventually come as the company finds a way to organize or, better, to make a decision on what to keep in a disorganized state.

This is the effectiveness versus efficiency trade off that is triggered by disorganization (Secchi, 2019). Traditional management theory would posit that efficiency will bring effectiveness, at least in the long run (a very short history covering also this can be found in Hendry, 2013). But this holds only if and when change is kept to a minimum, that is when environmental conditions are stable. Over the last three decades, we have never experienced stability and this means that the *ceteris paribus* assumption of traditional theory is only a case for speculation. The actual world of organizations is one of change, where action drives some of their processes toward a *functional* way of keeping formal and norm-bound organizing down.

The second aspect that Herath (2019) relates to disorganization is the *structural* effect. In fact, disorganization can have effects on the relations among employees, management, and executives in the typical organizational hierarchy. These can become loose depending on a stretch that is required by the environment, such as a sudden change in the

---

[3]This example comes from an actual business I visited in Cagliari, Sardinia (Italy).

workforce (a surge or a cut), the adoption of agile management practices (e.g., Worley, Williams, & Lawler III, 2014; Worley & Lawler, 2010), a restructuring process, a merger, or any other disruptive or more subtle change in the way in which work is typically distributed. One of the effects of disorganization is that of keeping resources that are typically distant somewhat closer. After a restructuring, the head of operations that used to only talk to his/her folk is now forced to share ideas, opinions, recommendations, and directions with others. This may make processes more cumbersome and take time to find a new re-alignment. At the same time, it may bring solutions, opportunities, and resources closer to problems and tasks.

10.1.2   Resilience

In contrast to that of disorganization and plasticity, the concept of *resilience* has a long history in MOR. From a broad perspective, it is "closely related with the capability and ability of an element to return to a stable state after a disruption" (Bhamra, Dani, & Burnard, 2011, p. 5376). This can be easily related to an organization facing turbulent or abrupt environmental conditions, and its needs to return, more or less quickly, to stable operations. There are multiple questions that surface this definition, mainly related to what *stability* means and to what *disruption* is. Let me start with the latter.

Disruption is a word that is often used among MOR scholars to indicate, for example, the impact of innovation on firms (e.g., Rogers, 2003) or the sudden change of conditions leading to individual misunderstanding (e.g., Weick, 1993). It is a situation that puts the typical operations of a system under threat, by making some of its elements disconnect and relocate, or simply by making the resources to function properly unavailable. This determines the system to become under pressure and even to fail. As I write these sentences, my mind goes to organizations that, during the COVID-19 pandemic, experience relocation of workers, layoffs, abrupt decrease in (or absence of) demand, lack supplies, or strain to keep teams together. The global pandemic is one of the major disruptions in organizational operations, probably since World War II.

While the standard interpretation relates to large unpredictable events, disruption can also manifest through minor and apparently insignificant events. The failure to "read" the market or a change in the environment may lead organizations to find themselves struggling to survive. This may happen, for example, in relation to a legislative change. The General Data Protection Regulation (GDPR) of the European Union was designed to protect citizens' data from the exploitation that many large so-called Internet companies practice.

It has, however, repercussions on the way several SMEs operate, for example, when dealing with personal information of their clients and employees. This legislation is notoriously difficult to interpret and sometimes to apply, leading organizations to learn from each other and from professional recommendations coming from their industry associations. Failure to apply GDPR correctly may imply, for SMEs, a fine so large it may disrupt operations as it drains resources.

The second aspect of the definition is that of *stability*. Holling (1973) indicates there are two viewpoints to consider, that of "resilience" and that of "stability." The first emphasizes the capacity of a system to handle deviations from the standard state and keep the existing connections between the component entities. The second is about consistently keeping an equilibrium state for a period of time, independent of perturbation. While resilience is about keeping the system working, stability is about maintaining a given condition. Occasionally, the second implies the first, meaning that the departure of the organization from its standard equilibrium may signify that there are no operations.

The picture is that of an organization that is able to restore its original state by absorbing shocks from the environment. This is certainly dynamic but, if one stops at this perspective then *resilience* may be insufficient to make the organization survive. This is simply because the environment might have changed as the organization strives to restore its original state. And changes in the environment may be due to the complexity of institutions (Greenwood, Raynard, Kodeih, Micelotta, & Lounsbury, 2011) and to organizational interventions. The point here is that the organization-environment relation is more similar to an organism in a niche (Hench & Secchi, 2009; Odling-Smee, Laland, & Feldman, 2003) than to anything else. For this reason, some claim that another take on resilience is that it forces the organization to change and develop to keep pace with the changes in the environment (Lengnick-Hall, Beck, & Lengnick-Hall, 2011).

This latter aspect highlights another dimension, that of considering resilience as a mere passive attitude of an organization to "bounce back" as it recovers from disruption as well as the active attitude to deal with disruption in a more constructive way (Somers, 2009).

10.1.3   Plasticity

While both disorganization and resilience share very relevant aspects with plasticity, they can also be used to make a few distinctions. On the one hand, both aspects have *change* at their core. Disorganization, as described above, is more a process, a driving force of change within the organization that may or may not match with external pressures.

In fact, it may happen for reasons that find roots in pressures from the environment or grow entirely within the organization (Herath, 2019). Resilience is, instead, something that has been typically considered as it emerges from external pressures. Whether it is active or passive, it still requires an external "disruptive event" to be triggered (Somers, 2009). It can be studied with an internal perspective (e.g., Lengnick-Hall et al., 2011), although it is still related to something happening externally to the organization.

Plasticity is about setting the working conditions in an organization such that it makes adaptation easier. Contrary to resilience, there is no requirement to "bounce back" to a pre-existing form, because plasticity is about evolution – better, co-evolution of the organization and its components with various elements of the environment. On the one hand, a plastic organization shows flexibility of the way in which its internal components are structured and operate. This aspect makes it close to disorganization, since the ability to keep resources close to where they are needed is more easily achievable with it (Herath et al., 2016). On the other hand, organizations are complex systems and are immersed in wider complex systems (e.g., institutions, markets, societies). For this reason, plasticity considers the multiple connections of the various elements within and around the organization as a ground for its existence. A plastic organization exploits the complex nexus of relationships that individuals, groups, teams, departments, and their workings have with the various and multifaceted aspects of the environment. The relation is not one-way, it is made of multiple double-feedback loops. In other words, the organization may have an overall strategy to deal with suppliers, for example. This macro structural aspect is, however, inevitably interpreted by a team, and by one or more individuals who deal with the actual suppliers. The interaction adjusts mutual expectations, refines orders, expands them, or drops them. The macro structural element connects plasticity to resilience while the micro and social interactivity create a link to disorganization. This makes it possible to describe plasticity as a key element of complex adaptive and dynamic social systems.

10.2 The Model

The paper on which this chapter is based (i.e. Secchi, 2020a) has been accepted for publication in a Special Issue that is completely dedicated to organizational *plasticity* and edited by Dinuka Herath and I (Herath & Secchi, 2021). The journal that hosts this paper is *Evidence-based Human Resource Management*, hence the emphasis of most papers is explicitly intra-organizational. My paper as well tackles on the effects of plasticity inside an organization, specifically on the ability of the workforce to contrast the effects of change on their work.

The model is designed to study how two different EDEC strategies – i.e. enaction and extended cognition – serve the ability of individuals to practice effective teamwork while their job-related tasks increase due to adaptation to shocks of various proportions. Stated differently, I am asking the following question: what are the organizational characteristics that allow workers to face change more effectively? The intra-organizational plasticity or `IOP2.1.2` model[4] implements some of the definitional aspects that have been described in the section above.

10.2.1   Parameters

The `IOP2.1.2` model is built with the premises above in mind and its parameters reflect the attempt to understand how the traditional internal and external elements of an organizations are, in fact, all working parts of the same system.

Table 10.1 presents all the parameters of the simulation, with notations, values, and a short description. This simulation model underwent a very intense series of calibration procedures, with $373,248$ experiments to ascertain the most appropriate values for the parameters. Not only this signals that the `IOP2.1.2` model has been thoroughly tested, but it also indicates that the number of parameters is relatively high. In fact, I classify this as one of the most complex models I have designed to date.

The other implication of the extensive rounds of tests is that I have produced a number of results and they are only partially reproduced in Secchi (2020a). In fact, Table 10.1 is a very close reproduction of what published in (Secchi, 2020a, pp. 197–198), because the parameters and values discussed in this chapter are substantially unchanged from those in the article.

The simulation consists of an organizational environment with rules of operation (or mechanisms, described in the next subsection) where three types of agents interact. While the environment is not to be intended as a physical space, as the reader of this book has learned with the simulations presented in the previous chapters, agents consist of *employees* that perform *tasks* through the use of *resources*.

The agent-employee is described by four characteristics. One is the parameter `competence` (c) intended as a knowledge-specific measure that is related to the professionalism of each agent. This is distributed at random with a normal distribution with mean $\bar{c}$ that varies in the range

---

[4]Available on the platform OpenABM at `https://www.comses.net/codebases/4ff566a6-c0f8-4ca2-aa5f-21d44705aea8/releases/2.1.2/`.

Table 10.1. Parameter Notations, Values and Descriptions for IOP2.1.2.

Parameter	Notation	Values	Description
Setup conditions			
Steps		300	The measure for time in the simulation, the value indicates the upper value at which the simulation stops. Each step represents the attempt that an employee makes to find or perform a task.
Number of employees	N_e	200	Number of employees e in the organization; this is kept constant throughout the simulation.
Proportion of tasks*	$P_{t,0}$	$\{x + 0.5 \mid 0.5 \leq x \leq 2\}$	Tasks t in the organization at time zero 0, expressed as a proportion P of N_e, such that the number of tasks $t = P_{t,0} \times N_e$.
Proportion of resources*	$P_{r,0}$	$\{x + 0.5 \mid 0.5 \leq x \leq 2\}$	As for the tasks t, resources r in the organization at time zero 0 are also $t = P_{r,0} \times N_e$.
Employee characteristics			
Competence	c	$\approx \mathcal{N}(\{x+0.5 \mid 0.5 \leq x \leq 2\}, 0.5)$	Each employee has some knowledge related to task performance, distributed random normally, with a fixed standard deviation 0.5 and a mean that can take three values.
Ability	a	$\approx \mathcal{N}(\{0.05, 0.1, 0.2\}, 0.25)$	This is the expertise with which employees use their knowledge; it is distributed random normally, with a fixed standard deviation 0.5 and a mean that can take three values.
Role	R	0, 1	The role gives access to different categories of resources (see below). Employees are randomly assigned to the two values.
Docility	d	$\approx \mathcal{N}(1, 0.5)$	The extent to which an employee uses the competence c coming from others to perform a task.
Task characteristics			
Difficulty	δ	$\approx R[\{0, 0.4, 0.8\}, 1]$	Tasks have a difficulty δ level that is attributed randomly, with a uniform distribution that ranges between the three values of min δ and an upper bound of $\delta_{max} = 1$.
Time	T_t	$\{T_t \in \mathbb{N} \mid 0 \leq T_t < 4\}$	Initially attributed as a random integer to all tasks, when at least one employee is working on the task, T_t decreases of 0.1 at every step.
Resource characteristics			
Dimensions	K	$\{0, 1, 2\}$	When dimension $K = 2$, a resource can be used to work on any task independent of its difficulty, but only highly competent employees would have the know-how to use such a resource. Various limitations operate when $K < 2$.
Proportion availability	P_A	$\{0.25, 0.5\}$	The parameter $A = 0$ when unavailable and 1 if available. The proportion of resources in the system that are available P_A to employees with role $R = 0$ varies between $\{0.25, 0.5\}$. All resources are always available for employees with $R = 1$.
Immediateness	I	$\approx \mathcal{N}(\{-0.5, 0, 0.5\}, 0.5)$	This parameter is the extent to which a resource can be used, when $A = 1$. When $I < 0$ then it takes time for the employee to utilize that resource. Immediateness increases with ability a.
Procedural parameters			
Docility enabler	d_{en}	$\{0, 1\}$	When $d_{en} = 1$ then employees with docility higher than the mean of docility of employees $(d > \bar{d})$, connect to other employees and use their ability to perform tasks.
Extended cognition	EC	$\{0, 1\}$	When activated, EC makes individuals use a resource again and again if it has been successful in the past.
Hit wave	t_w	$\{0, 0.1, 0.2\}$	Every 10 seconds, t_w percent tasks are added to the system. The percentage is calculated on the initial number of tasks $P_{t,0} \times N_e$.
Competence increase	Δc	$\{0.2, 0.4, 0.6\}$	Competence c increases of a value specified by the parameter Δc when a task is performed successfully.
Ability increment	ΔA	$\{0.1, 0.2, 0.3\}$	When $d_{en} = 1$ employees with $d > \bar{d}$ who complete a task receive an increase in their ability that equals ΔA.

Source: Secchi (2020a, pp. 197–198). *Note*. * The math notation here means that the proportion moves in the range described at intervals of 0.5.

[0.5, 2] and a fixed standard deviation $s_c = 0.5$. Ability (a) is related to the skill that an agent-employee has to perform a task, intended to refer mainly to experience. Its values are distributed normally at random following a pattern similar to the parameter above, with a mean $\bar{a} = [0.05, 0.1, 0.2]$ and a standard deviation that is $s_a = 0.25$. The inclusion of this model in Part II of the book implies that the agent-employee is equipped with a *docility* (d) disposition, simulated with values attributed normally in the population, with $\sim \mathcal{N}(1, 0.5)$. Docility is implemented through organizational enabling mechanisms, and it is controlled by a docility enabler, that can be switched ON/OFF. The parameter role (R) is binomial and takes value $R = 1$ to mean that some categories of agent-resources are made available to the agent-employee. When it is $R = 0$ the agent-employee has access to a limited number of resources. The values are distributed at random.

Agent-tasks are modeled through two essential characteristics, one being difficulty (δ) and the other time (T_t). The former indicates the level of complexity that the task has and it is something to be matched with some of the employee characteristics, according to the rules shown below. An agent-task with high difficulty may still be relatively "easy" depending on the combination of agent-employees and agent-resources employed. For each agent-task, δ is defined by

$$\delta_j = \min \delta + \mathcal{R}, \tag{10.1}$$

where δ_j is the level of difficulty for agent j, $\min \delta$ is a bottom value for δ that is defined as a parameter that takes values $\{0, 0.4, 0.8\}$, and $\mathcal{R}$ is a random uniform distribution that ranges between $[\min \delta, 1]$. With these rules in place, the modeler can control the minimum difficulty of the agent-tasks in the organization, while still allowing for variability.

The other parameter, time, sets the limit to which each task can be worked on by agent-employees. It is, in other words, the due date of a task. It is attributed at random to each agent-task in the system, with $\mathcal{R} = \{0, 1, 2, 3, 4, 5\}$. At every step, this value reduces of 0.1 until the agent-task is either performed or the agent-employee leaves it to others.

Agent-resources are instrumental to agent-employees to work on an agent-task (according to rules of operations specified below). They have three characteristics, one is their dimension, $K = \{0, 1, 2\}$, and it indicates whether the agent-resource can be used with any agent-task $(K = 2)$ or whether there are restrictions $(K < 2)$, depending on δ such that $K = 1 \Rightarrow \delta \le 0.75$ and $K = 0 \Rightarrow \delta \le 0.25$. This means that not all agent-resources are available for every agent-employee. The proportion of resources available, $P_A = \{0.25, 0.5\}$, can be controlled by the modeler and it is such that it defines how many resources are available to agent-employees with $R = 0$. In addition to the above, there is an `immediateness`, I, parameter to indicate that there may be a delay between the time a resource is deployed and that to which it is used. This is to replicate the effect of the time it takes by an unskilled (less competent and with reduced ability) employee to put the resource into effect. It is distributed normally at random, with $\sim \mathcal{N}(\bar{I}, s_I)$, where the standard deviation is fixed at $s_I = 0.5$ while the mean varies, $\bar{I} = \{-0.5, 0, 0.5\}$.

The number of agent-employees N_e is fixed at 200, while numbers for agent-resources, N_r, and agent-tasks, N_t, are defined as a proportion of N_e such that the initial number for these two are

$$N_{t,0} = N_e \cdot P_{t,0} \tag{10.2}$$

$$N_{r,0} = N_e \cdot P_{r,0}. \tag{10.3}$$

10.2.2 Procedures

At the beginning of the simulation, all agents appear in random locations in the environment. This is done to make sure that there is no direction in the way the modeler assigns tasks to given employees or groups. Tasks do not move in the environment, while resources move at random following one direction only, and employees move around without a clear direction.

The simulation stops automatically as steps $= 300$ or when tasks decrease to 10% or less of their initial number. Time in the simulation is counted by steps, and they are intended as an opportunity for agents to interact rather than representing a unit of actual time. They can be thought of as times in which some effort is infused on tasks by employees, with an opportunity of some performance improvement – major or minor. The number 300 was chosen after preliminary runs of the simulation showed that most effects were clearly visible already before this horizon.

As the simulation starts, the system is invaded by a `hit wave`, $t_w = \{0, 0.1, 0.2\}$, of new tasks. This represents a challenge to plasticity because the simulation studies how the system and employees react to various increases in the number of tasks. The tasks increase every J seconds, defined by a parameter `frequency` that is kept fixed for this study. If $N_{t,1} > t_w \cdot N_{t,0}$ then a random number $\mathcal{R} = [0, t_w]^5$ of new tasks appears in the organization, with random characteristics and at random locations.

---

[5]The wave is composed by two parts, one that is calculated on the equation in the text, and another that uses $N_{t,1} > w_t \cdot N_{t,0} \cdot 0.8$, such that uncertainty grows, because the impact of w_t can be almost double.

Agent-employees connect to agent-tasks and agent-resources when they are available in a radius, defined by a constant `range` (r) that is fixed at 6 for the current study. Once links are established according to the rules explained above (related to R, P_A, and K), agent-employees start performing the task they are connected to. The first step for the model is to distinguish between high and low c for employee-agents. Depending on the match between c, K, and δ, the task is either solved or is signaled as being "worked on." For example, if an agent-employee with low competence – i.e. $c_i < (\bar{c} - s_c)$ – finds an agent-resource with $K = 1$ to work on an agent-task with $\delta \leq 0.75$, the task is being "worked on," otherwise it is abandoned after time for that task reaches T_t.

After the above is checked, if agent-resources available to the agent-employee have $I > 0$, they leave a mark on the ground, to mean that the use of that resource has been successful, hence signaling that the same resource is up for repeated use. As one may remember from Chapter 3 this is a feature of extended cognition (Clark & Chalmers, 1998), that is the re-use of disposable resources.

The idea to operationalize work on a task is that the immediateness of a resource is put into effect by a capable employee through ability, hence:

$$IA_e = I_r \cdot a_e \qquad\qquad (10.4)$$

where I_r is `immediateness` of one of the resource, r, connected to an employee, e, and a_e is the `ability` of this employee.

When $IA_e > \delta_t$, then there is a `competence` increase that is proportional to δ_t such that it is the full value of parameter `increase` (Δ_c) when $\delta_t > 0.75$, and it decreases to $1/2 \cdot \Delta_c$ and $1/10 \cdot \Delta_c$ when, respectively, $\delta \leq 0.75$ and $\delta \leq 0.25$. Of course, the other implication of $IA_e > \delta_t$ is that agent-task t disappears from the system. It has been performed.

By working with an agent-resource, an agent-employee uses a portion of its a_e ($1/10^{th}$) to improve I_r, and this means that the resource's usability gradually increases.

At this point, there are two alternatives that may work together or separately. One is called `extended cognition` (EC). When turned ON, agent-employees only deal with resources that are located on a patch with a mark, meaning that they have been successfully used in the past. When the switch is OFF, then there is a much more frequent change in the use of resources and this means that agent-employees do not stick with one resource, even if proven successful in the past. In this setting, agent-resources relocate away from the agent-employee, at a distance where they cannot easily re-connect (it is $r \times 2$).

The other alternative is the binomial `docility enabler` (d_{en}) that allows for the effect of *social* rather than general resources to enter the task performance process. When ON, it allows those employee-agents with $d_e > \bar{d}$ to form a team with other employee-agents around a range r. The team then has an effect such as

$$a_{e,1} = a_{e,0} + \frac{\Delta_A \cdot \bar{a}_E}{s_{a,E}} \qquad (10.5)$$

where $a_{e,1}$ is the ability of agent-employee e at step= 1, $a_{e,0}$ has the same meaning for step= 0, Δ_A is the increment in a set for all agent-employees with $d > \bar{d}$, $\bar{a}_E$ is the mean ability of agent-employees in the team E, and $s_{a,E}$ is the standard deviation of ability for agents in team E.

The flow chart in Fig. 10.1 is an overview of the processes in IOP2.1.2. The chart presents mechanisms that can be summarized

Fig. 10.1. Flow Chart of the IOP2.1.2 Model.

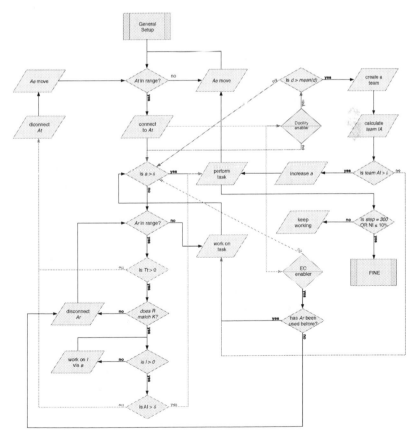

Note. At: agent-task; Ae: agent-employee; Ar: agent-resource; Nt: number of tasks.

into three main processes: (a) *individual* task performance, (b) *socially-oriented* task performance, and (c) *extended* cognitive task performance. These three processes may coexist or work independently.

The first process – letter (a), *individual* – is described by the vertical line departing from the box "General setup." This describes a series of conditions that must align in order for a task to be performed. All of these conditions have been already described above and, given the summary provided by Fig. 10.1, there is little to gain from repeating them. Perhaps, what can be highlighted is that many of these conditions apply to different combinations of the relations between the three types of agents. In this simulation, `competence` is a way for an agent-employee to align with an agent-task, while `ability` is designed to be the driver of performance.

The second main process under letter (b) refers to *socially-oriented* approaches and it relates to the parameter `docility enabler`, d_{en}. When activated, teams can perform together with a highly docile individual that is capable of successfully utilize the abilities of team members. As explained above, successful performance generates an increment to the ability a of highly docile agents.

The third process on *extended cognition*, *EC*, attaches the agent-employees to an agent-resource that is found in a knowledge area. This means that the resource has been successfully used before and there are evident synergies in their employment when it comes to task performance. Or, at least, this is what the precepts of extended cognition suggest. The `IOP2.1.2` simulation model puts this statement into a test and compares it to the procedures indicated in conditions (a) and (b).

10.3   Findings

Given the intricacies of the processes in this model, the calibration process was extensive. The $373,248$ experiments conducted led to a sensitivity analysis (Table 10.2) where parameters were tested using linear regressions. By comparing the R^2 and the β coefficients for all the configurations, I was able to exclude those values with limited effect on the outcome variable. The analysis allowed to eliminate some of the values and settle on a reduced number of configurations (864) for the main experiment.

Given the final value of 864 as reported in Table 10.2, the usual statistical power analysis was performed to estimate the number of times this simulation should have been performed. In this case this estimation is crucial, given the many stochastic components of the ABM. Given I performed several regressions, I had a fairly good idea of the effect

Table 10.2. Parameter Value Selection: From Sensitivity Analysis to the Main Simulation Experiment.

Parameter	Code	SA	SA Values	ME	ME Values
Proportion of tasks	$P_{t,0}$	4×	$\{0.5, 1, 1.5, 2\}$	2×	$\{0.5, 2.0\}$
Proportion of resources	$P_{r,0}$	4×	$\{0.5, 1, 1.5, 2\}$	3×	$\{0.5, 1.0, 2.0\}$
Mean competence	$\bar{c}$	4×	$\{0.5, 1, 1.5, 2\}$	1×	$\{1.0\}$
Mean ability	$\bar{a}$	3×	$\{0.05, 0.1, 0.2\}$	2×	$\{0.05, .2\}$
Minimum difficulty	δ_m	3×	$\{0, 0.4, 0.8\}$	3×	$\{0, 0.4, 0.8\}$
Proportion avail. res.	P_A	2×	$\{.25, .5\}$	1×	$\{0.5\}$
Mean immediateness	$\bar{I}$	3×	$\{-0.5, 0, 0.5\}$	2×	$\{-0.5, 0.5\}$
Docility enabler	d_{en}	2×	ON/OFF	2×	ON/OFF
Extended cognition	EC	2×	ON/OFF	2×	ON/OFF
Task wave hit	t_w	3×	$\{0, 0.1, 0.2\}$	3×	$\{0, 0.1, 0.2\}$
Competence increment	Δ_c	3×	$\{0.2, 0.4, 0.6\}$	1×	$\{0.4\}$
Ability increment	Δ_A	3×	$\{0.1, 0.2, 0.3\}$	1×	$\{0.2\}$
Number of Configurations of Parameters			$= 373,248$		$= 864$

Note. SA: sensitivity analysis, ME: main experiment.

size to consider for the main experiment.[6] Most effect sizes, f^2, are very large and, in an attempt to be cautious, I have selected the Smallest Effect Size of Interest (SESOI Lakens, 2013). The one I considered to be the benchmark was $f^2 = 0.15$, leading to $n = 2$. Hence, the total number of simulations performed was $864 \times 2 = 1,728$.

Fig. 10.2 compares a number of conditions in the simulation, and it shows the tasks performed in relation to those considered and left. This could be due to one or more unmet conditions (see Fig. 10.1). Probably, the most apparent difference is that of the increasing number of resources, P_r. This always leads to a higher number of tasks performed, independent of the other conditions. The result is hardly surprising, given that this is what A_r are there for. When, however, these artifacts, tools, and other material resources represented by A_r are matched with the social mechanism as enforced by d_{en}, something interesting happens. If one compares Fig. 10.2 (left pane) with Fig. 10.2 (right pane), not only a large use of resources, $P_r = 2$, lead to a larger number of tasks performed, but also a mid-size increase, $P_r = 1$ (or $N_e = N_r$) has similar effects. In some instances, even the deprived condition of $P_r = 0.5$ reaches high levels of performance. This means that, overall, the mechanism of considering social interactions through docility ($d_{en} = $ ON) is effective in dealing with tasks.

While there is an increase in task performance when $EC = $ ON, the largest increases can be visible when the opposite is selected. This means that sticking to resources that have been successful in the past – i.e. using the assumption of extended cognition with $EC = $ ON – is

---

[6]In the case of regressions one can use the R^2 to approximate the value of f^2, the effect size. In fact, the simple formula $\frac{R^2}{1-R^2}$ gives a valid enough reference (Seri & Secchi, 2018).

Fig. 10.2. Mean Tasks Considered and Performed Divided by EC, P_r and Split by d_{en}, with $P_t = 2$, min $\delta = 0$, $\bar{a} = 0.05$, $t_w = 0$.

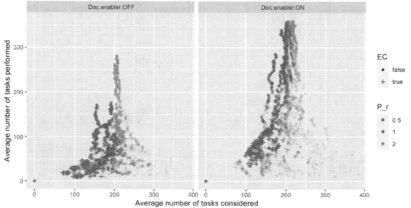

probably susceptible of being equated to a *status quo* bias (Kahneman, Knetsch, & Thaler, 1990; Silver & Mitchell, 1990). That is because re-use of the same resource with a new task, implies that one imagines the task is somehow similar to the one performed in the past. This may not always be the case, as the results of the simulation in Fig. 10.2 suggest.

A final comment on Fig. 10.2 is that the data follows different trends when one takes into account the relation between tasks considered and those performed. When $P_r = 0.5$, there is an increase that looks stable (red observations in the figure), as the number of tasks considered increases, there is also an increase in those performed. This seems to be the baseline for the other two P_r conditions although there are some instances in which higher numbers of tasks considered (> 250) show a low performance (< 100), meaning that A_e leave the task after a while. The hypothesis is that this is an effect caused by difficulty, δ. In Fig. 10.2, δ can vary from $[0, 1]$ for all A_t, and this leads to the need to consider this aspect further (see below).

But the data analyzed in Fig. 10.2 is that of a condition where the tasks are constant with $t_w = 0$, i.e. there are no waves of new tasks that are induced by a change event. What happens to the two main conditions tested here – i.e. EC and d_{en} – when the storm hit the farm? Which combination of strategies is more likely to deliver smart flexible coping strategies? Fig. 10.3 takes care of showing what happens when the tasks increase exponentially in the organization.

The split between EC and d_{en} is still visible although it takes a different turn. While the split in the use of A_r is clear as P_r grows in the case where $d_{en} = $ ON, it becomes blurred when $d_{en} = $ OFF

Fig. 10.3. Mean Tasks Considered and Performed Divided by EC, P_r and Split by d_{en} and $t_w > 0$, with $P_t = 2$, $\min \delta = 0$, $\bar{a} = 0.05$.

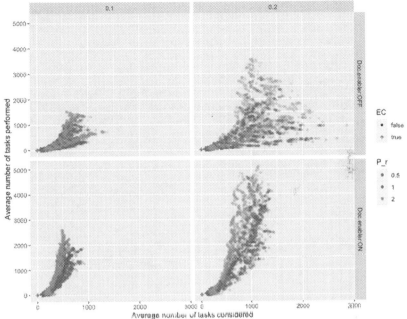

(upper panes). This effect is increasingly visible for $t_w = 0.2$, when the organization is under a "storm" of tasks. Another aspect to notice from Fig. 10.3 is that the trends are upward for the bottom panes with $d_{en} = $ ON, and they are more spread horizontally when $d_{en} = $ OFF. A third consideration is that an EC strategy is one that seems effective only with relatively low numbers of tasks considered and performed. In fact, $EC = $ ON is indicated by the $+$ sign in the plots. These signs are concentrated in the first quadrant on the bottom left of each pane, for $\approx x = y < 500$. This may lead an observer to believe that there are not many tasks considered but that most of these are performed. There seems to be less adaptation to the conditions of the environment (i.e. t_w) when $EC = $ ON, to the point that this condition somehow forces docile individuals into focusing on fewer tasks.

The vast majority of observations that are visible in Fig. 10.3 are those where there is an *individualistic* approach to task performance (upper right pane, circles) as opposed to a *social* approach (bottom right pane, circles). Besides the consideration that the *social* approach seems more effective, given it considers fewer tasks than it performs, there are many occasions where P_r does not matter much ($EC = $ OFF

and d_{en} = OFF). At the extremes, it is probably fair to state that there
are cases in which more resources (P_r = 2, green circles) help perform
more tasks and fewer resources (P_r = 0.5, red circles) are responsible
for a decreased performance. However, there are many cases in which
it is impossible to determine an impact of P_r, at least not as well as it
is when d_{en} = ON. This means that an *individualistic* approach to hit
waves of tasks (t_w) neglects the synergies deriving from teams as well as
from the extended cognition hypothesis, leading to confusing strategies.
When the only strategy to task performance is the use of resources and
their increase does not lead to better performance, then there must be
an inefficient use of this "surplus" of resources. This phenomenon does
not happen when d_{en} = ON.

Fig. 10.4. Task Efficiency Ratio E_t by Mean Change in Competence $\bar{c}$,
Considered by $\bar{a}$ and P_r, and Split by d_{en} and min δ, with EC = ON,
$P_t = 2, t_w = 0.2$.

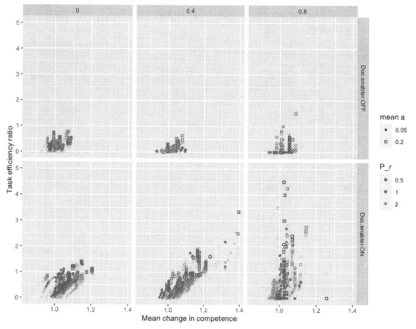

Fig. 10.4 changes the perspective a bit, in an attempt to address
the questions opened through the observation of the trends so far. In
particular, it is important to understand the role of competence on task
performance, especially in relation to the case when EC = ON. The y-
axis in Fig. 10.4 is the *Task efficiency ratio*, E_t, calculated as the number
of tasks performed as a proportion of those considered. This is indicative

of how much screening is done by A_e and of how much effective it is. Higher numbers of E_t mean that many tasks are performed immediately, by meeting all the conditions in Fig.10.1 and reducing to zero the time spent "considering" (i.e. working on) the task. This clearly indicates that more tasks are performed, hence the system is more efficient.[7]

Another disclaimer about Fig. 10.4 is that I have excluded 233 outlier observations (on 43,200) that showed values $E_t > 5$ and would have made discerning about the remaining 99.46% observations on the plot particularly difficult.

The two blocks of panes for $d_{en} = \text{ON/OFF}$ confirm what already seen above, with a higher E_t achievable when `docility enabler` is ON. The difference here is made by considering also the increase in mean `ability`, $\bar{a}$, as one of the initial conditions for the simulations. Given a is one of the components that is used to perform a task (combined with I in IA_e as seen in Equation 10.4 above), there is no surprise in observing that E_t increases when $a = 0.2$. However, this effect becomes more relevant when δ increases (see $\delta = 0.8$), and $\hat{c}$ – that is the increase in competence due to the interactions – becomes more effective when $d_{en} = ON$.

10.4   Two Coping Strategies

The data analyzed in this chapter support the findings reported in Secchi (2020a) and has been able to shed some additional light on the mechanisms that explain those findings with a finer granularity of details.

Results show that, in general, an organization that encourages exchanges between individuals in the form of cooperation, extra-role behavior, and citizenship behavior is more effective in facing increasing work demands. These behaviors are reflected in the simulation by social orientation (docility) enabled by parameter d_{en}. In the vast majority of cases, the network of interactions among members of a team working together is more effective in dealing with the tasks. This is apparent from both Figs. 10.3 and 10.4 where, respectively, the exponentially increasing number of tasks, $t_w = 0.2$, and the increase in average problem difficulty, $\min \delta > 0$, indicate a wider reach caused by the docile

---

[7]I have kept the same label for E_t I have used in the article (Secchi, 2020a). However, the more I think about this the more it seems to me that this is an *effectiveness ratio* because it does not tell much about the resources used in the process but only compares the final outcome – i.e. tasks performed – to the number of tasks that are in the process of being performed – i.e. tasks considered. The efficiency in the article relates to the use of time. In this respect, a high ratio indicates that the combination of A_e and A_r has been able to conclude the work on the tasks with relatively fewer tasks being under examination.

A_e. I call this organizational-wide effect derived by socially distributed cognition a *differentiation strategy*, for two reasons. One is obvious, and it is that employees are able to use a combination of social (other A_e) and non-social (A_r) resources. The other is that they can use a selection of resources that are not necessarily the same, when confronted with different tasks. When requirements for task performance increase, this strategy is particularly effective in securing performance for the mass of tasks.

The question is when a strategy that encourages the use of *extended cognition* becomes relevant and effective. To answer this question, we have considered both the evolution of competence in the system, $\hat{c}$, independent of the initial mean, $\bar{c}$, and task difficulty, δ. Fig. 10.4 is an attempt to present evidence that can answer the question. The general condition for that figure is that $EC = $ ON so that we are zooming in on *extended cognition* usage. The mean change in competence $\hat{c}$ is 1.239, with a very small standard deviation of 0.063, indicating that the effect of EC is that of constraining the work on a limited number of tasks, leading to a relatively narrow increase in competence. This reduces the number of tasks that the organization is capable of handling but it also produces another quite surprising result that is only implicitly visible in Fig. 10.4 while it clearly appears in Fig. 10.5. Here, all the conditions from Fig. 10.4 are repeated but they are used to produce two density curves for the distribution of E_t where $EC = $ ON and OFF.

Fig. 10.5. Density Curves for Task Efficiency Ratio E_t with $EC = $ ON (Blue Solid Line) and $EC = $ OFF (Red Dashed Line), with $P_t = 2, \min \delta = 0.8, t_w = 0.2, d_{en} = $ ON.

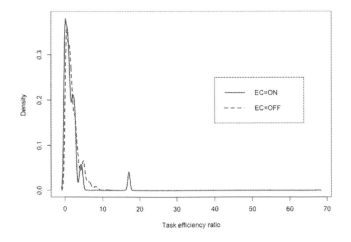

Both curves are skewed to the right, with the blue curve for $EC = $ ON having a very long tail compared to the red dashed curve for $EC = $ OFF. In fact, max $E_t = 11.24$ in the latter case while it is 67.5 in the former, means are similar for both curves, with $\bar{E}_{t,EC=\text{OFF}} = 1.92$ and $\bar{E}_{t,EC=\text{ON}} = 1.78$, and medians are respectively at 1.367 and 1.091. This means that the two distributions are similar, as far as efficiency is concerned, but that there is a minority of cases where agent-employees exploit resources to an extent that is exceptional, under $EC = $ ON. This may be due to the interaction of A_r and A_e in a team that become only possible under some circumstances. Further exploration on the data indicates that parameter $\bar{I} > 0$ is relevant for these agents to perform at such a high level. A key component is, hence, that resources can be used immediately by their users – it is easy to understand why this is important when the organization is hit by a very high number of additional tasks to perform. In this case, few highly docile agents do the work for many. For all these reasons, I have called this a *concentration strategy*.

10.5 Summary

This chapter has presented the IOP2.1.2 model in an attempt to extend findings from the INQ1.0.1 and DI01.0 models of Chapters 8 and 9. In light of the limitations found in the concept of docility, and of the attempts to extend its reach through *inquisitiveness*, the IOP2.1.2 model has multiplied the implementation of EDEC perspectives in an organization and matched them to turbulent conditions. In other words, the agent-based model presented in this chapter has studied factors that may help an organization show *plasticity*, that is a flexible adaptation to challenging times. In the first part of this chapter, I have exposed a very short conceptualization of the concept by comparing it to disorganization and resilience. The assumption of the model is that an organization that promotes and encourages EDEC – i.e. that provides employees with the tools to use their cognition to its fullest extent – may become more successful in implementing plasticity. The challenge given to agents in the model is that of an increase in the number of tasks.

Results are interesting in that they do not provide one single answer to the question on the effectiveness of EDEC perspectives, but indicate that (a) social distribution of cognition (i.e. docility or SDC) is the most successful strategy but that (b) the combination of SDC to extended cognitive use of artifacts may also be useful when difficulty of tasks increases. I have called the first a *differentiation strategy* while the second is a *concentration strategy*.

Part III
The Larger Picture

11

Understanding Organizational Cognition

You have reached the third and last part of this book. I assume (hope!) you have gotten here by reading the previous two parts. If so, I believe congratulations are in order: reading descriptions and results of four agent-based models can be extremely challenging. Instead, if you have skipped most of the pages before and landed on Part III because interested in getting a broader picture, you can still appreciate most of what follows. When necessary, I have made clear references to previous chapters and I have taken care of recalling those concepts that lie at the core of particular arguments below.

Especially after reading the pages up to this one, you are probably asking yourself something along the lines of "so, what?" Stated differently, after an overview of organizational cognition and of the EDEC perspectives (Part I) and a way to operationalize these views through computational means (Part II), one may be wondering about the implications of what written so far. Wonder no more, Part III is dedicated to establish a closer link between Part I and Part II, and to discuss implications.

This third part of the book is made of three chapters. In the current Chapter 11, I am set to connect the models in Part II together and discuss their implications in relation to the theories outlined in Part I. The following Chapter 12 is instead dedicated to define what I and a few colleagues have called the *theory of social organizing*, a conceptual framework that takes from the results of the simulations and from a more current reading of EDEC perspectives. The final Chapter 13 offers a

Computational Organizational Cognition:
A Study on Thinking and Action in Organizations, 165–178
Copyright © 2021 by Emerald Publishing Limited
All rights of reproduction in any form reserved
doi: 10.1108/978-1-83867-511-020211011

perspective on these theoretical developments that is focused on setting the agent-based computational research agenda.

11.1   From Theory to Modeling...

Before I can elaborate on findings, I think a short recap of what is in Part I and in Part II is due, in light of what written above. This way I am able to go over the reasons that brought me to study organizational cognition the way I have in this book. This section is dedicated to a recap and the next to a broader discussion that will continue in the following chapters.

11.1.1   The Organizational "Focus"

The book started with a review of the literature in MOC (Chapter 2) to show that the field has only now (and very slowly) started to consider unorthodox approaches. Even though these approaches – that I have called EDEC (embodied, distributed, and extended cognition; Chapter 3) – have been around for about 30 years, they have only recently started to surface the traditional organizational cognition literature (Healey, Hodgkinson, & Massaro, 2018; Hodgkinson, 2018). The idea that cognition cannot be understood, let alone studied, if confined only to the human skull is what these EDEC approaches broadly propose. They suggest that cognitive *systems* (Cowley & Vallée-Tourangeau, 2017) distribute to the environment to the point that the brain is shaped and develops in continuity with external resources (e.g., Hutchins, 1995a), often referred to as artifacts (e.g., Clark, 2003). This view has been criticized by cognitivists and brain-bound computational scientists (we have seen Miłkowski et al., 2018; Adams & Aizawa, 2008; Chapter 4).

In spite of the criticisms, I have argued (Chapter 5) that the EDEC perspectives need a more tight connection to *social* elements if they were to be connected to organizational research. Even though the work of Hutchins (1995a, 1995b) has been conducted inside an organization – e.g., the US military – and he mentions the social organization of cognition several times, that seems not to be the core of his contribution (see Chapter 4 on this). Hence, the need for a theory to explain how cognition deals with social resources in a way that is different to how it deals with artifacts and other non-social resources. As discussed elsewhere (Secchi, 2011), it is very difficult to define what is *not* a social resource, given that knowledge cannot be separated from the knower. As Maturana and Varela (1987) convincingly wrote, most if not all knowledge of an individual derives from another person. This social view of knowledge also reflects on cognition. Nevertheless, and other than a socialized view of the world, we can certainly make a distinction between dealing with a pencil or with another human being. But this is just commonsense. There is a distinction to make between the simple interaction and the knowledge that is embedded in that interaction.

Yes, using a pencil to take a note is different than asking your colleague to "please remember this when we get back to the office." At the same time, a pencil is full of social meaning that is embedded in the use one makes of it. Someone in a relatively distant past taught us how to use a pencil, and we have learned how to take notes over the years, becoming more skilled with practice and experience (and probably good role models).

Both processes serve the same goal that is, for example, to remember something for later. The first uses an externalization that is based on an artifact (a pencil), the second uses an externalization that is based on another human being. Cognition's re-projecting phase (Magnani, 2007, see Chapter 5) is where the difference weights the most. When we read the note again is where the phase starts and where we potentially confirm, change, or add meaning to it. This process is recursive in the sense that we might read the note multiple times, add some more notes, or even dismiss it as irrelevant. But the process is that of extending cognition to the note and dynamically interacting with it. The note is passive, the only dynamic is in the back and forth that we do with it.

When asking a colleague to remember a sentence or a detail of a company visit from a consulting team, for example, the nature of the re-projecting changes. The external resource is not passive any more. The colleague could ask questions, seek clarifications, take a note of what he/she understands of the comment, or simply use memory and report what he/she remembers. Instead of considering this as noise, from the perspective of communication and of information, it is a rich process that adds depth, meaning, and sense to the comment. The personal comment just became a social event, something to which context, interactions, words spoken, and history of relations contribute to qualify it.

In addition to the above, the externalization is probably different as well. Sometimes taking notes for the self may be intelligible only to the person who wrote that note. Instead, when communicating the same information to another person, we usually take care of making the comment understandable, to frame it in a way that is intelligible – not by a large number of people but just – to the special dynamic that is established by a pair of colleagues working together. So, in the end, while re-projecting is the core of the matter, one cannot (and should not) exclude the externalization phase as well.

11.1.2   Where Docility Comes in

If the above makes sense and we cannot discard the fact that the type of externalization (or distribution) is relevant to define the type of cognitive processes, then the claim above that EDEC perspectives need a *social* focus is justified. While artifacts are used extensively in organizations, it is teamwork, cooperation, collaboration, as well as the attitudes and perceptions toward the organization that qualifies organizational day-to-day operations. An EDEC theory of cognition that wants to explain organizational dynamics and processes needs to revert around these social aspects to effectively capture what happens.

Coming from this train of thoughts, Emanuele Bardone and I found in the concept of *docility* our way to connect EDEC to social aspects of organizational behavior (Secchi & Bardone, 2009). As mentioned in Chapter 5, we have modified the concept as originally formulated by Simon (1993) to become an active/passive mechanism that allows individuals to successfully exchange information, advice, recommendations as well as exercise persuasion. This concept is particularly powerful in that it allows to factor in elements that are typical of human behavior in organizations such as altruism, cooperation, social responsibility, among others (Secchi, 2009). As per the conceptualization we have proposed (Secchi & Bardone, 2009; Bardone & Secchi, 2009 and Chapter 5), this active/passive mechanism is only effective when individuals feel part of a community that encourages public circulation of information and supports a way of sharing this information (we called it a "code"). These preconditions for the emergence of docile behavior are very close to what happens in a team, a group, a department or an organization.

Without delving into the motivations that bring an individual to share and exchange information with others in a team/department/organization (a detailed discussion on these is in Secchi, 2011), I have proposed that this prosocial disposition is essential to understand how most cognition happens in organizations. The theory of socially distributed cognition (SDC) assumes that *prosocial information exchanges*:

(a) happen as a natural disposition necessary to live in a social environment,

(b) are distributed differently, i.e. individuals show different disposition levels, depending on various sets of circumstances such as personal histories, past experience, knowledge/training, organizational roles, expertise,

(c) determine gains in terms of fit to the community of reference, depending on the number of other docile individuals in the system, and also

(d) indicate there are costs of prosocial behavior.

The assumptions outlined in this short recap of the theory have been tested in the four simulation studies presented in Part II.

11.1.3   What Have We Learned so far

In order to test the assumptions of this *socially distributed cognition* theory, I have used a series of agent-based computational simulation models. A selection of these agent-based models have been presented in Part II (Chapters 6–10). ABM allows for the study of complex systems and I have argued earlier that organizational cognition falls within this domain (Chapter 1).

Previously, I have presented each of the models as a logical companion to each other. OrgBand2.0 (Chapter 7) is the first model to explore SDC in organizations by using it to enquire about rapid diffusion processes within organizations. The findings show that docility mechanisms do not limit the rapid and mindless spread of information but seem to speed it up. At first, this seems to contradict the theory, in that it postulated that docility is a mechanism to gain mindfulness because it should support the distribution of cognition over the most powerful resources, i.e. human beings.

Given the puzzling results of this model, what seemed an obvious step to follow was that of building a model to test the assumptions of the theory. This was done in the DIO1.0 model, with which it became apparent that docility mechanisms need organizational support in order for them to enable mindfulness or intelligent agency, *à la* Simon.

If that is the case, then one of the incentives would be for an organization to operate on the relaxation of one (or more) of the conditions that structure docility, as defined by the theory. This was the approach followed in the INQ1.0.1 model, where some individuals are let free to break the exclusive relations with their team (i.e. community) and have the option to establish cooperation (or docile-oriented mechanisms) with members of other teams. Emanuele Bardone and I have called these cooperative mechanisms "inquisitive." The model shows that there is a clear advantage in problem solving brought by these individuals to the organization as a whole and to their team in particular.

Another way to understand how organizations can enable mindful cognitive processes through SDC is to explore flexible behavior such as *inquisitiveness* further. Model IOP2.1.2 is an attempt to understand this by putting into practice the opposition between EDEC and SDC as described before. Consistently with this approach, the model explores whether there are conditions in which SDC allows the organization a higher degree of plasticity while, at the same time, it tries to understand whether the use of artifacts – as per the standard EDEC perspective – increases organizational performance or not. Findings have shown that there are two cognitive strategies that come into play depending on the situation; I called them the *differentiation* and the *concentration* strategy.

11.2   ...and from Modeling Back to Theory

As it is apparent from the above and from Part II, it is fair to write that agent-based simulations have significantly supported my research enquiry on organizational cognition. At this point, however, it is unclear how exactly they achieved that outcome. While it is probably evident that the models followed one another, inspired by a rational quest to address the questions raised by findings, it may not be so apparent where all these results lead the discourse on cognition.

The data from the four agent-based models have highlighted a series of aspects that need to be addressed when going back to both EDEC perspectives and, in particular, to SDC theory and docility. This section is dedicated to an attempt to systematize these findings and outline the concepts to consider. The models and the sets of results are considered together, since they are part of the same research enquiry, kept together by the underlying thread of docility and SDC.

There are many directions that can be pursued and, overall, it is possible to group them into three: (a) types of prosocial dispositions, (b) cognitive strategies, and (c) organizational enabling mechanisms. Each one of these is considered separately in the following pages.

11.2.1   Types of Prosocial Dispositions

The first two simulations, OrgBand2.0 (Chapter 7) and DIO1.0 (Chapter 8), specify and clarify Simon's original intuition (Simon, 1993). He did not have the power of ABM nor he seemed too interested in building a theory around the concept of docility, and this is probably why he indicated only two types, called *unintelligent* and *intelligent* docile individuals. While the former type is unable to discriminate the extent to which prosocial behavior is exercised, the latter is. An unintelligent behavior would be to be altruistic independent of the person to which this altruism is directed to, while an example of the other type would be to cooperate only with those that are able to reciprocate altruistic behaviors. This simple specification serves to limit the costs of prosocial behavior for one, while increase them for the other. Yet, they both gain in social fitness for being docile over those who are not docile.

If I had to point at one only thing I have learned from the simulations is that this picture is perhaps too simplistic. Instead of considering the extremes and hypothesize that individual prosocial dispositions are stable and the same for everyone, the simulations have adopted the strategy of assigning the values to the agents at random, using a normal distribution. This allows for the majority of individuals ($\approx 68\%$) to have an average docility level – still not fixed but distributed one standard deviation $\pm$ the mean – with peaks of docility for some ($\approx 16\%$) and very low levels for others (the remaining $\approx 16\%$). This allows for a range of behaviors that are connected to varying levels of the disposition.

Instead of using the word intelligence,[1] I have preferred referring to an attentive and proactive state of *mindfulness* (Fiol & O'Connor, 2003; Langer, 1989) and its opposite, i.e. a *mindlessness* state. These states, however, depend as much from the individual as from the environment. This is something that the original formulations of docility did not consider (e.g., Simon, 1993; Secchi & Bardone, 2009; Secchi, 2011). In fact, no matter how the distribution of docile dispositions is conceived, a behavior, thought or else will diffuse in an organization when docility is unconstrained (OrgBand2.0, Chapter 7). Why?

There are two basic reasons. One is that docility is a prosocial disposition and this should never be forgotten nor underplayed. As such, it functions within the core of human beings' attitudes and, as such, it enables imitation. A key feature of a cohesive organization (or a team, for example) is that members trust each other and sometimes believe that what the others are doing or thinking is right, without giving too much weight to it (Ossola, 2013). This is sometimes referred to as groupthink (Janis, 1972; Moorhead & Montanari, 1986) or it can be framed as a way to give trusted others the benefit of the doubt, when one has not set the mind on something. But imitation does not last forever. Under many circumstances, either the test of performance or that of other facts may lead to an unexpected outcome such that it breaks expectations and, in turn, the imitation pattern. In other words, a fact-based test may transform *mechanic* decision making into *choice-based* (Secchi, 2011). The first are automatic, immediate, sometimes unconscious, not deliberate, and happen "without thinking" (Secchi, 2011, pp. 9–10) while the second "imply a conscious, deliberate choice [...] *that allow to* evaluate possible alternatives and then select one" (Secchi, 2011, p. 10; italics added). The transition is very important in terms of gaining mindfulness. In the original formulation of SDC, docility was thought to address exactly this point and allow for mindfulness to see a choice where there seemed to be none.

The swing between a more or less mindful state is not embedded in the docility mechanism, instead. In fact, this seems to be a default cognitive mechanism that reiterates previous behavior. In other words, inside docility there is no stop nor regulatory condition that interferes with trust. These, in fact, come from a complex mix of interactions with

---

[1] I have started to deprecate the use of this word. Too much emphasis has been put in the past to intelligence by equating it to the measurement of controversial tests. We know enough right now to consider human capacity for thinking in different terms. My inspiration for this is Gould (1996).

others and with the organizational environment. It is the *local* social environment that serves as a condition for docility and prosocial behavior to materialize. At the same time, the organizational environment as a whole – the set of structural conditions in which work happens – has an effect on shaping possibilities of behavior. Let me take these two conditions one at a time.

From the data of all the simulations in Part II, it is very clear that the extent to which one is able to exercise a more or less mindful activity depends on *local* interactions. For example, the teams in the INQ1.0.1 model are responsible for both a narrow view of the task or problem and, at the same time, for a more open perspective on it. In this last case, the problem is solved more effectively. The extent to which this effectiveness is possible depends on the ties that agents have so that a more mindful approach to the problem depends on the sociality that develops around it. The swing between a more or less mindful state is partially dependent upon personal characteristics as well as those of the people around each worker.

The other condition is relative to structural organizational elements. These have been identified in OrgBand2.0, for example, as *conformity* norms. These are aspects of organizational culture that support or reject autonomous thinking and behavior by workers. To use a very broad theoretical frame, one may claim that an organization that is structured around tight control of its members would consider all workers as belonging to McGregor's *Theory X* (McGregor, 1960). A more permissive culture, one where workers are able to improvise and experiment may be considered in line with *Theory Y*. While the first does not constitute a break in the imitation patters that docility mechanisms come with, the second is a suggestion to think or re-think about what one is doing (possibly before doing it!). Considering this and other macro organizational aspects when identifying cognitive mechanisms seem to be particularly relevant, if not essential.

In short, the raise of one type or the other depends on a mix of organizational structural, local, and personal conditions. The lack of appreciation of this complex mix of conditions altered the expectations I had for the model of diffusion I presented, hence making them unrealistic.

Before moving to the next set of implications, there is one last note on imitation that I believe it is important. When I referred to it in the model OrgBand2.0 in Chapter 7 and in the paper (Secchi & Gullekson, 2016), I have implicitly considered it as negative. The reason is that whenever something spreads rapidly in an organization there is a risk of unexpected consequences deriving from a lack of reasoned choice. It may be that the implications of switching to a fancier intra-organizational messaging system may, in the long run, distract many as opposed to making them more efficient, for example. However, there are also bandwagon diffusion processes that are harmless, and there is a limit to the amount of conscious choice-based decisions organizations can require from their managers and employees. Some diffusion processes are inevitable, while others have no clear negative repercussions. Some others have positive repercussions instead. Results from simulations after `OrgBand2.0` suggest that the function of control that intra-organizational diffusion processes are not hurting the business can be performed by an inquisitive individual and/or by an organization-wide support for such behaviors. The following subsection is dedicated to the strategies workers can put in place while the next takes on organization-wide support mechanisms.

11.2.2 Cognitive Strategies

If we regard organizations to be complex systems, then we are also open to the possibility that the configuration of a small number of their elements have meaningful impacts to the organization as a whole and, sometimes, to the external environment as well. This is a transposition of the loose dependence on initial conditions that defines complex systems (e.g., Prigogine & Stengers, 1986). Not only this works upward, that is from the elements within the organization up, it also works downward, from the system to its components. In the context of the enquiry this is extremely relevant because it recognizes that specific cognitive patterns that appear *locally* (a) may still affect the entire organization and they (b) may be disproportionally affected by decisions made centrally.

It is possible to make sense of some of the results in light of the above. The simulation that most of all is in line with the above is the `IOP2.1.2` model, where different cognitive strategies adopted locally have implications for the organization and, at the same time, the pressures coming from the organization (in terms of an increasing workload). The idea portrayed by that model is that of an organization that faces increasing demands – it does not matter whether they come in the form of pressures from the market or internally. These demands are then translated within the organization by a multiplication of tasks to which employees have to cope with. In order to understand what would make a better strategy to achieve this coping, I have designed a number of computational experiments that turn on and off a series of characteristics belonging to the EDEC perspective and to SDC theory. With this systematic approach, it is easier to isolate the effects of these characteristics. This way, the simulation has suggested that workers may adopt two strategies, one called *differentiation*, the other *concentration*.

Differentiation Strategy

When the organization faces the highest pressure in terms of tasks that need to be performed, workers usually strive to stay tuned to the requirements and only few succeed. One of the aspects that has been made clear by the data analysis is that an individual working in isolation is not a viable cognitive strategy, unless resources become quickly available. One of the aspects that matters in those cases is that the *efficiency ratio* E_t (problems solved over those considered) is extremely poor, with fewer tasks performed in relation to the number of those considered.

In almost all circumstances reviewed in the simulation, it seems that an organization is able to perform better when workers are encouraged to form teams and work together on a task. This implies that SDC theory is actively encouraged, such that docile individuals do not face constraints in their activities and are able to channel the resources of the team (or those team members to whom they are connected with and that constitute their social network). By exploiting a selection of social and material resources, workers are able to perform more tasks, hence adapt to the increasing work demands. In this case, it is variety that plays a major role. In front of an increasing variety of tasks to which workers are confronted with, a viable cognitive strategy – the most successful, if one considers quantity as a benchmark – is that of diversifying the number of resources.

This is a path that indicates cognitive flexibility, because an individual and a team are always in search of different resources and solutions to the problems they face. In this perspective, it is less effective to stick to what one knows, even though the time spent to *learn* how the new resource works can be considered a high cost to pay. The simulation shows that this is not the case, especially when tasks increase. Quite the opposite, variety in handling resources gives an edge to the employee, such that they can deal with a wider variety of tasks. This *learning* process also leaves some marks in the individual and the team that successfully performs the task. And this is a cognitive advantage when it comes at dealing with new tasks, new resources, new colleagues (or new configurations of team members).

In summary, the essence of this *differentiation strategy* is that of providing individuals with the liberty to adapt and become flexible. This way it is possible for the organization as a whole to plastically address the various issues that have generated a dramatic multiplication of tasks.

Concentration Strategy

The differentiation strategy discussed above seems particularly effective when quantity is the issue, but what happens to addressing those issues that are more urgent? Not all tasks carry the same weight and sometimes prioritization is essential to keep an organization alive. Think of a start up that has no clear procedures in place for its operations. Failure to assess which tasks are to perform first may result in de-structuring the core of the organization and ultimately make it unreliable and unresponsive. For this reason, it is sometimes important that a selection of urgent and important tasks are prioritized by a small but effective group of people. Those who embrace this perspective are using a cognitive *concentration strategy*.

These individuals are very effective in solving a limited typology of problems, those that fall within their particular skills. From the data shown in Chapter 10, it can be seen that an EDEC perspective on artifacts allows for a few agents to specialize and perform a very high number of tasks, at an *efficiency ratio* E_t that is $\approx$ 35 times higher than the average. This exceptional performance is the result of cutting the costs of adapting to new resources all the time. Here, cognition specializes on the excellent use of what is available and repetition becomes particularly effective. Of course, this happens only for some tasks and a differentiation strategy remains the one that has more widely recognizable effects.

A *concentration strategy* derives from an organization-wide effect that affects a relatively small number of workers. These, in turn, have a meaningful impact to the organization as a whole. Even though in the simulation the computational experiments exclude or include one condition (parameter) at a time to study its effect relative to the other conditions, these two differentiation and concentration strategies may – probably should – coexist. In fact, the organizational path toward plasticity passes through allowing workers to flexibly organize their work depending on the conditions they are facing. The skillful combination of these two strategies, both within the same individual and across teams, may bring plasticity to the fore.

Inquisitiveness and Competence

A strategy that is different from the two above, but that is related to the SDC theory emerges from the findings of INQ1.0.1. This is the model that extends the use of docility to work across teams in an organization. In this case, I have studied cognition as it pertains to those individuals that reach out to teams other than their own. The focus, as seen in Chapter 9, is the problem that requires a solution rather than the loyalty to one's team. An individual that is driven by problem solving more than anything else is applying an *inquisitive* strategy to their own cognition.

Results show that one of the effects of this strategy is that the extent to which competence is combined to fit a particular solution to a problem are less than those necessary in absence of this strategy. An inquisitive strategy is, in other words, a way to pull resources together in a *systemic* way, such that the synergies are more important that individual contributions. This is an unexpected effect of docile behavior that extends to wider communities and it probably relies on a particular set of skills that fall within the set of competences of those who pull resources together. These individuals serve as cognitive mediators to the others, more than what the average worker can do. The mediation that happens is probably a mix of synthesis and information flow from one team to the other, such that the organization as a whole is better off, not just the individual teams.

The above allows me to give a more nuanced read to the findings of the original paper where Emanuele Bardone and I introduced and discussed *super-docility* (Secchi & Bardone, 2009). That idea was about someone who reaches out more than the average worker. To do so, this person works more than average, is particularly knowledgeable, and more effective. The *inquisitive* strategy adds direction to the action, in that we now understand that working across teams is essential as well as pulling competences and having a focus on problems.

11.2.3   Enabling Mechanisms

If one wants to understand how the cognitive strategies above as well as the types of docile behaviors materialize, one must not forget to consider the *structural elements* that make an organization what it is. From a cognitive point of view, these structural elements are essential as they shape some of the boundaries within which action and thinking happen. At the same time, they evolve continuously under the effect of the actions of the various individuals that are members of the organization.

One of the computational simulations in particular – the `DIO1.0` model – has been able to highlight the role of organizational structures. In that model each agent has a fitness equation that indicates alignment with the social environment of their organization. An element of these equations is the *cost* that individuals pay when behaving prosocially. This is a very old concept that derives from a utilitarian view on altruism, specifically (Khalil, 2004; Knudsen, 2003; Simon, 1993). From a self-centered perspective, an act of altruism deprives the doer of resources (e.g., time, money), hence it costs something. This is undoubtedly true however, from a cognitive perspective, things may be completely different. The clear reference – the reason why Simon inserted a "cost" in the fitness equation – was that the concept of altruism he had in mind was coming from economics (Becker, 1976). In that frame an act of altruism would be a money donation to the homeless, to a charity or, to use a classic example, a fat tip to a waiter of an on-the-road restaurant to which one knows it is very unlikely to dine again. In these cases, there is a cost – i.e. the money handed in – but no gain. To some, this indicates a breach of the neoclassical economics rationalistic view of individual choice (Khalil, 2004).

Especially if considered under an EDEC perspective, the cognition of altruism (and of many other prosocial behaviors) is difficult to reduce to a narrow economic/accounting view, where outputs are justified or clearly stem out of given inputs. For cognition, the dynamic of the system is what matters. In this respect, cognition concerns both the micro (what I called *local*) and the macro (called *structural* above). It relates to the micro domain when one considers the action that constitutes altruism and, at the same time, it refers to a macro domain since the action need to find a frame in which it makes sense. In fact, it is relatively unimportant how much time one spends to help a new hire to get acquainted with the job through actions outside one's own responsibilities (this is called extra-role behavior or organizational citizenship; Ocampo et al., 2018; Podsakoff, MacKenzie, Paine, & Bachrach, 2000). This action feeds into cognition as it informs the *local* (micro) dynamic between the two colleagues and, at the same time, there is a *structural* organizational frame that legitimizes and encourages such actions.

In this perspective, the "cost" that I have factored in the DIO1.0 simulation is not necessarily related to the specific prosocial behavior in which employees are engaged in. Instead, it can be considered a structural limit that is super-imposed to workers such that the cognitive dynamic enables docility or not. In other words, the "cost" is a lever that favors the social distribution of cognition or that defines its boundaries within the organization. While the cost affects single employees and it is experienced by them, it comes from an organizational source and intends to be uniform.[2] However, it is perceived differently by each worker because it relates to their own docility disposition so that its impact exercises a diversity of effects. In other words, the "cost" represents something to which it is difficult to assign a fixed value, hence it escapes the accounting view of prosocial behavior, to some extent.

Some organizations make no mystery about their propensity toward or against behaviors that stem out of SDC. There are banks that notoriously encourage competition among their employees, by discouraging exchange of information and cooperation among colleagues. This has *de facto* the effect of disabling SDC among co-workers. By discouraging the use of one of the richest cognitive resources potentially available in the organization, these banks block prosocial behavior. At the other end of the spectrum, there are tech companies that are famous for encouraging the widest cooperation by setting the ground for employees

---

[2]This is why it is modeled as a value that enters the fitness equation similarly for every agent.

to work across departments, teams, and even with external partner organizations. The effect is opposite here in that the tech company works as an enabler of SDC by promoting its outcomes. It goes without saying, the organization cannot "force" employees to cooperate nor it has a tight control of the conditions that define interpersonal exchanges in a team or in a department. At the same time, it can set the general tone for these exchanges, by setting policies, standard operating procedures, processes, routines, and rewards for behaviors that can be considered to fall within the frame of a cost for certain actions.

In the DIO1.0 model, "cost" is the single most important factor in determining the way in which socially distributed cognition is able to establish prosocial behaviors in the organization. It is by imposing a high or low "cost" that different types of prosocial behavior (docility) prevail. What is interesting from the findings is that it was not clear why certain types of docility would emerge, given the initial conditions set. This is due to the mix of *local* and *structural* conditions that have been discussed in this section. What is relevant for the discourse here is that (a) the macro/structural enabling conditions shall not be disregarded and (b) their effect depends on the a combination of other conditions, including micro/local dynamics.

11.3   Summary

This chapter has been dedicated to an interpretation (yet another!) of what was done in Parts I and II so that it would have been easier to comment on and draw implications from the models' findings. The first section of Chapter 11 presents the most salient points of the SDC theory to show how they have been parametrized and included in the four agent-based models. Long story short, the social side is (a) core to understand and analyze organizational dynamics and (b) it is almost completely missing in the EDEC perspectives. The four models presented in Part II are an attempt to study how this social side can affects these organizational dynamics.

Implications have been discussed in a way such that I can connect them back to the theory that generated them, called SDC. This chapter has been concerned with three set of implications:

(a) the importance of distinguishing the types of docile dispositions that may lead to very different prosocial behavior,

(b) the array of cognitive strategies in place, as they depend on the *local* conditions and affect the organization differently, and

(c) the relevance of enabling SDC conditions that operate at the macro or *structural* organizational level to set the limits of prosocial behavior.

12

A New Paradigm

"We're all together again for the first time"
         − Album title. Dave Brubeck et al., *1973, Atlantic*

I have written Chapter 11 with the clear purpose of keeping the theoretical and the simulation part of the book together. This way I could read the results of Part II in relation to what had been previously exposed in Part I. What remains implicit in Chapter 11 is the extent to which the findings modify and advance SDC theory. The direction in which the findings take the theory is probably clear at this point: I have set a course for the study of organizational cognition as a complex system[1] by means of computational simulation. In reflecting further on a theory I am also attempting to answer the question "what is organizational cognition."

This chapter starts with recalling selected aspects of the EDEC perspectives in light of the findings discussed previously in Chapter 11, and then moves to outline the *theory of social organizing* as a specification of the SDC theory. The discussion continues in the last Chapter 13, dedicated to the *agent-based approach* to the study of cognition in organizations.

In Chapter 3, I have reviewed a selection of foundational EDEC research and I have shown how they have been extended in recent years in Chapter 4. Since the book has been mainly built around the EDEC perspectives, it is not necessary to summarize them in detail again here. In the following, I refer to selected aspects of them as I outline the way

---

[1]A discussion on complexity in organizations and cognition can be found in Chapter 1, while complexity in ABM is presented in Chapter 6.

Computational Organizational Cognition:
A Study on Thinking and Action in Organizations, 179–189
Copyright © 2021 by Emerald Publishing Limited
All rights of reproduction in any form reserved
doi: 10.1108/978-1-83867-511-020211012

in which they can be updated. There are three aspects covered here: coordination, direction, and social organizing.

12.1   Coordination

From one of the traditional EDEC perspectives (Hutchins, 1995a) and from a few of its more recent updates (Cowley, 2011; Steffensen, 2013), *coordination* is a fundamental aspect of cognition. According to these authors, this is an essential element for understanding how distributed cognitive processes materialize as well as to characterize interactivity between external resources and the individual. In describing language (better, languaging) as distributed, Cowley (2011) extends this concept of coordination to the way in which two or more people make sense of each other through words and sentences.

12.1.1   A Classic EDEC View

The reasoning behind the need for coordination is intuitively clear: if there are two elements that are tied together by cognitive links, then there must be a way in which the activity of one falls "in line" with the activity of the other so that they function efficiently. There are two parts in this reasoning. When considering the activity of the two elements, A and B, for example a human being (A) and the steering wheel of a car (B), the actions of one (A) need to be skilled as to produce an effect on the action of the other (B). By exercising a force with both hands, the wheel rotates clockwise or anti-clockwise, depending on whether the force applied is going down or up. The relation described is *prima facie* of the type $A \to B$, where element A exercises an effect on element B. However, at a closer look, for coordination to be in place, there must be a feedback loop such that $A \leftarrow B$, that is the force exercised from A to B depends on how B responds to it. When the car is parked, one needs to exercise more force because the wheel may be stuck or more difficult to move. As a result of this, for coordination to be in place, the relation is actually of the type $A \rightleftarrows B$. If described this way, it becomes apparent what it is meant by the concept of *coupling* between cognitive resources (Clark & Chalmers, 1998) and how their relation is easily represented by System Dynamics (called "dynamical systems" in Chemero, 2009).

The second part of the reasoning above leads to reflect on the system. The fact that there is coordination between two elements of a cognitive process does not make either one or the other more efficient. Instead it is the system – i.e. cognition – that is the recipient of the effects of the two working together, by virtue of which it is made more efficient. These systemic effects are the essence of the distributed cognition discourse, because the claim is to steer away from focusing on either of the elements but to appreciate the synergies that they produce and the effects these have on the system. The feedback loop above is an example of this. As seen above, the force on the steering wheel is adjusted depending on its resistance to the exercised pressure. The result of the wheel movement is not that the force is more efficient, nor that the wheel is more efficient, but the system of the two combined – that make turning a car possible – is made more efficient by this *coordination*. Now, one may ask what would a lack of coordination be like. When learning to drive it is difficult to find the exact force to exercise on the wheel to make it turn the way one wants. Also, the right timing in which this is best done may not be clear, resulting in several adjustments before the car moves the way the driver wants. These actions point at coordination to be found or in the making. If the system is the benchmark to assess whether there is efficiency, then the means employed to reach the end goal of the process are to consider. In the case of someone learning how to drive, it is fair to write that the system is less efficient (less coordinated) than, say, in a Formula 1 pilot. When the end result is not achieved – e.g., the wheel does not steer as it should have because of either the angle or the timing – then there is no coordination because it was insufficient or inefficient.

To add to the formulation above, it is fair to add that the two elements have to establish a feedback loop and, at the same time, this feedback loop has to drive the system's efficiency. Hence, we can write that

$$C_{A,B} = (E(S)|A \rightleftarrows B) \tag{12.1}$$

where $C_{A,B}$ is the coordination between element A and element B, that depends on the system's efficiency $E(S)$, given the feedback loop $A \rightleftarrows B$.

The above is a simple – perhaps not too simple – representation of basic coordination and I believe it is fair in spite of its simplicity. The example I have used is probably clearer than another where, for example, multiple individuals are involved. In fact, I am using such an example later in this chapter to consolidate my point further. One aspect to clarify is whether steering a wheel can be considered a cognitive activity. This activity does not happen in a vacuum: one does not steer a wheel unless there is a need for it, either to park a car, or drive the car any place. As such, the coordination is not *just* between the person's body, brain, and the wheel but it involves deciphering other cars and pedestrians' movements around, as well as interpreting the horizontal and vertical signs on the road, traffic lights, etc. The system is complicated. Similar examples are used in the EDEC tradition, such as specific instruments used to conduce a ship into port (Hutchins, 1995a), instruments and tools used to land a plane (Hutchins, 1995b), or moving objects in a game of Tetris (Kirsh & Maglio, 1994).

12.1.2   The SDC View

Is coordination necessary to describe cognition? Or, to use its opposite, does absence of coordination mean absence of cognition? These are fundamental questions that have to be carefully considered. My take is that it is a sufficient condition but it is not necessary.

If efficient performance of a system is needed to describe coordination, then the question of *when* coordination appears becomes relevant. There are two possible interpretations here. One could claim that coordination between the elements of the system is achieved only when efficiency becomes visible, but that up to that point the elements were not aligned and were inefficient. In this case, if coordination is necessary, then cognition is only happening when efficiency is achieved, not before. A more relaxed view would be to claim that the process to achieve efficiency and the various attempts to coordinate are also to be considered. In this case, cognition is the process of achieving efficiency through coordination. These two views – coordination as an *end state* and coordination as a *process* – have radical implications on the interpretations of what cognition is. While the first is consistent with the EDEC literature, the latter is not (if one holds to coordination as a core aspect). In fact, with the *process* view one is extending coordination to states of the system where it is not actually present. Although this is a better view of cognition and what most EDEC scholars who explicitly mention coordination refer to (see, e.g., the many instances of this in Cowley & Vallée-Tourangeau, 2017), it is not coordination.

Let us go back to the example of the steering wheel. When drivers are using their own car, and know how the system works, then we assume there is coordination. When the driver is using a new car, or is learning how to drive then there are several instances in which the actions are not coordinated. These are instances in which cognition cannot be detached from the body and the activity one is exercising on the wheel. I have mentioned this before (Chapter 5) using the expression *through doing* cognition (in line with Magnani, 2007). In this respect, cognition lies in the connection between the two elements, no matter how coordinated.

The case of an experienced driver can be equated to that of employees using the same resources again and again to perform a task or solve a problem, as they do in the IOP2.1.2 model. In those cases, one may claim there is a higher degree of coordination and efficiency in the system created by these employees and their "preferred" resources. Albeit successful, that is not the only possible way in which cognition is exercised and an employee may well decide to choose different resources to tackle with an increasing number of tasks or problems. This second solution is less efficient in terms of the time one needs to attune oneself with the new resource, but it is quantitatively more effective. These are both instances of cognitive processes, one where coordination is key, the other where learning is key.

It would also be unsatisfactory to state that the system strives to obtain efficiency through coordination of its elements. This is probably a fair statement, but it only moves the problem to the end state. In fact, many cognitive systems do not depend on whether coordination is achieved or not. In the INQ1.0.1 model results indicate that the way in which competence (information) is channeled toward a problem is more relevant than how individuals coordinate around it. In fact, one may assume that the member of another team that is involved by the inquisitive employee does not necessarily need to coordinate with the team from which the inquisitive employee comes from. The burden is on the inquisitive employee to make the various competences and skills match the needs of a problem.

A corollary of what written above relates to the concept of efficiency. Especially when there are tasks and goals to consider it is fair to assume that efficiency through coordination relates to a successful execution of the task. If, while driving a car, one steers the wheel by applying too much force to end up on a wall, then where is efficiency and where coordination? The unsuccessful coordination led to failure. If coordination is a necessary condition then errors are not cognitive. This is a radical interpretation of coordination, but it serves the purpose of exposing the difficulty in using this concept the way EDEC scholars have over the last years. An unsolved problem or unsuccessful task performance are still related to cognitive activities that support the attempts toward finding solutions or performing a task. In many cases, one learns from these failures to attune cognition and perform better later (as agents do in the IOP2.1.2 Model).

In summary, the *end goal* view on coordination is particularly daunting because it excludes too much of cognition. The *process* view is slightly better, because it includes at least the way in which coordination is achieved. However, it still excludes messy, non teleological processes and, in other words, processes typical of complex systems. In light of the above arguments, this excludes most of organizational cognition. Hence, I can write that when there is coordination there is cognition but when there is cognition there may be no coordination.

12.2 Direction

Most EDEC studies consider cognition in very precise settings (e.g., Hutchins, 1995a, 1995b; Clark, 2003; Pedersen and Steffensen 2014; Kirsh and Maglio, 1994). The golden standard for these studies is to consider task-oriented behavior as a setting on which cognition can be

effectively studied. This point is related to the one on coordination above
so, some of the arguments produced in the previous section are not
repeated here.

Cognition is a very wide concept, it spans across disciplines (Hodgkinson, 2015; Varela, Thompson, & Rosch, 1991), and is applied to various
aspects of work and life in general. Not all that we do is oriented toward
a goal or is a task. Yet, it is extremely convenient to study tasks and
especially work tasks (or problems) as settings in which it is easier
to observe cognitive activities. I have done the same in some of the
models presented in this book. The INQ1.0.1 model and the IOP2.1.2
model consider workers as they deal with, respectively, problems and
tasks. After all, many activities in the workplace are organized around
problems to solve and tasks to execute (March, 1994; Simon, 1997), this
is nothing surprising.

The elements of a task make the study of cognition fit an easy
schema. A task is there to be performed, hence there is an end goal
to be achieved. The task of preparing slides for a presentation has the
clear goal to have a presentation at the end of the process. Typically, a
task is performed by applying a number of resources to it, hence there is
a functional element that makes the process easily mappable. In the case
of a presentation, there is software, a computer, maybe colleagues to be
involved to gather the necessary information. At the same time, a task
can be measured in terms of effectiveness – i.e. how well the goal has been
achieved – and efficiency – i.e. how well the resources have been used.
Time to completion is one element. Finally, a task may be associated
to limits in its execution, meaning that it may be only performed by
using certain tools. In many circumstances, companies provide their
workers with specific software to perform specific tasks (e.g., sending
messages, assessing performance, calculating resource use). This allows
for precision when studying cognition.

The above points at various elements that constitute the toolkit of
the EDEC scholar. For example, the functional interrelation (coupling)
between an artifact and the person working with it, the coordination
between them, the way in which cognition is shaped by the dynamic
interactivity, the meaning of the external resource, but also the skills
and competence applied, tacit knowledge, and the action exercised on
the resource as a further way to shape cognition. When considering all
these and other aspects, the service that task-oriented activities have
done for EDEC is truly exceptional.

Now that I think I have cleared the waters from any criticism of
studies on task-orientation, I can add that cognition does not start and
end with them. Especially research on cognition in organizations should
be partly driven by an interest on non-task-oriented (or problem-solving-
oriented) activities. What are these?

A good starting point is to define a *task*. In MOR, there are several definitions of a task (Hackman, 1969; Wood, 1986). In Secchi (2020a), I have offered the following conceptualization and highlighted links to EDEC perspectives:

> we define a task as an abstract, manual or repetitive proce-
> dure that calls for execution from an actor (e.g., Bosio and
> Cristini, 2018). From this perspective, a task is conditional
> on the *local* variables that define its execution, and that are
> specified by a sentient individual or by a team, and by the
> resources available. In other words, it is claimed that tasks
> are (1) enacted, meaning that they are inseparable from the
> individual that performs them (Hærem et al., 2015); and
> they are (2) a function of the context in which they are
> performed (e.g., Schatzki, 2005). The combination of these
> two elements implies that the resources employed to perform
> a task also serve a definitional function. (p. 4)

The spectrum of activities that are left off the ones described in the quote are many, even though the description above is very broad. To use the same words of the quote, an abstract, manual or repetitive procedure that does *not* call for execution is not a task. Also, something that is performed *una tantum*, hence it is not a procedure, is not a task. For example, attending a meeting, taking notes, talking to a colleague, asking questions without a clear connection to a procedure, using an unorthodox process to address an issue, or improvising in the face of a sudden challenge are all examples of activities that are not tasks.

The simulation `OrgBand2.0` is based on behavior that is not con-nected to a task. Adopting a thought, a behavior, or something else that does not necessarily require execution or is not necessarily tied to a procedure is not a task. The study of the cognitive determinants of intra-organizational diffusion, while not related to a task it is still a study of cognition. Actually, this agent-based model has been particularly important. From `OrgBand2.0` I have learned that SDC and docility have counterproductive effects on the emergence of bandwagons. This signaled that (a) further enquiries were necessary to understand why and (b) SDC exercises effects outside of task-oriented activities.

The following subsection takes these considerations further by pre-senting a new theoretical framework that reconciles these findings with EDEC and SDC theory.

12.3   The Theory of Social Organizing

The idea of systemic cognition (Cowley & Vallée-Tourangeau, 2013) is fascinating because it is potentially appealing to most cognitive processes. At the same time, in its first formulation (Cowley & Vallée-Tourangeau, 2013) it seems to lack precision and it certainly does not show clear focus. As such, it remains a very broad and useful as a philosophical framework rather than as an approach to cognition.

The main concern with systemic cognition is that it does not hold a firm grip on a specific concept. This is apparent by the use of the word "thinking" by its authors (Cowley & Vallée-Tourangeau, 2013); while this word is evocative of cognitive processes, it is also loose in its meaning, unless further details are offered. This is understandable because the chapter in which Cowley & Vallée-Tourangeau (2013) outline this perspective serves the purpose of establishing connections with a wide range of concepts (and related literature), including: artifacts, individuals, groups, culture/cultural activity, the physical environment, epistemic values, organisms/biology, complexity, simplexity, dynamic change, judgment, action, cooperation/competition, coordination, functions/functionality, processing, and interactivity. Each one of these concepts would have probably required an entire paper if one wanted to begin to understand how systemic cognition is capable of truly developing our knowledge. But that was not the purpose of the book chapter by Cowley & Vallée-Tourangeau (2013). In fact, that is the place where the two authors introduce this concept for the first time and it is understandable that they have been trying to play the evocative value of the perspective. Yet, without a clear grip, the essence, meaning and implications of applying a systemic approach to cognition remained extremely vague.

The *theory of social organizing* (Secchi & Cowley, 2018, 2020) is an attempt to demonstrate the effectiveness of using a systemic cognition approach and, at the same time, to define what organizational cognition is and how it works. Stephen Cowley and I have started discussing about this approach[2] in light of a general dissatisfaction with the state-of-the-art in the MOC field (mainly after Secchi & Adamsen, 2017). As it will become apparent very soon, this theory has very strong ties with what can be learned from the findings of the agent-based simulations presented in Part II and to what discussed previously in Chapter 11.

The theory is explained by a model where *micro* and *macro* domains interact to define several *meso* domains in which cognition materializes. A succinct representation of the model is given in Table 12.1, where the three domains are described and a number of references are offered to connect them to the extant literature.

---

[2]We have called it a theory as we started working on our book *Organizational Cognition: The Theory of Social Organizing* (Secchi, Gahrn-Andersen, & Cowley, 2022, forthcoming).

Table 12.1. The 3M Model of Organizational Cognition.

Domain	Description	Conceptual Affinities	References
Micro	The biological individual is featured in this domain. Non distributed activities can be allocated here.	Cognitivism Computationalism Mainstream MOC	Fodor (1975); Chomsky (1980) Newell and Simon (1972); Simon (1996) Hodgkinson and Healey (2008a)
Macro	Organizational structural elements are framed within this domain. They include culture, norms, routines, procedures, processes and all other characteristics that are institutionalized and affect workers.	Holism Strategic management	Luhmann (1995) Ghosal (1993); Ansoff (1965)
Meso	The intersection of macro and micro aspects converge when individuals establish exchange mechanisms with others, artifacts, and when they engage with ideas that pertain to the organization.	Sensemaking (only partially) EDEC perspectives	Weick (1993); Weick and Sutcliffe (2006); Gioia and Chittipeddi (1991) Varela et al. (1991); Hutchins (1995a); Clark and Chalmers (1998)

Note. The references are to be intended as either focusing exclusively on the relevant domain or, in the case of the *meso* domain, as sources *ante litteram*.

What I previously called *micro* by referring to the *local* conditions in the models (Chapter 11) is here split into two parts. The domain that pertains to the micro is here the biological individual or, as Stephen Cowley would say, neurophysiology. Considering the micro separated from the other two domains means to approach cognition with a cognitivist angle (*à la* Fodor, 1975; Newell & Simon, 1972). Building on the review of the MOC literature in Chapter 2, it is fair to write that the mainstream organizational cognition approach still holds a strong grip on the individual, hence falling within the micro domain. Everything else that derives from various exchanges between the self and artifacts, other human beings and ideas belong to the *meso* domain. Almost every action that happens in an organization is related to a single or multiple meso domains. It is this perspective in which EDEC scholars typically frame their conceptualizations of cognition.

The *macro* domain is also something that I have described in Chapter 11. The stable structural and infrastructural elements that make an organization and are institutionalized in its procedures, norms, processes, routines, and culture (to name a few) constitute a general reference for every employee to operate in their jobs.

The combination of these three domains makes the micro-meso-macro model of organizational cognition (*3M model* for short). The 3M model is an instantiation of the *theory of social organizing*, that relates to the way in which the meso domain is structured and comes to existence, mainly through people working together. The main contribution of the model is at least twofold. On the one hand, the 3M model is an attempt to bridge these three domains together in a coherent systemic perspective. In fact, what we are claiming is that there is no understanding of cognition unless these three are considered in the way they mutually affect each other. On the other hand, the model is putting the 'social' (or organizational) at the core of cognition. By highlighting that one should look at these three domains at once, we are pointing at the need to always factor in a wide range of actual and latent factors that shape cognition. At this point, an example is probably worth more than further abstract conceptualizations.

In Secchi and Cowley (2020), we use peer-review to exemplify how the 3M model works so to identify ways in which *social organizing* happens. In another work (Secchi & Cowley, 2018), we model a computational simulation of a review process to identify the functioning mechanisms of the theory and in yet another (Secchi & Cowley, 2019), we create another agent-based model of how peer-reviewers are affected, in their assessment, by journal metrics such as the Impact Factor. I invite interested readers to use these publications to have a precise idea of how the 3M model and the theory work. In this book, instead of insisting with the same example, it is probably better to find one that is tied to a more traditional organizational framework.

A consulting company that helps small enterprises to grow can be used as an example. In practice, the 3M model is able to unveil social organizing when specific occurrences or events happen but it can also be used to describe a typical interaction in abstract terms. There are many types of consulting companies, some of them send their consultants to work for a period of time in the organization they provide their services to. When this happens, the consultant needs to be acquainted with the general ways in which business is conducted in that organization or, in other words, just like any new hire, she/he needs to learn how a typical work day is. This is mainly done through the *macro* structure, by reading some of the relevant procedures and observing how these are actually practiced. Of course, when they are practiced, then understanding behavioral and socialization aspects become essential. And they can only happen in a *meso* domain. The consultant may spend the first days or weeks, if necessary, observing, studying, and asking how things are done while also contributing with her/his unique expertise (the value of consultancy). The way in which consultancy comes to life is though working with others in the company, by feeling embedded in the company, being committed to improving their work, hence by knowing who they are and how they work. While performing these activities, consultants also re-define their role, adjust their performance, fine-tune their interventions and, if good, they necessarily question who they are and what they do. Any consultancy cannot work unless customized to the company they offer their services to. This result is achieved through discussions, meetings, and other types of exchanges that are necessary to establish knowledge and the basis for communicating further. These are instances of *social organizing*, as they are limited (and enhanced, sometimes) by the macro structural elements and by the characteristics of the individuals involved (the micro domain). It is the intertwined links between these three domains that make *social organizing* possible, providing a frame for cognitive processes to happen by increasing SDC.

The quotation at the beginning of the chapter is a sentence taken from a record by a famous jazz pianist, Dave Brubeck. I have always liked the sentence because it is so ambiguous that it is a good representation of what happens in the meso domain. On the one hand, workers get together again and again, day in and day out and, on the other hand, circumstances are almost never the same, so that there is both an element of novelty and one that belongs to the past. Hence, one could claim they "are all together again for the first time." It is a wonderful accent on one of the constituents of cognition, i.e. change.

Through the book, it has been apparent that ABM is a method that can be used for the study of complex systems. As such, not only it has been used to show how the 3M model reflects actual work in organizations (Cowley, 2016; Secchi & Cowley, 2018, 2019), but it has inspired the way in which the *theory of social organizing* has come to the fore (Part II). For this reason, the next chapter presents some reflections on an agent-based computational *approach*, rather than just as a tool for research.

12.4   Summary

This chapter has outlined the *new paradigm* for the study of cognition in organizations. Not only cognition in organizations needs EDEC perspectives, but it does so in a way that requires the understanding of complex social dynamics. These are articulated in three domain – i.e. micro, meso, and macro – as they enmesh in each other. Under an SDC umbrella, the *theory of social organizing* is an exemplar of how this new paradigm unfolds.

13

Final Remarks: Pushing the Boundaries

> *"Against any evidence, it is often simply hoped that the details of the individuals' cognitive model will not matter once embedded within a network of interaction. This is an understandable hope, since having to deal with both individual cognitive complexity and social complexity makes the job of modelling social complexity much harder [...]."*
>
> – Edmonds and Meyer (2017a, p. 6)

The final chapter of a book is very difficult to write. One should avoid repetitions yet summarize content, draw conclusions while attempting not to be conclusive, reflect on the messages of the book and set an agenda for future research at the same time. In other words, final chapters are a contradiction in terms.

There are still at least two important aspects that need to find place in this book. One is to elaborate on the legacy of studying cognition in organizations using computational agent-based simulations (the section below). The other is to reflect more broadly on the research avenues that are opened up by a computational approach, and on how to take it further (the other section in this chapter).

Before you start reading, it is probably worth mentioning something obvious. The use of agent-based computational simulations to study cognition is not an immutable choice. ABM has been an obvious choice, given the advantages already described in the previous chapters and what you will find below. At the same time, the approaches, tools,

Computational Organizational Cognition:
A Study on Thinking and Action in Organizations, 191–207
Copyright © 2021 by Emerald Publishing Limited
All rights of reproduction in any form reserved
doi: 10.1108/978-1-83867-511-020211013

and instruments of science advance constantly and this means that one cannot exclude improved versions of what we currently use. Would those approaches, tools, and instruments become available, they can be made to serve the study of organizational cognition. A scientist need to be pragmatic, not dogmatic. What I can write is that computational social science – no matter with which means it is pursued – is probably here to stay. Today, the most promising approach, tool, and instrument for the study of organizational cognition is offered by ABM.

13.1   The Agent-based Approach

The idea here is that bounded rationality, docility, plasticity, and all the other concepts theorized in this book can and should be defined computationally with an agent-based approach. If one assumes and agrees that organizational cognition is complex (and part of a wider complex system), with different elements autonomously interacting with each other with both down- and up-ward causation patterns, then ABM is probably the best option we have to study it. SDC and the *theory of social organizing* provide a roadmap to guide this research effort.

As it is clear from the models reviewed in Part II, ABM coding is a mix of mathematics, statistics, and single and double loops in which the modeler only defines the starting conditions and the mechanisms for interaction in an environment, leaving the system to produce patterns (emergent properties) as it evolves.

This is different than, for example, a mathematical or a statistical approach. Mathematical modeling can include dynamic elements but it is mainly a static tool that works with relatively strict assumptions, as the field of economics and mathematical sociology has taught us. Statistical modeling can, instead, allow for a higher degree of stochastic processes (e.g., Monte Carlo simulations) but, due to the needs to mathematically formalize its workings it is still bound to strict assumptions. Both methods are de facto not used (or used seldom) in management and organization research (MOR) and in managerial and organizational cognition (MOC) and, for this reason, a finer discussion of their details may lack an audience.

While organizational cognition scholars have used a wide range of qualitative methodologies, statistical modeling in both MOR and MOC has been mainly used to make inference and estimate variable effects in connection with empirical data. The nature of inference is based on probability theory, since it reverts around comparing a sample to its population to determine whether the effects in the former are attributable to the latter. In so doing, it produces estimates that are usually interpreted as effects of one variable to another. The assumptions that undergo such models are still particularly strict, especially in the

MOR field, as it is apparent to anyone who has used OLS regression analysis (e.g., normality, independence of observations, homoscedasticity, no multicollinearity, no endogeneity). When one or more of these assumptions are not met, statistics offers various options (e.g., multilevel random coefficient models, polynomial regressions, PLS-SEM, Bayesian models), still within a rigid frame that needs to fit the data. Most importantly, these statistical models based on empirical data are not simulations. Those that get close to simulations are techniques that employ random resampling or bootstrapping, but they are still bound to the data in a way that fits the underlying mathematics. They can be flexible and are now used although not as widely as one would hope, given the sample sizes of empirical data in MOR (and especially MOC) and the availability of computer power.

Agent-based modeling appears as a compromise between the need of formalization – that we still have in MOR, MOC and organizational cognition as well as in any other scientific field – and the opening to the unavoidable ambiguity, uncertainty, and unpredictability of organizational thinking and behavior. ABM forces researchers to be more precise about the way in which variables interact. Statistical modeling based on empirical data works well because the effect between variables is not determined in advance, but it becomes so through means of the statistical technique one selects for the analysis. For example, when a vague hypothesis such as "A positively affects B" is formulated, the selection of a linear model makes this effect to be

$$\hat{B}_1 = \alpha + \beta \cdot A + \epsilon, \tag{13.1}$$

where $\hat{B}_1$ is the estimated dependent variable, α is the intercept, β is the coefficient, and ϵ the error. Alternatively, given no specific indications in the hypothesis, one could model the relation differently, as in

$$\hat{B}_2 = \frac{\gamma + A^\eta}{\mu \cdot C} + \epsilon, \tag{13.2}$$

where γ is a constant, η is a coefficient that indicates a wider effect, μ a coefficient for another variable C that discounts the effects of A on B. One could rightly claim that there are at least another two hypotheses one should write to specify the relation between A and C and B and C. Fine, but the point is that, even when researchers specify these relations in the broad (ambiguous) way indicated above, I am almost certain you have probably never seen a statistical model based on Equation 13.2 and tested in a MOR paper. However, if you think about Equation 13.2, it is something likely to appear among typical variables studied in organizations. Take cognition, the subject of this book, as an example.

Elements of task performance B, can be explained through cognitive distributions, A, in a way such that the coupling with external resources makes the effects exponentially higher, and can be estimated by coefficient η, given a common ground on which performance can start (the constant γ). These effects can be reduced by the repeated use of a given resource C, that has a discount effect μ on A and a reverse effect on B. How to produce a statistically reliable estimate is beyond the purpose of this chapter and of this book. The point here is to understand how an advanced computational approach can help us understand cognition with finer granularity and insight. And I would go one step further with this and state that, given the instability of relations among variables in a typical organizational frame, ABM is probably the most effective tool to theorize about these relations.

The above tackles on a series of points, some are similar, while others significantly different. In the following pages of this section, I move the discussion further by presenting reflections on the importance of time, the chronic poverty of data in the MOR/MOC field, the absence of a mathematical (or statistical) framework, and what the unique features of an agent-based approach entails. The objective is that of establishing ABM as the most natural basis for the study of organizational cognition or what can be referred to as *computational organizational cognition*.

13.1.1   Time: The Big Absentee

One of the chronic problems of social science is the difficulty (and precision) of data collection (see, e.g., Westland, 2015). In much of MOR and MOC these problems are exacerbated by the use of primary data (Scandura and Williams, 2000), where researchers collect data samples through methods that are designed to be employed only once – in that specific setting and with those participants. Of course interview questions in qualitative research and measurement scales in quantitative surveys, for example, can be (and are) used many times by multiple researchers. But they are also attached to other measures, in a different configuration/structure, sometimes adapted or translated to fit the context in which they are deployed. Participants are almost always different, meaning that the typical study is cross-sectional – this is in MOR (Aguinis, Pierce, Bosco, & Muslin, 2009; Scandura & Williams, 2000). Only recently academic journals have started to publish data that are collected in waves such that it allows for longitudinal analytical techniques (Jebb & Tay, 2017; Zaheer, Albert, & Zaheer, 1999). Even when this is the case, data collection instances are limited to two or three.

These are, of course, issues pertinent to empirical data analysis, not to theory and modeling. In general, some have claimed that MOR (and organizational cognition as part of it) lacks consistent reference to time scales (Zaheer et al., 1999) and there is little evidence that this trend is changing.

Timescales

One of the most relevant features of ABM is that it is about how any given set of interdependencies are generated, develop, and progress over time. In one word, one could refer to these as *dynamics* (Miller & Page, 2007). I claim that ABM is one of the most appropriate tools to address the concerns of MOR and MOC scholars, especially when theory development or "testing" (see below) is concerned. This book is an example of how theoretical assumptions in organizational cognition (and EDEC) can be modeled to gain meaningful data that inform reflections, suggest further enquiries, expand the discourse, and help to refine assumptions and conceptualizations.

First of all, one should be clear about "time." What I mean is that there is a need to understand what is meant by time in a computational simulation context as opposed to time in a theory or in the actual world.[1] Time in a computational simulation is not – it cannot be – the same as "natural" time. In fact, if that were the case, a simulation would run in the same amount of time it takes to referent counterpart to perform the processes under examination. This is to state that, to simulate the adjustment of a company to a market pressure would take the same time that it actually does for an organization to do that. Not only this would make simulations very time consuming and almost impossible to perform but it also would make them worthless. Why study an exact replica if the actual phenomenon is there to be studied? From this simple consideration, it is clear that simulation time is not natural time. The dynamics as studied in a computational simulation are defined by the modeler to represent an occurrence in the observed phenomenon. For example, in the `DIO1.0` model they represent opportunities to interact. As the time counter in the simulation "ticks" and moves one unit at a time, it represents the likelihood that an agent (an employee) has to meet and interact with another agent (employee). If the situation is that of an office and interactions have to deal with work-related exchange of information then it may be that these interactions occur 10 times a day, on average. It is clear that the reference to time takes a different form in the simulation. There are cases in which the reference to time is more direct. For example, some models may use the simulation time unit to represent a year, a day, a minute or any other natural time reference. All that counts is that these are simulation's times.

---

[1] This expression is to avoid the word "real" that is bound to certain philosophical assumptions that are not necessarily subscribed by the reasonings in this book. The expression belongs to my friend and colleague Bill Adamsen.

The various elements of ABM can come into play differently. This is because they can be made to advance more or less slow (or fast) as the time unit goes by. There is a here-and-now dimension that affects the elements of the simulation simultaneously and as the time progresses. Other elements are, instead, affected by the slow movement of other factors. While the first are typical of the micro and meso, the latter are visible in the macro domain. Think of how a norm affects the behavior of employees in an organization. It is usually framed in the long run, because it needs time to form and it affects individuals and their actions only indirectly (or by means of subtle processes). These have been framed as *slow timescales* (Neumann and Cowley, 2016). But the behavior we have been referring to happens here-and-now as it happens in a much *faster timescale*. The ABM logic allows for these aspects to be counted on, such that it is not just "time" to be factored in but its effects on the system's dynamics.

More than slow and fast timescales (Neumann & Cowley, 2016), ABM allows for the interaction between the two. Just like the slow is affected by the fast, the simulation may be coded to allow for these intersections. Clearly, the way in which these two affect each other is never linear and it requires a very careful consideration of how their effects play out. The case of agents moving from one cognitive frame to another can be an example of slowly changing the macro structure of reference for the organization. This is what happened, for example, in a model where Stephen Cowley and I allowed for agent-academics to embrace certain beliefs on paper assessment during peer review (Secchi & Cowley, 2019), hence changing the institutional frame of reference.

Besides being able to work with time and organizational dynamics, the two ABM features – (a) the slow and the fast timescales and (b) the influence they have on each other – constitute a very clear bridge toward the needs of MOR (and MOC).

Theory Development

The other aspect that is mentioned in Zaheer et al. (1999) is the use of time in theory development. This is a relatively widely debated issue, since it appears in multiple disciplines and in relation to ABM (e.g., Grimm et al., 2019). The general point is that computational simulation can (and should) be used for theory development purposes. This is because of its ability to represent aspects of a theory in a relatively straightforward way, allowing for assumptions to be checked. Mainly, some argue, ABM can be considered as a heuristics for reasoning about theory (Cowley, 2016).

There have been calls in this direction from MOR scholars (Davis, Eisenhardt, & Bingham, 2007), but their appeal has not been too specific, does not refer to ABM, and it has been mainly overlooked. Instead, others have advocated for the use of ABM as a theory development instrument. Edmonds et al. (2019) indicate that theoretical exploration is one of the main purposes for these types of models. In an inspiring chapter, Gajary (2020) highlights how the hybrid combination of System Dynamics and ABM can lead to develop theory. Most noticeably, Smaldino, Calanchini, & Pickett (2015) also argue very strongly in that same direction. After a series of workshops funded by the Volkswagen Foundation in Hanover, a group of modelers have attempted to give a set of guidelines for the use of ABM as theory development tools (Grimm et al., 2019).

In a recent publication Nuno Oliveira and I have shown that ABM can be used as a meta-theoretical tool, to help researchers reflect on the choices they make. We use ABM to suggest how scholars should reflect on independence of cases when dealing with multiple case research (Oliveira & Secchi, 2020). In a completely different case, I have developed an ABM to study the typology of information, and outline a theory of non-functional information (Secchi, 2020b, 2020c).

In short, it seems that the second "call for action" in Zaheer et al. (1999) can be even more easily dealt with by embracing ABM. As far as organizational cognition is concerned, time and dynamics are even more relevant than the average MOR, and this book has demonstrated a few ABM applications.

13.1.2   What About Data?

The absence of empirical data to start a computational simulation is not a mandatory state. There are examples of agent-based models built around data gathered prior to the coding of the model. In economics, for example, models that are created using data on record for a given phenomenon are called "history friendly" (Malerba et al., 2001). Other models are build by using empirical data as a benchmark to which some agent characteristics have to adhere to. Herath, Costello, & Homberg (2017) use descriptive statistics of motivation, for example, taken from data collected among volunteers to create a simulation model of the dynamics with which they solve problems in more or less organized hierarchical structures. In yet another case (Lotzmann & Neumann, 2017), qualitative data is used to create alternative virtual worlds in which different narratives can be examined and compared.

ABM is an extremely flexible approach that allows for the use of different types of data as model inputs, to better specify and define the characteristics of the agents, the environment or, sometimes, the rules of interaction (i.e. the mechanisms). Data could also be used in the stage of calibration of the model – in that case it is called *verification* (Boero and Squazzoni, 2005; Seri, Martinoli, Secchi, & Centorrino, 2020) – or to benchmark the behavior of the model's output variable (Fagiolo, Moneta, & Windrum, 2007).

The MOR field's chronic problems with data collection (see above) has also close connections with the ease with which ABM integrates with data. Independent of sample size, ABM can use data to characterize its agents, replicate features of the empirical data, define relations, or parametrize the model's elements. No matter how the empirical data maps on the model, there are choices and assumptions the modeler needs to make to establish the dynamics and observe how the established relations evolve as time goes by. Using the example above in Equation 13.2, one could apply the measurements of the variables task performance B, cognitive distributions A, and the effectiveness in the repeated use of resources C. The simulation needs the mechanisms of operation to be specified. One could implement a version of Equation 13.2 as a guideline for agent behavior to estimate $\hat{B}$ and then compare the simulated data with the measurements of B. Performance would depend on *local* conditions, for example on how many resources are consistently and repeatedly utilized and on how many tasks the agent finds. If the modeler leaves A and C to reflect the data, at least initially, she/he also needs to estimate the coefficients γ, η, and μ. These become parameters that take different values as the simulation is performed. A typical approach would be to fix a baseline with the parameters values that get a closer match between $\hat{B}$ and B, and then explore what happens when they take different values. This is a way in which computational experiments explore alternative realities or *counterfactuals.*

Among the mechanisms a modeler does not find in the common MOR (and MOC) data is what happens over time. That would be part of the assumptions that are necessary for the simulation to perform. If the data reflect the most popular cross-sectional or qualitative design, then a question to answer when designing and coding an agent-based simulation would be what happens after the initial conditions are set and after the agents are done with their first set of tasks, to stick with the example above. Whether they find other tasks and how, whether there is an adjustment in their cognition A after they perform, and how does performance actually work, specifying whether tasks B have values for difficulty or complexity. All these questions (and many others) require an answer when a computational simulation is planned, designed, and programmed. These questions are tied to the purpose of the model, and are crucial to make the data have a dynamic application, even if the starting point was static.

A key issue in Equation 13.2 is the modeling of the error term, ϵ. This is a derivative of the inferential technique one uses when performing statistics, and it is a factor that needs to be thought in detail when programmed into the computational model. By all means, this is essential because it is one of the many ways to add stochasticity to the processes such that agent actions are never univocal and deterministic. Using the simulations in Part II, I have shown a number of different random components and how they can be modeled. Ambiguity and uncertainty are key elements of social life and they are unavoidable in complex systems. ABM is designed to take these elements into account.

The mechanisms in ABM can derive from observations, other models, or theory. In the case of MOR and MOC, theories are never specified in such a way that they have a, more or less, unambiguous modeling solution. Muelder and Filatova (2018) have analyzed models of the Theory of Planned Behavior (Ajzen, 1991) and found that there are a plethora of coding solutions to incorporate its elements computationally. This is one of many examples but probably an eye opener to those who believe path models are precise enough. This is both a problem and a strength. It is a problem because, in principle, any researcher can interpret the connections between elements of a theory their own way and still be within the frame of the theory. When a theory has multiple instantiations – i.e. multiple models – then one could start reflecting on which model is actually a better fit to the theory from which it was generated (Gelfert, 2017). While this can be a problem because it means that there is inner vagueness in the theory, it can also be a strength because it forces researchers to ask more questions and improve the original theory. This is, of course, if there is a loop that feeds back into the theory.

A final point concerning ABM and data relates to the type of data one generates. Being a computational product, every single element as well as everything that happens in a simulation generates a measure. If the modeler is "greedy" and wants to download the data from all possible simulation sources, then the file is likely to be large. Even if the computational model is of moderate complexity and the researcher needs data from all calculated variables measured at every time unit (tick or step) until the end, the data is likely a large file. Granularity of results mean that a researcher using ABM needs to be acquainted with techniques of data mining that are typical of big data handling (e.g., Arroyo, Hassan, Gutiérrez, & Pavón, 2010).

13.1.3   A Reverse Logic

A shared understanding of ABM is that they should be analyzed by the patterns they outline with their behavior (Grimm et al., 2005). This derives precisely from the understanding that the simulations generated by ABM are complex and, as such, it is extremely difficult to predict the final state of the system from its initial conditions. This means that patterns emerge from given configurations and that is where the researcher attempts to find regularities, if any.

The scientific logic is, in some sense, reverse from normal in that mathematical expressions may come at the end of the process to describe the configurations of the data, rather than inform the setting. As seen in the previous pages, mathematics and statistics can inform the way in which agents of a simulation relate to each other, but the purpose there is not to outline a deterministic rule, but to set a possible direction that comes to life only if and when other conditions are satisfied. Using the example above, cognition can be distributed, giving raise to A only when resources C do not disappear after their use. Hence performance abides to Equation 13.2 only when resources are of a certain kind, otherwise other rules may apply. To be more precise, even the execution of the rule can be subject to a randomization effect in that the modeler could decide to add variability to the two variables A and B. An example of this is the way in which the spin off condition has been modeled in IOP2.1.2 (see Chapter 10).

The mathematical expressions used to describe patterns are likely to be supported by the use of statistical inference. This is because the data (see above) is sometimes difficult to interpret and paths are not clear, if they are there at all. A good approach to make sense of data when confronted with complex systems is that of using statistics. In other words, it is possible that the mathematical expressions derive from the analysis of the data that is inspired by the use of statistics.

Why is this a *reverse logic*? After all, MOR and MOC do not use mathematics at the onset of their research. This statement is correct, but the assumptions one makes with a testable statistical model are very much imposing a mathematical frame to the data gathered empirically. With ABM the computational frame is also there, but it is more flexible, to the point that it does not necessarily produce the same results, given the same parameter values. If you perform the same statistical model used to make inference on empirical data[2] multiple times with the same set of data the result does not vary; in fact, there is no point in such an exercise. By starting with a more flexible design a modeler arrives at data that then needs interpretation. A very popular mean to do this is one I have used in Part II, that is, graphical analysis.[3] The fact that one arrives at a possible statistical model to define the patterns in the data

---

[2]I am referring to the typical inference made by MOR/MOC scholars and found in any management journal.

[3]I had performed regressions and other statistical analyses when I commented results of these models before (see, e.g., Bardone & Secchi, 2017; Secchi & Gullekson, 2016).

instead of starting with it means applying an upside down logic to the enquiry. Exploration seems to be a broad strategy in ABM research, as opposed to hypotheses testing typical of MOR and MOC quantitative research.

13.1.4 ABM Uniqueness

Not all computational modeling is of this kind and I claim that ABM offers unique options to those who use it, especially when studying cognition. Other computational techniques have a clearer path to the conditions from which they start. For example, NK Models (Kauffman & Weinberger, 1989) are tied to the mathematical structure that defines the two main parameters, N and K. These are models that are useful to study how certain combination of characteristics fit a particular set of conditions (e.g., an environment). Given their relatively simple design, they have been implemented in MOR (starting with the seminal Levinthal, 1997) at a pace that seems higher than that of ABM (Baumann, Schmidt, & Stieglitz, 2019). Another technique that is relatively grounded in its math is System Dynamics (Forrester, 1958, 1961). I have mentioned this technique before (especially Chapter 5 and Chapter 6) as based on sets of differential equations that allow for the definition of stocks and flows in the system of reference. Both these simulation techniques, like many others (e.g., cellular automata, neural networks), have a sharp dependence on their initial conditions and can be used to study selected aspects of given phenomena. In light of how tight these techniques are with their mathematical upbringing, some have claimed recently that computational simulation is no different than mathematical modeling (Knudsen, Levinthal, & Puranam, 2019).[4]

ABM is a different kind of technique. Not only it generates systems that reflect aspects of complexity, hence departing almost completely from classic mathematical modeling, but its overall structure outlines a new *approach* to the study of social phenomena. The interest here is limited to organizational cognition. The points above clearly demarcate the extent to which ABM can and should be used more in cognition research. By forcing the researcher to express relations in terms of cognitive dynamics, thus having time as an unavoidable factor, by having to define the operating mechanisms between the elements of these cognitive dynamics, and by embedding ambiguity as a constitutive element of their reasoning, researchers are approaching cognition from a very different angle.

---

[4]As argued elsewhere (Secchi, 2021), I cannot disagree more with these colleagues. But it would be too long to repeat my arguments here and I believe it would be too long a digression.

The review of the MOC literature in Chapter 2 has indicated that the field is somewhat far from the approach outlined in this book. At the same time, the EDEC perspectives as defined in Chapter 3 and in Chapter 4 are more in line with treating cognition as a complex phenomenon, although they are generally far from organizational phenomena as well as from the ABM approach as described in this book (with noticeable exceptions, such as Cowley, 2016).

This book is an attempt to demonstrate not only the way in which organizational cognition can be theoretically identified, but it is also an attempt to outline how it can be structured computationally.

13.2 Computational Organizational Cognition

The previous pages in this chapter and the entire book have been dedicated to the use of computational simulation to study various aspects of cognition in organization. This is well reflected in the subtitle of the book that repeats this is a study of "thinking and action" in organizations. As far as my knowledge is concerned, there are very few attempts to study organizational cognition through means of ABM. The reasons may vary, but one claim of this book is that the social/organizational aspect of cognition has often been overlooked, even by those who refer to their research domain as MOC.

This section of Chapter 13 is also the final section of this book and it is dedicated to broader reflections on the research avenues that may open up.

13.2.1 The Meaning of Computation

As seen throughout the book and actually explicitly referred to earlier (Chapters 5, 6, and 12), the use of computation in this book is very different from that of cognitive computationalists, mainly referred to as cognitivists (Varela, Thompson, & Rosch, 1991). It is possible to summarize these differences in the instrumental use of computation[5] that has been proposed in these pages.

Contrary to the early cognitivists (Newell & Simon, 1972; Simon, 1979) and to some more recent revivals (Miłkowski, 2012),[6] this book does not claim that computation describes the way in which humans reason. The workings of cognition are represented computationally, since

---

[5]This is, according to the interpretation of Pinna (2017) and Wells (1998), similar to the idea that Turing had of computation.

[6]Cognition as studied in artificial intelligence has remained anchored to computations, for obvious reasons.

that is an effective way to analyze them. At the same time, there is no need (nor evidence) to claim that cognitive processing maps on what happens on a computer. In short, this book still rejects the computer metaphor of the mind (Gigerenzer & Goldstein, 1996; Ibáñez & Cosmelli, 2008; Patokorpi, 2008).

It is important to specify this point further. Agent-based computational organizational cognition (AOC) serves the purpose of studying the complexities of cognition as intertwined with action. As made apparent throughout this book, especially when considered in organizational settings, there is no restless cognition but one that is always tied or that makes reference to an incoming action. To write this differently, solipsistic cognition, if at all possible, plays a marginal role in organizations. Hence, AOC is always systemic in the sense that it is undetachable from all the elements typical of socially-based EDEC perspectives. Viewed under this angle AOC is the perfect companion to the study of SDC.

There are at least two implications of this activity-based definition of organizational cognition. One is that the point of reference for research in the field becomes *action* as opposed to the more traditional *behavior*. The way I have intended the former above is wider than the latter, in the sense that *action* includes some *behavior*, but *behavior* does not necessarily mean *action*. The reason is relatively simple and it deals with the fact that the first presupposes mindful presence and some level of involvement while the second can be interpreted as the simple registration of a change of state (e.g., in the position of a body). The other implication relates to the idea that most cognitivist perspectives are tied to functionalism in some shape or form. On the contrary, the present interpretation of organizational cognition (and of cognition, more generally) escapes from this characterization. This is due to the fact that – and this should probably be clear to the reader by now – cognition is lived through action, hence the functionality of the various resources involved is necessarily process-based and flexible. In this sense, there is a way in which subjectivity and practice cannot be escaped from any description of organizational cognition. Both of these implications would require in-depth consideration. At this point of the book, I believe it is sufficient to just mention them as aspects of interest rather than engage in a long discussion of their role and importance. I leave this to further research.

Does the above exclude a computational account of brain activities? The straightforward answer is negative in the sense that it may be possible to describe a brain's functioning with ABM. At the same time, it is not the focus of the stream of research described in this book. A neuroscience approach to cognition may be interested in developing an agent-based computational account of brain activity. And that may become relevant to AOC when and if it is tied to organizational processes. So far, I am not aware of such an attempt being convincingly made since most scholars using ABM in neuroscience have used it often to explore broader social components of cognition (Farrell & Lewandowsky, 2015; Goldstone & Janssen, 2005).

Another question, related to the one in the previous paragraph, is how complex an agent should actually be modeled. This point constitutes a very interesting challenge because the choices made in relation to agent cognition and behavior have repercussions on the overall model results. The approach followed in this book has been inspired by pragmatism, in relation to the functional elements necessary to make certain interactions work. An example of this point is the relative understanding an agent (in a simulation) has of the problem or task in front of it. In all the simulations presented in Part II – and more explicitly in DIO1.0 and INQ1.0.1 – the agent does not have a univocal understanding of the problem/task it is dealing with. Even though the problem/task may have a value to represent its complexity (or task difficulty), this is then *read* by the agent. It is this *reading* that makes the problem/task complex or simple for the agent that is interacting with it. In addition to this individual take on problem solving (and task performance), there is also the use of other cognitive resources. In fact, in all the models above, the agent has the opportunity to reach out and "consult" other agents or exploit other resources to address the problem or task. This action is also what characterizes complexity. Once again, the problem/task is deemed complex when all the efforts, individual, team, and solution-bound (artifacts), are not successful. Hence, it can be stated that the value assigned to a problem/task to represent its complexity is not *objective*, but relative to the characteristics of the agent(s) that approach it.

To rephrase the question above, how much more complex should this interaction between the agent and the problem/task be? Would modeling long and short term memory or learning mechanisms more effectively, for example, make a difference? And is it worth pursuing these "complexifications"? I do not have an answer to these questions, only speculations hence, these are questions that may inform future research.

13.2.2   A Final Thought on Rationality

The idea that rationality – a short for individual cognitive processing abilities – is limited is considered a truism by most. The fact that Simon, March, Williamson, and others (including most of us, computational modelers; see Edmonds and Meyer, 2017a) have been defining rationality as "bounded" (or limited, as it is translated in many languages Secchi,

2011) derives from economics. This is not surprising, given the cultural dominance that economics has on most of the social sciences. No need to explain why here, just recall that math and formal expressions made, over the years, a very significant impact. But, in benchmarking rationality to neoclassical economics one has also accepted the constraints that some of that cultural milieu brought. Emanuele Bardone and I have written this in a paper, still unpublished, but presented to two conferences over the years (Secchi & Bardone, 2010, 2014), where we indicate that there are at least four problems. Namely, bounded rationality presents a negative perspective, is rationalistic, isolationist, and computationalist in the narrowest possible sense.

These problems can be related to the fact that scientists have to connect their own to previous studies on a topic or problem. This is how science mainly works and the work of Simon was not an exception. At the same time, when scientists operate this connection to previous studies, they also inherit a series of constraints. This happened to Simon and the others while they developed the concept of bounded rationality. It also happened to all those who took this idea for granted and worked on it, taking some of its inheritance with it.

Now, are we limited? Is our rationality limited? If the question is whether we "fall short of omniscience" (as Simon once put it 1979, p. 502) then, the answer is, obviously, positive. If the question means to ask whether there are specific limits to human abilities to make decisions such that they allow them to adjust to particular situations, then the answer is probably different. Or, at least, it can be stated that these limits are unforeseeable because they depend on interactions (exchanges) between the resources at play (artifacts), the social environment, perceptions, dispositions, the material environment and, most importantly, other individuals. One may say, the limits to our rationality are only those we decide to put in front of us. Of course, this means that our ability to cognize depends on the set of resources available and, most importantly, on the interplay between them and us (Clark & Chalmers, 1998; Magnani, 2007).

The question is whether AOC is an approach that is in line with the classic accounts of bounded rationality or whether it helps move beyond those accounts. I believe the latter is where I and this book stand.

One need not to forget the importance of individual "stocks" of cognitive resources (those belonging to one's brain). However, these are only relevant the same way initial conditions are to a complex system. This is to say that what comes from these resources is uncertain and depends very much by the "interplay." And this is given mainly by *local* conditions or the way in which the domains in the 3M model are nested into the *meso* domain.

In a way I am detaching myself from the idea that we need to picture ourselves as necessarily "bounded." The reason seems to be that these bounds are extremely difficult to place. As I have shown in *Extendable Rationality* (Secchi, 2011), the bounds are not static and they do move depending on various circumstances, most of all the social environment and the interactions that stem from it. However, can one still call rationality bounded if the bounds cannot be outlined ex ante? Even outlining them ex post could be an intellectual exercise that depends, very much, on the mental frames of the one who is analyzing the case. This looks like calling something by a name it does not represent what it actually is. Does this mean that AOC and this book present theories of unbounded rationality? Not really.

We shall probably move away from the idea of limits or bounds because it is misleading. It is not the most interesting (nor the most important) feature of cognitive processing. It is a truism, I would agree with that. Any system has boundaries, limits. Does it mean that those are its most important characteristics? Probably not. It is now evident that this is a call to depart from the negative view of human rationality, that belongs to a tradition of thoughts that has constrained its conceptualizations.

If not bounds, what then? The question is, in different terms, what is (are) the most relevant features of human cognition? What amazes me, in cognition as well as other aspects of human action, is the way we constantly adapt. Now, the word "adapt" may not be the most appropriate, given its biological appeal. But constant adjustments to situations and local conditions is one of the typical traits of a human mind. Most of all, this is apparent when observing social interactions, especially in a work setting. So, I would say, something along the lines of "plasticity" or complex adaptability is what may be described as one of the most (probably the most) important aspect of human cognition and rationality.

The formulation of these concepts can be rendered computationally. This is the core of AOC and this book; it is probably now clear that the various models discussed in Part II expose a feature of the adaptive side of cognition, rather than of its bounds. If cognition is a complex system then it needs tools apt to describe complexity. This is a computational theory of cognition in organizations, the place where it is possible to explain, describe, and analyze how we do make most of our decisions, thinking, and action.

13.3   Summary

This chapter has described an agent-based approach to the study of organizational cognition and attempted to presents its potentials. In so doing, the chapter has outlined that agent-based computational organizational cognition (or AOC) offers clear advantages to the study of cognition in organizations by covering a ground that no other approach can. In particular, it (a) is a companion to and extends mathematic/statistic modeling, (b) takes multiple timescales under consideration, (c) is a powerful tool to develop theory, (d) supports various uses of data, (e) arrives at formalizations rather than requires them to start computations, and (f) offers features that are not matched by any other technique.

The last part of the chapter has instead focused on the meaning of computation and on the implications that this has on the main theme of rationality and bounded rationality. Contrary to the general understanding of ABM as a way to study bounded rationality, this book argues that AOC does not actually show bounds but it is able to turn the table by showing the positive (potentials) of human cognition. This way agent-based computational organizational cognition is an exemplification of socially distributed cognition theory that serves to re-discuss some of the taken-for-granted assumptions that are at the core of most cognitive approaches, including EDEC and MOC.

References

Abrahamson, E. (2002). Disorganization theory and disorganizational behavior. *Research in Organizational Behavior, 24*, 139–180.

Abrahamson, E., & Freeman, D. H. (2007). *A perfect mess: The hidden benefits of disorder.* New York, NY: Little Brown.

Abrahamson, E., & Rosenkopf, L. (1997). Social network effects on the extent of innovation diffusion: A computer simulation. *Organization Science, 8*(3), 289–309.

Adams, F., & Aizawa, K. (2008). *The bounds of cognition.* Malden, MA: Blackwell Publishing.

Adner, R., & Helfat, C. E. (2003). Corporate effects and dynamic managerial capabilities. *Strategic Management Journal, 24*(10), 1011–1025.

Aguinis, H., Pierce, C. A., Bosco, F. A., & Muslin, I. S. (2009). First decade of organizational research methods: Trends in design, measurement, and data-analysis topics. *Organizational Research Methods, 12*(1), 69–112.

Ajzen, I. (1991). The theory of planned behavior. *Organizational Behavior and Human Decision Processes, 50*, 179–211.

Akgün, A. E., Lynn, G. S., & Byrne, J. C. (2003). Organizational learning: A socio-cognitive framework. *Human Relations, 56*(7), 839–868.

Ansoff, H. I. (1965). *Corporate strategy.* New York, NY: McGraw-Hill.

Argyris, C., & Schön, D. A. (1978). *Organizational learning: A theory of action perspective.* Reading, MA: Addison-Wesley.

Arroyo, J., Hassan, S., Gutiérrez, C., & Pavón, J. (2010). Re-thinking simulation: A methodological approach for the application of data mining in agent-based modelling. *Computational and Mathematical Organization Theory, 16*(4), 416–435.

Ashforth, B. E., & Mael, F. (1989). Social identity theory and the organization. *Academy of Management Review, 14*(1), 20–39.

Bardone, E. (2011). *Seeking chances. From biased rationality to distributed cognition*, volume 13 of *Cognitive Systems Monographs*. New York, NY: Springer.

Bardone, E., & Secchi, D. (2009). Distributed cognition: A research agenda for management. In M. A. Rahim (Ed.), *Current topics in management. Organizational behavior, performance, and effectiveness* (Vol. 14, pp. 183–207). New Brunswick, NJ: Transaction Publishers.

Bardone, E., & Secchi, D. (2017). Inquisitiveness: Distributing rational thinking. *Team Performance Management, 23*(1/2), 66–81.

Barnard, C. I. (1938). *The functions of the executive*. Cambridge, MA: Harvard University Press.

Baumann, O., Schmidt, J., & Stieglitz, N. (2019). Effective search in rugged performance landscapes: A review and outlook. *Journal of Management, 45*(1), 285 – 318.

Becker, G. S. (1976). Altruism, egoism, and genetic fitness: Economics and sociobiology. *Journal of Economic Literature, 14*(3), 817–826.

Becker, W. J., Cropanzano, R., & Sanfey, A. G. (2011). Organizational neuroscience: Taking organizational theory inside the neural black box. *Journal of Management, 37*(4), 933–961.

Becker, G. S., Murphy, K. M., & Tamura, R. (1990). Human capital, fertility, and economic growth. *Journal of Political Economy, 98*(5, Part 2), S12–S37.

Benartzi, S., & Thaler, R. H. (1999). Risk aversion or myopia? Choices in repeated gambles and retirement investments. *Management Science, 45*, 364–381.

Berthoz, A. (2012). *Simplexity: Simplifying principles for a complex world*. London: Yale University Press.

Bhamra, R., Dani, S., & Burnard, K. (2011). Resilience: The concept, a literature review and future directions. *International Journal of Production Research, 49*(18), 5375–5393.

Bliese, P. D. (2002). Multilevel random coefficient modeling in organizational research: Examples using sas and s-plus. In F. Dragsow & N. Schmitt (Eds.), *The Jossey-Bass business & management series. Measuring and analyzing behavior in organizations: Advances in measurement and data analysis* (pp. 401–445). San Francisco, CA: Jossey-Bass.

Boero, R., & Squazzoni, F. (2005). Does empirical embeddedness matter? Methodological issues on agent-based models for analytical social science. *Journal of Artificial Societies and Social Simulation, 8*(4), 6.

Borghini, S. (2005). Organizational creativity: Breaking equilibrium and order to innovate. *Journal of Knowledge Management, 9*(4), 19–33.

Borkar, V. S. (2005). Controlled diffusion processes. *Probability Surveys, 2*, 213–244.

Bosio, G., & Cristini, A. (2018). Is the nature of jobs changing? The role of technological progress and structural change in the labour market. In G. Bosio, T. Minola, F. Origo, & S. Tomelleri (Eds.), *Rethinking Entrepreneurial Human Capital* (pp. 15–41). Cham: Springer.

Bozeman, B., & Feeney, M. K. (2011). *Rules and red tape: A prism for public administration theory and research.* Armonk, NY: ME Sharpe.

Breslin, D., Romano, D., & Percival, J. (2016). Conceptualizing and modeling multi-level organizational co-evolution. In D. Secchi & M. Neumann (Eds.), *Agent-based simulation of organizational behavior* (pp. 137–157). Cham: Springer.

Busby, J. S., & Hibberd, R. E. (2006). The coordinating role of organisational artefacts in distributed cognitions-and how it fails in maritime operations. *Travail Humain, 69*(1), 25–47.

Cacioppo, J. T., Petty, R. E., & Feng Kao, C. (1984). The efficient assessment of need for cognition. *Journal of Personality Assessment, 48*(3), 306–307.

Campbell, T. T., & Armstrong, S. J. (2013). A longitudinal study of individual and organisational learning. *Learning Organization, 20*(3), 240–258.

Cannon-Bowers, J. A., & Salas, E. (2001). Reflections on shared cognition. *Journal of Organizational Behavior, 22*, 195–202.

Carley, K. M. (2009). Computational modeling for reasoning about the social behavior of humans. *Computational and Mathematical Organization Theory, 15*(1), 47–59.

Carley, K. M., Prietula, M. J., & Lin, Z. (1998). Design versus cognition: The interaction of agent cognition and organizational design on organizational performance. *Journal of Artificial Societies and Social Simulation, 1*(3), 4.

Chemero, A. (2009). *Radical embodied cognitive science.* Cambridge, MA: MIT Press.

Chiang, Y.-S. (2007). Birds of moderately different feathers: Bandwagon dynamics and the threshold heterogeneity of network neighbors. *Journal of Mathematical Sociology, 31*, 47–69.

Chomsky, N. (1980). *Rules and representations.* New York, NY: Columbia University Press.

Clark, A. (1998). *Being there: Putting brain, body, and world together again.* Cambridge, MA: MIT Press.

Clark, A. (2003). *Natural-born cyborgs. Minds, technologies, and the future of human intelligence.* Oxford: Oxford University Press.

Clark, A., & Chalmers, D. J. (1998). The extended mind. *Analysis, 58,* 7–19.

Cohen, W. M., & Levinthal, D. A. (1990). Absorptive capacity: A new perspective on learning and innovation. *Administrative Science Quarterly,* 128–152.

Cohen, M. D., March, J. G., & Olsen, H. P. (1972). A garbage can model of organizational choice. *Administrative Science Quarterly, 17*(1), 1–25.

Coleman, J. S. (1988). Social capital in the creation of human capital. *American Journal of Sociology, 94,* S95–S120.

Colquitt, J. A., Lepine, J. A., Piccolo, R. F., Zapata, C. P., & Rich, B. L. (2012). Explaining the justice-performance relationship: Trust as exchange deepener or trust as uncertainty reducer? *Journal of Applied Psychology, 97*(1), 1–15.

Colquitt, J. A., Noe, R. A., & Jackson, C. L. (2002). Justice in teams: Antecedents and consequences of procedural justice climate. *Personnel Psychology, 55*(1), 83 – 109.

Colquitt, J. A., & Rodell, J. B. (2011). Justice, trust, and trustworthiness: A longitudinal analysis integrating three theoretical perspectives. *Academy of Management Journal*, *54*(6), 1183 – 1206.

Conte, R. (1999). Social intelligence among autonomous agents. *Computational and Mathematical Organization Theory*, *5*(3), 203–228.

Conte, R., Hegselmann, R., & Terna, P. (1997). *Simulating social phenomena*. New York, NY: Springer-Verlag.

Cowley, S. J. (Ed.) (2011). *Distributed language*. Amsterdam: Benjamins.

Cowley, S. J. (2016). Cognition beyond the body: Using ABM to explore cultural ecosystems. In D. Secchi & M. Neumann (Eds.), *Agent-based simulation of organizational behavior. New frontiers of social science research* (pp. 43–60). New York, NY: Springer.

Cowley, S. J., & Harvey, M. I. (2016). The illusion of common ground. *New Ideas in Psychology*, *42*, 56–63.

Cowley, S. J., & Vallée-Tourangeau, F. (2013). Systemic cognition: Human artifice in life and language. In S. J. Cowley & F. Vallée-Tourangeau (Eds.), *Cognition beyond the brain* (pp. 255–273). Dordrecht: Springer.

Cowley, S. J., & Vallée-Tourangeau, F. (Eds.) (2017). *Cognition beyond the brain. Computation, interactivity and human artifice* (2nd ed.). London: Springer.

Csardi, G., & Nepusz, T. (2006). The igraph software package for complex network research. *InterJournal, Complex Systems*, 1695.

Cyert, R. M., & March, J. G. (1963). *A behavioral theory of the firm*. Englewood Cliffs, NJ: Prentice-Hall.

Davis, J. P., Eisenhardt, K. M., & Bingham, C. B. (2007). Developing theory through simulation methods. *Academy of Management Review*, *32*(2), 480–499.

Eberlen, J., Scholz, G., & Gagliolo, M. (2017). Simulate this! an introduction to agent-based models and their power to improve your research practice. *International Review of Social Psychology*, *30*(1), 149–160.

Edmonds, B., & Meyer, R. (2017a). Introduction to the handbook. In B. Edmonds & R. Meyer (Eds.), *Simulating social complexity. A Handbook* chapter 1 (2nd ed., pp. 3–12). Heidelberg: Springer.

Edmonds, B., & Meyer, R. (Eds.) (2017b). *Simulating social complexity. A handbook* (2nd ed.). Heidelberg: Springer.

Edmonds, B., & Moss, S. (2005). From KISS to KIDS — An 'anti-simplistic' modelling approach. In P. Davidson (Ed.), *Multi agent based simulation*, volume 3415 of *Lecture Notes in Artificial Intelligence* (pp. 130–144). New York, NY: Springer.

Edmonds, B., Page, C. L., Bithell, M., Chattoe-Brown, E., Grimm, V., Meyer, R., ... Squazzoni, F. (2019). Different modelling purposes. *Journal of Artificial Societies and Social Simulation, 22*(3), 6.

Edwards, J. R. (2008). Person–environment fit in organizations: An assessment of theoretical progress. *Academy of Management Annals, 2*(1), 167–230.

Fagiolo, G., Moneta, A., & Windrum, P. (2007). A critical guide to empirical validation of agent-based models in economics: Methodologies, procedures, and open problems. *Computational Economics, 30*, 195–226.

Farrell, S., & Lewandowsky, S. (2015). An introduction to cognitive modeling. In B. U. Forstmann & E.-J. Wagenmakers (Eds.), *An introduction to model-based cognitive neuroscience* (pp. 3–24). New York, NY: Springer.

Fiol, C. M., & O'Connor, E. J. (2003). Waking up! Mindfulness in the face of bandwagon. *Academy of Management Review, 28*(1), 54–70.

Fioretti, G. (2013). Agent-based simulation models in organization science. *Organizational Research Methods, 16*(2), 227–242.

Fioretti, G., & Lomi, A. (2010). Passing the buck in the garbage can model of organizational choice. *Computational and Mathematical Organization Theory, 16*(2), 113–143.

Fodor, J. A. (1975). *The language of thought.* Cambridge MA: Harvard University Press.

Fodor, J. A. (1987). *Psychosemantics. The problem of meaning in the philosophy of mind.* Cambridge, MA: MIT Press.

Forrester, J. W. (1958). Industrial dynamics. A major breakthrough for decision makers. *Harvard Business Review, 36*(4), 37–66.

Forrester, J. W. (1961). *Industrial dynamics.* Mit Press.

Forrester, J. W. (1971). *World dynamics.* Cambridge, MA: MIT Press.

Forrester, J. W. (1994). System dynamics, systems thinking, and soft or. *System Dynamics Review, 10*(2–3), 245–256.

Foss, N. J. (2003). Bounded rationality in the economics of organizations: 'much cited and little used'. *Journal of Economic Psychology, 24*, 245–264.

Gabbay, D. M., & Woods, J. (2009). Fallacies as cognitive virtues. In O. Majer, A.-V. Pietarinen, & T. Tulenheimo (Eds.), *Games: Unifying logic, language, and philosophy* (pp. 57–98). Springer Netherlands.

Gajary, L. (2020). Hybridizing agent-based with system dynamics models: Principles for theory development in public policy and management research. In E. Vigoda-Gadot & D. R. Vashdi (Eds.), *Handbook of research methods in public administration, management and policy: Towards new frontiers* (pp. forthcoming). Cheltenham: Edward Elgar.

Gavetti, G., Levinthal, D., & Ocasio, W. (2007). Neo-carnegie: The carnegie school's past, present, and reconstructing for the future. *Organization Science, 18*(3), 523–536.

Gelfert, A. (2017). The ontology of models. In L. Magnani & T. Bertolotti (Eds.), *Springer handbook of model-based science*, Springer Handbooks book series (SHB) (pp. 5–23). Cham: Springer.

Ghosal, A. (1993). Cognitive revolution in management. *Kybernetes, 22*(6), 100–104.

Gigerenzer, G., & Goldstein, D. (1996). Mind as a computer: Birth of a metaphor. *Creativity Research Journal, 9*(2–3), 131–144.

Gigerenzer, G., & Selten, R. (2001). *Bounded rationality. The adaptive toolbox.* Cambridge, MA: MIT Press.

Gigerenzer, G., Todd, P., & Group, A. R. (1999). *Simple heuristics that make us smart.* New York, NY: Oxford University Press.

Gilbert, N. (2008). *Agent-Based Models*, volume 153 of *Quantitative Applications in the Social Sciences.* Thousand Oaks, CA: Sage.

Gilbert, N., & Troitzsch, K. G. (2005). *Simulation for the social scientist.* Maidenhead: Open University Press.

Gioia, D. A., & Chittipeddi, K. (1991). Sensemaking and sensegiving in strategic change initiation. *Strategic Management Journal, 12*(6), 433–448.

Gnyawali, D. R., Stewart, A. C., & Grant, J. H. (2005). Differentiated learning processes for enhancing organizational knowledge across environmental contexts. *International Journal of Organizational Analysis*, *13*(3), 216–243.

Goldstein, J., Hazy, J., & Lichtenstein, B. (2010). *Complexity and the nexus of leadership: Leveraging nonlinear science to create ecologies of innovation.* New York, NY: Palgrave McMillan.

Goldstone, R. L., & Janssen, M. A. (2005). Computational models of collective behavior. *Trends in Cognitive Science*, *9*(9), 424–430.

Gould, S. J. (1996). *The mismeasure of man.* New York, NY: WW Norton & Company.

Grandori, A., & Cholakova, M. (2013). Unbounding bounded rationality: Heuristics as the logic of economic discovery. *International Journal of Organization Theory and Behavior*, *16*(3), 368–392.

Granovetter, M. (1978). Threshold models of collective behavior. *American Journal of Sociology*, *83*(6), 1420–1443.

Greenwood, R., Raynard, M., Kodeih, F., Micelotta, E. R., & Lounsbury, M. (2011). Institutional complexity and organizational responses. *Academy of Management Annals*, *5*(1), 317–371.

Grewatsch, S., & Kleindienst, I. (2018). How organizational cognitive frames affect organizational capabilities: The context of corporate sustainability. *Long Range Planning*, *51*(4), 607–624. Cited By :11.

Grimm, V., Lorscheid, I., Railsback, S., Achter, S., Ahrweiler, P., Backmann, P., . . . Meyer, M. (2019). Agent-based theory development for a changing world. Unpublished Manuscript.

Grimm, V., & Railsback, S. F. (2013). *Individual-based modeling and ecology.* Princeton: Princeton University Press.

Grimm, V., Revilla, E., Berger, U., Jeltsch, F., Mooij, W. M., Railsback, . . . DeAngelis, D. L. (2005). Pattern-oriented modeling of agent-based complex systems: Lessons from ecology. *Science*, *310*(5750), 987–991.

Guiette, A., & Vandenbempt, K. (2013). Exploring team mental model dynamics during strategic change implementation in professional service organizations: A sensemaking perspective. *European Management Journal*, *31*(6), 728–744.

Hackman, J. R. (1969). Toward understanding the role of tasks in behavioral research. *Acta Psychologica*, *31*, 97–128.

Hærem, T., Pentland, B. T., & Miller, K. D. (2015). Task complexity: Extending a core concept. *Academy of Management Review, 40*(3), 446–460.

Harrison, J. R., Lin, Z., Carroll, G. R., & Carley, K. M. (2007). Simulation modeling in organizational and management research. *Academy of Management Review, 32*(4), 1229–1245.

Hayek, F. A. (1980). *Individualism and economic order.* University of Chicago Press.

Healey, M. P., Hodgkinson, G. P., & Massaro, S. (2018). Can brains manage? The brain, emotion, and cognition in organizations. *Individual, Relational, and Contextual Dynamics of Emotions,* 27–58.

Heavey, C., & Simsek, Z. (2017). Distributed cognition in top management teams and organizational ambidexterity. The influence of transactive memory systems. *Journal of Management, 43*(3), 919–945.

Heckbert, S. (2013). MayaSim: An agent-based model of the ancient Maya social-ecological system. *Journal of Artificial Societies and Social Simulation, 16*(4), 11.

Hench, T., & Secchi, D. (2009). Organizational niche-construction and stakeholder analysis: Concepts and implications. *Philosophy of Management, 8*(3), 47–64.

Hendry, J. (2013). *Management: A very short introduction* (Vol. 368). Oxford: Oxford University Press.

Herath, D. B. (2019). *Business plasticity through disorganization.* Bingley: Emerald.

Herath, D., Costello, J., & Homberg, F. (2017). Team problem solving and motivation under disorganization – An agent-based modeling approach. *Team Performance Management, 23*(1/2), 46–65.

Herath, D. B., Homberg, F., & Secchi, D. (2021). Agent-based models as a lever for the power of simulations in third sector research: Opening the toolbox. *Voluntas, forthcoming.*

Herath, D.B. and Secchi, D. (2021), "Editorial", Evidence-based HRM, Vol. 9 No. 2, pp. 121–125.

Herath, D., Secchi, D., & Homberg, F. (2016). The effects of disorganization on goals and problem solving. In D. Secchi & M. Neumann (Eds.), *Agent-based simulation of organizational behavior. New frontiers of social science research* (pp. 63–84). New York, NY: Springer.

Hodgkinson, G. P. (2015). Managerial and organizational cognition. In J. D. Wright (Ed.), *International encyclopedia of the social & behavioral sciences* (2nd ed., pp. 479–483). Oxford: Elsevier.

Hodgkinson, G. P., & Healey, M. P. (2008a). Cognition in organizations. *Annual Review of Psychology, 59*, 387–417.

Hodgkinson, G. P., & Healey, M. P. (2011). Psychological foundations of dynamic capabilities: Reflexion and reflection in strategic management. *Strategic Management Journal, 32*(13), 1500–1516.

Holling, C. S. (1973). Resilience and stability of ecological systems. *Annual Review of Ecology and Systematics, 4*(1), 1–23.

Homberg, F., Secchi, D., & Herath, D. B. (2020). Agent-based modeling as a tool for public management research. In E. Vigoda-Gadot & D. R. Vashdi (Eds.), *Handbook of research methods in public administration, management and policy: Towards new frontiers* (pp. 42–62). Cheltenham: Edward Elgar.

Huber, P. (1991). Organizational learning: The contributing processes and the literatures. *Organization Science, 2*(1), 88–115.

Hutchins, E. (1995a). *Cognition in the wild.* Cambridge, MA: MIT Press.

Hutchins, E. (1995b). How a cockpit remembers its speeds. *Cognitive Science, 19*(3), 265–288.

Hutchins, E. (2010). Cognitive ecology. *Topics in Cognitive Science, 2*(4), 705–715.

Hutchins, E. (2014). The cultural ecosystem of human cognition. *Philosophical Psychology, 27*(1), 34–49.

Hutto, D. D. (2008). *Folk psychological narratives. The Sociocultural Basis of Understanding Reasons.* Cambridge, MA: MIT Press.

Ibáñez, A., & Cosmelli, D. (2008). Moving beyond computational cognitivism: Understanding intentionality, intersubjectivity and ecology of mind. *Integrative Psychological & Behavioral Science, 42*(2), 129–136.

Ilgen, D. R., Major, D. A., & Spencer, L. (1994). The cognitive revolution in organizational behavior. In J. Greenberg (Ed.), *Organizational behavior: The state of the science* (pp. 1–22). Mahwah, NJ: Lawrence Erlbaum.

Jackson, J. C., Rand, D., Lewis, K., Norton, M. I., & Gray, K. (2017). Agent-based modeling: A guide for social psychologists. *Social Psychological and Personality Science, 8*(4), 387–395.

Janis, I. L. (1972). *Victims of groupthink: A psychological study of foreign-policy decisions and fiascoes*. Boston, MA: Houghton Mifflin.

Jebb, A. T., & Tay, L. (2017). Introduction to time series analysis for organizational research: Methods for longitudinal analyses. *Organizational Research Methods, 20*(1), 61–94.

Jensen, A., Secchi, D., & Jensen, T. W. (2019). A distributed framework for the study of organizational cognition. In *European Academy of Management Annual Conference*, Lisbon, Portugal.

Kahneman, D. (2003). A perspective of judgement and choice. mapping bounded rationality. *American Psychologist, 58*(9), 697–721.

Kahneman, D., Knetsch, J. L., & Thaler, R. H. (1990). Anomalies. the endowment effect, loss aversion, and status quo bias. *Journal of Economic Perspectives, 5*, 193–206.

Kahneman, D., & Tversky, A. (1979). Prospect theory: An analysis of decision under risk. *Econometrica, 47*(2), 263–292.

Kauffman, S. A., & Weinberger, E. D. (1989). The NK model of rugged fitness landscapes and its application to maturation of the immune response. *Journal of Theoretical Biology, 141*(2), 211–245.

Kaufmann, W., Taggart, G., & Bozeman, B. (2019). Administrative delay, red tape, and organizational performance. *Public Performance & Management Review, 42*(3), 529–553.

Khalil, E. L. (2004). What is altruism? *Journal of Economic Psychology, 25*, 97–123.

Kiesling, E., Günther, M., Stummer, C., & Wakolbinger, L. M. (2012). Agent-based simulation of innovation diffusion: A review. *Central European Journal of Operations Research, 20*(2), 183–230.

Kirsh, D. (1997). Interactivity and multimedia interfaces. *Instructional Science, 25*(2), 79–96.

Kirsh, D., & Maglio, P. (1994). On distinguishing epistemic from pragmatic action. *Cognitive Science, 18*(4), 513–549.

Kiverstein, J., & Clark, A. (2009). Introduction: Mind embodied, embedded, enacted: One church or many? *Topoi, 28*(1), 1–7.

Klein, K., & Kozlowski, S. (2000). From micro to meso: Critical steps in conceptualizing and conducting multilevel research. *Organizational Research Methods, 21*(1/2), 211–236.

Knudsen, T. (2003). Simon's selection theory: Why docility evolves to breed successful altruism. *Journal of Economic Psychology*, *24*, 229–244.

Knudsen, T., Levinthal, D., & Puranam, P. (2019). Editorial: A model is a model. *Strategy Science*, *4*(1), 1–3.

Kozhevnikov, M. (2007). Cognitive styles in the context of modern psychology: Toward an integrated framework of cognitive style. *Psychological Bulletin*, *133*(3), 464.

Kurakin, A., Swistowski, A., Wu, S. C., & Bredesen, D. E. (2007). The pdz domain as a complex adaptive system. *PloS one*, *2*(9), e953.

Lakens, D. (2013). Calculating and reporting effect sizes to facilitate cumulative science: a practical primer for t-tests and anovas. *Frontiers in Psychology*, *4*, 863.

Langan-Fox, J., Wirth, A., Code, S., Langfield-Smith, K., & Wirth, A. (2001). Analyzing shared mental models. *International Journal of Industrial Ergonomics*, *28*, 99–112.

Langer, E. J. (1989). Minding matters: The consequences of mindlessness-mindfulness. In L. Berkowitz (Ed.), *Advances in experimental social psychology* (Vol. 22, pp. 137–173). San Diego, CA: Academic Press.

Lant, T. K., & Shapira, Z. (2000). *Organizational cognition: Computation and interpretation*. New York, NY: Taylor & Francis.

Lengnick-Hall, C. A., Beck, T. E., & Lengnick-Hall, M. L. (2011). Developing a capacity for organizational resilience through strategic human resource management. *Human Resource Management Review*, *21*(3), 243–255.

Levinthal, D. (1997). Adaptation on rugged landscapes. *Management Science*, *43*, 934–950.

Levitt, B., & March, J. G. (1988). Organizational learning. *Annual Review of Sociology*, *14*(1), 319–338.

Lotzmann, U., & Neumann, M. (2017). Simulation for interpretation: A methodology for growing virtual cultures. *Journal of Artificial Societies and Social Simulation*, *20*(3), 13.

Luhmann, N. (1995). *Social systems*. Stanford, CA: Stanford University Press.

Magnani, L. (2007). *Morality in a technological world. Knowledge as a duty.* New York, NY: Cambridge University Press.

Magnani, L., Secchi, D., & Bardone, E. (2007). The docile hacker: The open source model as a way of creating knowledge. In C. Schmidt (Ed.), *Proceedings from the international conference on computers and philosophy 2006* (pp. 583–596). Laval: i-C&P.

Malerba, F., Nelson, R., Orsenigo, L., & Winter, S. (2001). History-friendly models: an overview of the case of the computer industry. *Journal of Artificial Societies and Social Simulation, 4*(3), 6.

Manral, L. (2011). Managerial cognition as bases of innovation in organization. *Management Research Review, 34*(5), 576–594.

March, J. G. (1991). Exploration and exploitation in organizational learning. *Organization Science, 2*(1), 71–87.

March, J. G. (1994). *A primer on decision making.* New York, NY: Free Press.

Maturana, H., & Varela, F. J. (1987). *The three of knowledge: The biological roots of human understanding* (1st ed.). Boston, MA: New Science Library.

McGregor, D. M. (1960). *The human side of enterprise.* New York, NY: McGraw-Hill.

Menary, R. (2010). Introduction to the special issue on 4e cognition. *Phenomenological Cognitive Science, 9,* 459–463.

Merleau-Ponty, M. (1982). *Phenomenology of perception.* Abingdon: Routledge.

Merleau-Ponty, M., & Fisher, A. L. (1963). *The structure of behavior.* Boston, MA: Beacon Press.

Meyer, J. P., & Allen, N. J. (1988). Links between work experiences and organizational commitment during the first year of employment: A longitudinal analysis. *Journal of Occupational Psychology, 61,* 195–209.

Michel, A. A. (2007). A distributed cognition perspective on newcomers' change processes: The management of cognitive uncertainty in two investment banks. *Administrative Science Quarterly, 52*(4), 507–557.

Miłkowski, M. (2012). Limits of computational explanation of cognition. In V. C. Müller (Ed.), *Philosophy and theory of artificial intelligence* (pp. 69–84). Heidelberg: Springer.

Miłkowski, M. (2017). Situatedness and embodiment of computational systems. *Entropy, 19*(4), 162.

Miłkowski, M., Clowes, R., Rucińska, Z., Przegalińska, A., Zawidzki, T., Krueger, J., ... Hohol, M. (2018). From wide cognition to mechanisms: A silent revolution. *Frontiers in Psychology, 9*, 2393.

Miłkowski, M., & Nowakowski, P. (2019). Representational unification in cognitive science: Is embodied cognition a unifying perspective? *Synthese*, 1–22.

Miller, K. D., & Lin, S.-J. (2010). Different truths in different worlds. *Organization Science, 21*(1), 97–114.

Miller, J. H., & Page, S. E. (2007). *Complex adaptive systems. An introduction to computational models of social life.* Princeton, NJ: Princeton University Press.

Moorhead, G., & Montanari, J. R. (1986). An empirical investigation of the groupthink phenomenon. *Human Relations, 39*(5), 399–410.

Moss, S. (1998). Critical incident management: An empirically derived computational model. *Journal of Artificial Societies and Social Simulation, 1*(4), 1.

Muelder, H., & Filatova, T. (2018). One theory-many formalizations: Testing different code implementations of the theory of planned behaviour in energy agent-based models. *Journal of Artificial Societies and Social Simulation, 21*(4), 5.

Narayanan, V. K., Zane, L. J., & Kemmerer, B. (2011). The cognitive perspective in strategy: An integrative review. *Journal of Management, 37*(1), 305–351.

Neale, M. A., & Bazerman, M. H. (1991). *Cognition and rationality in negotiation.* New York, NY: Free Press.

Neill, S., & Rose, G. M. (2006). The effect of strategic complexity on marketing strategy and organizational performance. *Journal of Business Research, 59*(1), 1–10.

Nelson, R., & Winter, S. (1982). *An evolutionary theory of economic change* (1st ed.). Cambridge, MA: Belknap Press.

Neumann, M., & Cowley, S. J. (2016). Modelling social agency using diachronic cognition: Learning from the Mafia. In D. Secchi & M. Neumann (Eds.), *Agent-based simulation of organizational behavior. New frontiers of social science research* (pp. 289–310). New York, NY: Springer.

Newell, A. (1973). You can't play 20 questions with nature and win: Projective comments on the papers of this symposium. In W. G. Chase (Ed.), *Visual information processing* (pp. 283–308). New York, NY: Academic Press.

Newell, A., & Simon, H. A. (1972). *Human problem solving*. Englewood Cliffs, NJ: Prentice-Hall.

Nicholson, N. (2001). Managing the human animal. *Industrial Management & Data Systems, 101*(2), 90–91. doi: 10.1108/imds.2001.101.2.90.4

Nobre, F. S., & Walker, D. S. (2011). A dynamic ability-based view of the organization. *International Journal of Knowledge Management, 7*(2), 86–101.

Nooteboom, B. (2008). Cognitive distance in and between communities of practice and firms: Where do exploitation and exploration take place, and how are they connected? In A. Amin & J. Roberts (Eds.), *Community, economic creativity, and organization* (pp. 123–147). Oxford: Oxford University Press.

Norman, D. (1993). *Things that make us smart* (1st ed.). New York, NY. Addison Wesley.

Ocampo, L., Acedillo, V., Bacunador, A. M., Balo, C. C., Lagdameo, Y. J., & Tupa, N. S. (2018). A historical review of the development of organizational citizenship behavior (ocb) and its implications for the twenty-first century. *Personnel Review, 47*(4), 821–862.

Odling-Smee, F. J., Laland, K. N., & Feldman, M. W. (2003). *Niche construction: The neglected process in evolution*. Cambridge, MA: Princeton University Press.

Oliveira, N. R. B. D., & Secchi, D. (2020). Theory building, case development, and researchers' bounded rationality in innovation diffusion research: An illustration from studies of innovation diffusion. *Sociological Methods and Research, forthcoming*.

Ossola, P. (2013). Trust as a mechanism to increase 'docility.' A theoretical approach. *International Journal of Organization Theory and Behavior, 16*(4), 495–520.

Patokorpi, E. (2008). Simon's paradox: Bounded rationality and the computer metaphor of the mind. *Human Systems Management, 27*, 285–294.

Pedersen, S. B. (2012). Interactivity in health care: Bodies, values and dynamics. *Language Sciences, 34*(5), 532–542.

Pedersen, S., & Steffensen, S. (2014). Temporal dynamics in medical visual systems. *Cybernetics & Human Knowing, 21*(1-2), 143–157.

Pinna, S. (2017). Turing's theory of computation. In *Extended cognition and the dynamics of algorithmic skills* (Vol. 35, pp. 1–17). Cham: Springer.

Podsakoff, P. M., MacKenzie, S. B., Paine, J. B., & Bachrach, D. G. (2000). Organizational citizenship behaviors: A critical review of the theoretical and empirical literature and suggestions for future research. *Journal of Management, 26*(3), 513–563.

Premack, D., & Woodruff, G. (1978). Does the chimpanzee have a theory of mind? *Behavioral and brain sciences, 1*(4), 515–526.

Prigogine, I., & Stengers, I. (1986). *La nouvelle alliance.* Paris: Gallimard.

R Core Team. (2019). *R: A language and environment for statistical computing.* R Foundation for Statistical Computing, Vienna, Austria, http://www.r-project.org/ edition. Vienna, Austria: R Foundation for Statistical Computing. Retrieved from http://www.r-project.org/edition

Rafferty, P. (2001). The representation of knowledge in library classification schemes. *Knowledge Organization, 28*(4), 180–191.

Raudenbush, S. W., & Bryk, A. S. (2002). *Hierarchical linear models: Applications and data analysis methods.* Thousand Oaks, CA: Sage.

Rogers, E. M. (2003). *Diffusion of innovation* (5th ed.). New York, NY: Free Press.

Rohlfs, J. H. (2003). *Bandwagon effects in high-technology industries.* Cambridge, MA: MIT Press.

Rosenkopf, L., & Abrahamson, E. (1999). Modeling reputational and informational influences in threshold models of bandwagon innovation diffusion. *Computational and Mathematical Organization Theory, 5*(4), 361–384.

Rubinstein, A. (1998). *Modeling bounded rationality* (1st ed.). Cambridge, MA: MIT Press.

Salaman, G. (2001). A response to Snell 'the learning organization: Fact or fiction?'. *Human Relations, 54*(3), 343–359.

Salomon, G. (1993). No distribution without individuals' cognition: A dynamic interactional view. In G. Salomon (Ed.), *Distributed cognitions: Psychological and educational considerations* (pp. 111–138). Cambridge: Cambridge University Press.

Scandura, T. A., & Williams, E. A. (2000). Research methodology in management: Current practices, trends, and implications for future research. *Academy of Management Journal, 43*(6), 1248–1264.

Schaafsma, S. M., Pfaff, D. W., Spunt, R. P., & Adolphs, R. (2015). Deconstructing and reconstructing theory of mind. *Trends in cognitive sciences, 19*(2), 65–72.

Schatzki, T. R. (2005). Peripheral vision: The sites of organizations. *Organization Studies, 26*(3), 465–484.

Schultz, T. W. (1961). Investment in human capital. *The American Economic Review,* 1–17.

Secchi, D. (2007). A theory of docile society: The role of altruism in human behavior. *Journal of the Academy of Business and Economics, 7*(2), 146–160.

Secchi, D. (2009). The cognitive side of social responsibility. *Journal of Business Ethics, 88*(3), 565–581.

Secchi, D. (2011). *Extendable rationality. Understanding decision making in organizations.* New York, NY: Springer.

Secchi, D. (2015). A case for agent-based models in organizational behavior and team research. *Team Performance Management, 21*(1/2), 37–50.

Secchi, D. (2016). Boundary conditions for the emergence of 'docility:' An agent-based model and simulation. In D. Secchi & M. Neumann (Eds.), *Agent-based simulation of organizational behavior. New frontiers of social science research* (pp. 175–200). New York, NY: Springer.

Secchi, D. (2019). Foreword. In D. B. Herath (Ed.), *Organizational plasticity. How disorganization can be leveraged for better organizational performance* (pp. xv–xxiii). Bingley: Emerald.

Secchi, D. (2020a). Cognitive attunement in the face of organizational plasticity. *Evidence-Based Human Resource Management, 9*(2), 192–208.

Secchi, D. (2020b). A typology of non-functional information. In C. Stephanidis, D. Harris, W.-C. Li, D. D. Schmorrow, C. M. Fidopiastis, P. Zaphiris, ... J. Schwarz (Eds.), *HCI International 2020 - Late Breaking Papers: Cognition, Learning and Games*, volume 12425 of *Lecture Notes in Computer Science* (pp. 240–254). Cham: Springer Nature.

Secchi, D. (2020c). What is non-functional information? Theory development through agent-based simulation. In *European Academy of Management Annual Conference*, Dublin, Ireland.

Secchi, D. (2021). *How do I develop an agent-based model?* Elgar Dissertation Companions. Edward Elgar (forthcoming).

Secchi, D., & Adamsen, B. (2017). Organizational cognition: A critical perspective on the theory in use. In S. J. Cowley & F. Vallee-Tourangeau (Eds.), *Cognition beyond the brain: Computation, interactivity and human artifice* (2nd ed., pp. 305–331). Heidelberg: Springer.

Secchi, D., & Bardone, E. (2009). Super-docility in organizations. An evolutionary model. *International Journal of Organization Theory and Behavior, 12*(3), 339–379.

Secchi, D., & Bardone, E. (2010). Does bounded rationality need an update? In *Behavioral Decision Research in Management Conference*, Carnegie Mellon University, Pittsburgh, PA (USA).

Secchi, D., & Bardone, E. (2013). Socially distributed cognition and intra-organizational bandwagons: Theoretical framework, model, and simulation. *International Journal of Organization Theory and Behavior, 16*(4), 521–572.

Secchi, D., & Bardone, E. (2014). Bounded rationality: Four critiques and an update. In *Second International conference on interactivity, language, and cognition*, Jyväskylä, Finland.

Secchi, D., & Cowley, S. J. (2018). Modeling organizational cognition: The case of impact factor. *Journal of Artificial Societies and Social Simulation, 21*(1), 13.

Secchi, D., & Cowley, S. J. (2019). Improbable fairness: Reviewing under the lenses of impact factor. *RASK, 50*(Autumn), 191–209.

Secchi, D., & Cowley, S. J. (2020). Organisational cognition: What it is and how it works. *European Management Review, forthcoming.*

Secchi, D., Gahrn-Andersen, R., & Cowley, S. J. (Eds.) (2022). *Organizational cognition: The theory of social organizing.* Routledge (forthcoming).

Secchi, D., & Gullekson, N. (2016). Individual and organizational conditions for the emergence and evolution of bandwagons. *Computational and Mathematical Organization Theory, 22*(1), 88–133.

Secchi, D., & Neumann, M. (Eds.) (2016). *Agent-based simulation of organizational behavior. New frontiers of social science research.* New York, NY: Springer.

Secchi, D., & Seri, R. (2017). Controlling for 'false negatives' in agent-based models: A review of power analysis in organizational research. *Computational and Mathematical Organization Theory, 23*(1), 94–121.

Seri, R., Martinoli, M., Secchi, D., & Centorrino, S. (2020). Model calibration and validation via confidence sets. *Econometrics and Statistics, forthcoming.*

Seri, R., & Secchi, D. (2017). How many times should one run a computational simulation? In B. Edmonds & R. Meyer (Eds.), *Simulating social complexity. A handbook* (2nd ed., pp. 229–251). Heidelberg: Springer.

Seri, R., & Secchi, D. (2018). A power primer for agent-based simulation models. Determining the number of runs in linear and polynomial regression. In *European Academy of Management Annual Conference*, Reykjavik, Island.

Seri, R., Secchi, D., & Martinoli, M. (2020). Randomness, emergence and causation: A historical perspective of simulation in the social sciences. In S. Albeverio & E. Mastrogiacomo (Eds.), *Complexity and Emergence*, Springer Proceedings in Mathematics and Statistics (pp. in press). Springer.

Siebers, P.-O., Herath, D., Bardone, E., Farahbakhsh, S., Knudsen, P., Madsen, J., ... Secchi, D. (2020). On the quest for defining organisational plasticity: A community modelling experiment. *Evidence-Based Human Resource Management, 9*(2), 126–138.

Siebers, P.-O., & Klügl, F. (2017). What software engineering has to offer to agent-based social simulation. In B. Edmonds & R. Meyer (Eds.), *Simulating social complexity. A handbook* (2nd ed., pp. 81–117). New York, NY: Springer.

Silver, W. S., & Mitchell, T. R. (1990). The status quo tendency in decision making. *Organizational Dynamics, 18*(4), 34–46.

Simon, H. A. (1955). A behavioral theory of rational choice. *Quarterly Journal of Economics, 69*(1), 99–118.

Simon, H. A. (1978). Rationality as process and a product of thought. *American Economic Review, 68*, 1–14.

Simon, H. A. (1979). Rational decision making in business organizations. *American Economic Review, 69*(4), 493–513.

Simon, H. A. (1993). Altruism and economics. *American Economic Review, 83*(2), 156–161.

Simon, H. A. (1996). *The sciences of the artificial.* Cambridge, MA: MIT Press.

Simon, H. A. (1997). *Administrative behavior* (4th ed.). New York, NY: The Free Press.

Smaldino, P. E., Calanchini, J., & Pickett, C. L. (2015). Theory development with agent-based models. *Organizational Psychology Review, 5*(4), 300–317.

Somers, S. (2009). Measuring resilience potential: An adaptive strategy for organizational crisis planning. *Journal of contingencies and crisis management, 17*(1), 12–23.

Squazzoni, F. (2012). *Agent-based computational sociology.* Chichester: Wiley.

Steffensen, S. V. (2011). Beyond mind: An extended ecology of languaging. In S. J. Cowley (Ed.), *Distributed language* (pp. 185–210). Philadelphia, PA: John Benjamins.

Steffensen, S. V. (2013). Human interactivity: Problem-solving, solution-probing and verbal patterns in the wild. In S. J. Cowley & F. Vallee-Tourangeau (Eds.), *Cognition beyond the brain: Computation, interactivity and human artifice* (pp. 195–221). Dordrecht: Springer.

Strang, D., & Meyer, J. W. (1993). Institutional conditions for diffusion. *Theory and Society, 22*(4), 487–511.

Strang, D., & Soule, S. A. (1998). Diffusion in organizations and social movements: From hybrid corn to poison pills. *Annual Review of Sociology, 24*, 266–290.

Strang, D., & Tuma, N. B. (1993). Spatial and temporal heterogeneity in diffusion. *American Journal of Sociology*, *99*, 614–639.

Teece, D. J. (2007). Explicating dynamic capabilities: The nature and microfoundations of (sustainable) enterprise performance. *Strategic Management Journal*, *28*(13), 1319–1350.

Teece, D. J., Pisano, G., & Shuen, A. (1997). Dynamic capabilities and strategic management. *Strategic Management Journal*, *18*(7), 509–533.

Tesfatsion, L., & Judd, K. L. (2006). *Handbook of computational economics: Agent-based computational economics* (Vol. 2). Amsterdam: Elsevier.

Thomas, N., Randolph, A., & Marin, A. (2019). A network view of entrepreneurial cognition in corporate entrepreneurship contexts: A socially situated approach. *Management Decision*, *58*(7), 1331–1354.

Thompson, E. (2007). *Mind in life: Biology, phenomenology, and the sciences of mind*. Cambridge, MA: Harvard University Press.

Todd, P. M., & Gigerenzer, G. (2003). Bounding rationality to the world. *Journal of Economic Psychology*, *24*, 143–165.

Tolman, E. C. (1948). Cognitive maps in rats and men. *Psychological review*, *55*(4), 189.

Tripsas, M., & Gavetti, G. (2000). Capabilities, cognition, and inertia: Evidence from digital imaging. *Strategic Management Journal*, *21*(10-11), 1147–1161.

Tversky, A., & Kahneman, D. (1974). Judgment under uncertainty: Heuristics and biases. *Science*, *185*, 1124–1130.

Van Eck, N. J., & Waltman, L. (2010). Software survey: Vosviewer, a computer program for bibliometric mapping. *Scientometrics*, *84*(2), 523–538.

Van Eck, N. J., & Waltman, L. (2014). Visualizing bibliometric networks. In Y. Ding, R. Rousseau, & D. Wolfram (Eds.), *Measuring scholarly impact* (pp. 285–320). Cham: Springer.

Varela, F. J., Thompson, E., & Rosch, E. (1991). *The embodied mind: Cognitive science and human experience*. Cambridge, MA: MIT Press.

Von Bertalanffy, L. (1968). *General system theory*. New York, NY: Braziller.

Walsh, J. P. (1995). Managerial and organizational cognition: Notes from a trip down memory lane. *Organization Science, 6*(3), 280–321.

Walsh, J. P., & Ungson, G. R. (1991). Organizational memory. *Academy of Management Review, 16*(1), 57–91.

Weick, K. E. (1993). The collapse of sensemaking in organizations: The mann gulch disaster. *Administrative Science Quarterly, 38*(4), 628–652.

Weick, K. E. (1995). *Sensemaking in organizations* (1st ed.). Thousand Oaks, CA: Sage.

Weick, K. E., & Roberts, K. H. (1993). Collective mind and organizational reliability: The case of flight operations on an aircraft carrier deck. *Administrative Science Quarterly, 38*, 357–381.

Weick, K. E., & Sutcliffe, K. M. (2006). Mindfulness and the quality of organizational attention. *Organization Science, 17*(4), 514–524.

Weick, K. E., Sutcliffe, K. M., & Obstfeld, D. (2005). Organizing and the process of sensemaking. *Organization Science, 16*(4), 409–421.

Weiss, M., & Wittmann, C. (2018). Objective environmental conditions and perceived environmental uncertainty: Cognitive models as explanation for a perceptual gap. *Journal of Accounting and Organizational Change, 14*(1), 33–60.

Wells, A. (1998). Turing's analysis of computation and theories of cognitive architecture. *Cognitive Science, 22*(3), 269–294.

Westland, J. C. (2015). Data collection, control, and sample size. In J. C. Westland (Ed.), *Structural equation models. Studies in systems, decision and control* (Vol. 22, pp. 83–115). Cham: Springer.

Wheeler, M. (2010). In defense of extended functionalism. In R. Menary (Ed.), *The extended mind* (pp. 245–270). Cambridge, MA: MIT Press.

Wilensky, U. (1999). *Netlogo.* Evanston, IL: Center for Connected Learning and Computer-Based Modeling, Northwestern University.

Wood, R. E. (1986). Task complexity: Definition of the construct. *Organizational Behavior and Human Decision Processes, 37*(1), 60–82.

Worley, C. G., & Lawler, E. E. (2010). Agility and organization design: A diagnostic framework. *Organizational Dynamics, 39*(2), 194–204.

Worley, C. G., Williams, T. D., & Lawler III, E. E. (2014). *The agility factor: Building adaptable organizations for superior performance*. San Francisco, CA: Jossey-Bass.

Yaniv, I. (2004). Receiving other people's advice: Influence and benefit. *Organizational Behavior and Human Decision Processes, 93*, 1–13.

Yaniv, I., & Kleinberger, E. (2000). Advice taking in decision making: Egocentric discounting and reputation formation. *Organizational Behavior and Human Decision Processes, 83*, 260–281.

Yu, T., & Glynn, M. A. (2015). *Competitive memory: Bringing the strategic past into the present*, volume 32 of *Advances in Strategic Management*. Bingley: Emerald.

Zaheer, S., Albert, S., & Zaheer, A. (1999). Time scales and organizational theory. *Academy of Management Review, 24*(4), 725–741.

Index

Note: Page numbers followed by "*n*" indicate notes.

Printed in the United States
by Baker & Taylor Publisher Services